Crime Scene Investigation
Case Studies

Crime Scene Investigation Case Studies

Step by Step from the Crime Scene to the Courtroom

Jacqueline T. Fish and Jonathon Fish

AMSTERDAM • BOSTON • HEIDELBERG • LONDON
NEW YORK • OXFORD • PARIS • SAN DIEGO
SAN FRANCISCO • SINGAPORE • SYDNEY • TOKYO
Anderson publishing is an imprint of Elsevier

ELSEVIER

Anderson publishing is an imprint of Elsevier
225 Wyman Street, Waltham, MA 02451, USA
The Boulevard, Langford Lane, Kidlington, Oxford, OX5 1GB, UK

Notices

Knowledge and best practice in this field are constantly changing. As new research and experience broaden our understanding, changes in research methods, professional practices, or medical treatment may become necessary.

Practitioners and researchers must always rely on their own experience and knowledge in evaluating and using any information, methods, compounds, or experiments described herein. In using such information or methods they should be mindful of their own safety and the safety of others, including parties for whom they have a professional responsibility.

To the fullest extent of the law, neither the Publisher nor the authors, contributors, or editors, assume any liability for any injury and/or damage to persons or property as a matter of products liability, negligence or otherwise, or from any use or operation of any methods, products, instructions, or ideas contained in the material herein.

Library of Congress Cataloging-in-Publication Data
A catalog record for this book is available from the Library of Congress.

British Library Cataloguing-in-Publication Data
A catalogue record for this book is available from the British Library.

ISBN: 978-1-4557-3123-7

Printed in the United States of America

14 15 16   10 9 8 7 6 5 4 3 2 1

Working together to grow
libraries in developing countries

www.elsevier.com | www.bookaid.org | www.sabre.org

ELSEVIER   BOOK AID International   Sabre Foundation

Contents

Foreword

Have you ever heard the adage, "The job isn't finished until the paperwork is done"? Without question, nowhere is this truer than in the field of criminal investigations. It is also true that the paperwork of any criminal investigation is absolutely vital for the proper administration of justice, where the innocent are protected and the guilty are held responsible for their illegal actions. You may be the greatest criminal investigator on the face of the earth, but if the paperwork in your case files is disorganized, incoherent, and doesn't accurately, truthfully, and concisely reflect every aspect of your criminal investigation, then all of your hard work may be for naught and justice may be averted. When you are a criminal investigator, what you do or fail to do with your assigned criminal investigations, and this includes your paperwork, can have life or death consequences. The public has entrusted a great responsibility to our criminal investigators, and it is our sworn duty to do everything, within the law, to protect that trust.

With regards to the who, what, where, why, and how of criminal investigative paperwork, many jurisdictions provide only "in house" training, specific to their jurisdiction. Much of this training is "informal", "on the job" training and is administered by senior investigators, who are assigned to tutor the new investigator. This type of training typically has inconsistent effects, and has the potential of passing on the habits, good and bad, of the senior investigator providing the training. While there will always be some jurisdictional differences involved in criminal investigative paperwork, there are far more universal aspects of criminal investigative paperwork that will be found in all criminal case files, regardless of the jurisdiction, and this text will highlight these best practices.

This text will provide readers with validated, standardized methodologies for completing thorough criminal investigative case files, regardless of the type of crime and jurisdiction, by highlighting actual case studies of different crimes and their associated investigative paperwork. The information presented in this text will form the ideal, non-bias foundation for future criminal investigators and newly assigned criminal investigators, as well as acting as a great refresher for experienced criminal investigators. When you are the criminal investigator, it is your name that will appear at the bottom of the case files, so remember, "garbage in, garbage out."

Edward William Wallace Jr.
Certified Senior Crime Scene Analyst,
NYPD First Grade Detective (Retired)

CSU Graduate Student Contributors

Charleston Southern University graduate students enrolled in the Master of Science in Criminal Justice program are responsible for the creativity of the case scenarios, development of the case files, preparation of the documentation, and presentation of the completed case files to colleagues for review. What started out as a graduate course assignment resulted in this newest textbook! Congratulations to every student for your perseverance and determination to earn your graduate degrees!

Chapter Two
Jamar Meadows, Bruce Powers, Amanda Sisson

Chapter Three
Amanda Albright, Tiffany Coleman, Lachelle Joyner

Chapter Four
Connie Davis, Kenisha Woods

Chapter Five
Kierstin Flores, Alison Harrison, Sade' Nelson
Molly Bentley, Jessica Bogstad, Jeremy Dalton, Stevie Simmons

Chapter Six
Courtney Barriere, Jennifer Drizis Mosher, Brittany Richardson

Preface

WIFM—what does that mean? Are they radio or television station call letters? Is it an abbreviation for a federal agency or a military acronym? Would you believe these letters stand for something you ask yourself every day: What's In it For Me? No matter what decision you are about to make, you inevitably weigh the outcome by asking, "What's in it for me?" You considered that question when deciding whether or not to take this class, and this textbook is the simple answer to that question. Students identified a need for a step-by-step manual as they seek to enhance their job performance as investigators.

Each chapter of this book involves a different type of criminal offense. After reading the opening section of the case, you will assume the role of investigator. Read the case narrative, and then identify the steps you will take to conduct the investigation (investigative strategy) and the accompanying documentation that must be completed. What criminal offenses have occurred? What are the elements of the crime? As you review the narrative, create a chronological timeline. You will find this extremely useful as events unfold throughout the investigation, and you are the primary person responsible for making sure every step is identified and examined throughout the case.

This book was created by students for students, and it is designed to teach you how to successfully complete investigative case files for criminal activities. Eighteen graduate students collaborated to create this collection of case studies. The events reflect criminal investigations that are conducted every day.

Small and large agencies alike create case files that eventually are reviewed for prosecutorial decisions. A variety of reports is available and an equal number of writing styles, required forms, standard operating procedures, and types of offenders exist. No two reports or files are the same. Every investigation is unique—and each of these case files is also quite different. However, every criminal investigation has commonalities, including chronological sequencing, constitutional guarantees, investigative strategies, and the capacity of the American criminal justice system to effectively identify the guilty and exonerate the innocent.

The criminal justice graduate students at Charleston Southern University offer you these case files to assist in your studies, provide valuable training experiences, and lead to justice being served.

Digital Assets

Thank you for selecting Anderson Publishing's *Crime Scene Investigation Case Studies: Step by Step from the Crime Scene to the Courtroom.* To complement the learning experience, we have provided a number of online tools to accompany this edition. Two distinct packages of interactive digital assets are available: one for instructors and one for students.

Please consult your local sales representative with any additional questions.

For the Instructor

Qualified adopters and instructors need to register at this link for access: http://textbooks.elsevier.com/web/manuals.aspx?isbn=9781455731237.

- **Test Bank** Compose, customize, and deliver exams using an online assessment package in a free Windows-based authoring tool that makes it easy to build tests using the unique multiple-choice and true or false questions created for *Crime Scene Investigation Case Studies.* What's more, this authoring tool allows you to export customized exams directly to Blackboard, WebCT, eCollege, Angel, and other leading systems. All test bank files are also conveniently offered in Word format.
- **PowerPoint Lecture Slides** Reinforce key topics with focused PowerPoint slides, which provide a perfect visual outline with which to augment your lecture. Each individual book chapter has its own dedicated slideshow.
- **Lesson Plans** Design your course around customized lesson plans. Each individual lesson plan acts as a separate syllabus containing a content synopsis, key terms, directions to supplementary websites, and more open-ended critical-thinking questions designed to spur class discussion. These lesson plans also delineate and connect chapter-based learning objectives to specific teaching resources, making it easy to catalog the resources at your disposal.

For the Student

Students will need to visit this link in order to access the ancillaries listed here: www.elsevierdirect.com/companion.jsp?ISBN=9781455731237.

- **Self-Assessment Question Bank** Enhance, review, and study sessions with the help of this online self-quizzing asset. Each question is presented in an interactive format that allows for immediate feedback.
- **Forms for Filling Out Reports**
- **Video Resources for Select Cases**
- **Image Bank** Full-color images of the photos in the book.

1

Introduction
From the Scene of the Crime to the Desk of the Prosecutor

OBJECTIVE

This opening chapter introduces the methodologies of investigating and reporting criminal offenses beyond the initial response. It includes a sample case for illustrative purposes.

KEY TERMS

case file	investigation	opinions
chronological order	jargon	reports
complainant	linkage	solvability factors
corpus delecti	Locards Exchange Principle	suspect
credibility	*modus operandi*	victim
elements	narrative	
fact	objective	

What You Will Learn
LEARNING OUTCOMES

- Describe the differences between facts and opinions
- Explain the goals of an investigation
- Examine case narratives to determine investigative strategies
- Identify the elements of the crime under investigation
- Review case file documents for accuracy
- Recognize areas for improvement in case files

Introduction

Millions of words have been written in an effort to educate and train law enforcement personnel to become well-prepared police officers, show crime scene technicians how to process crime scenes, help law school students to complete bar examinations, and equip judges to

Crime Scene Investigation Case Studies

fairly administer justice in the courtroom. What is the single tie that binds all these phases of the criminal justice system together? Investigative case files. First responders deal with emergency situations, and then they must begin the paperwork process that may cross dozens of desks and linger in the courts for many years. That initial preliminary investigation sets in motion a comprehensive course of action culminating in the completion of the inquiry process that may not end for decades. As with all systems, a strategy must be in place to guide the development of the investigation.

Poor police reporting can jeopardize effective criminal prosecution. Who is going to read your reports and case files? There is a wide spectrum of people contained in this audience, and first to view the report is your supervisor. Once the report is approved and becomes an official record, the list of readers expands: lawyers, prosecutors, judges, jurors, social workers, government officials, insurance adjustors and investigators, citizens, defendants, media representatives, crime lab analysts, and other investigating agencies. Is your work of sufficient quality to withstand all this scrutiny? Did you verify the information contained in the reports and subsequent forms? Can a person who is not familiar with investigative techniques read your report and develop a clear understanding of the events that have been documented?

This publication has been compiled to assist investigators and students in the various methodologies required to construct solid, factual investigative case files. These very different cases are presented for review, along with the required paperwork and an informative narrative that will provide details not apparent in the traditional reporting format. These types of investigations are conducted every day in agencies of every size across the United States and throughout the world. There is no "one size fits all" approach to acquiring the knowledge and skills that are required for successful case prosecution. We present the scenarios and the forms; you develop the timeline and the investigative strategy for completing the case file.

Investigation is successful when all the gaps are filled between the statements, alternative explanations are considered but then eliminated, and a solid prosecutable case file is presented to the state's attorney for review. Not all investigations will result in arrests. Not all arrests will result in prosecutions. Certainly not all prosecutions will produce a conviction. The goal is to achieve justice. Were guilty perpetrators identified and prosecuted? Equally important, were the innocent exonerated and not wrongfully prosecuted?

Overview

In the United States, more than 16,000 law enforcement agencies generate reports on a daily basis. Since 1838 when the Boston Police Department became the first official police agency in the United States, crime and offense reports have been written. After more than 170 years of compiling reports, there is still no uniform or consistent method of collecting information when officers are called to provide assistance and begin an investigation. Most law enforcement agencies have now moved to the use of standardized reports, but no matter how far technology advances, there will always be reporting requirements for law enforcement functions.

There are not many proficient criminal investigators available for hire by police agencies. The diverse skills that must be developed and honed for one to become a highly effective detective consume years of service and require a commitment, both of which are necessary to produce a high-quality, documented case file that accurately reflects every aspect of a case. Depending on the circumstances of the event, a few routine forms may need to be completed. Every action taken must be recorded. If a crime has been committed, the appropriate response actions will be initiated. Most actions taken by police officers and other first responders do not, in fact, involve criminal activity.

Regardless of whether the reports are completed on a keyboard or with an ink pen, the content must be complete, clear, concise, and accurate. Sometimes it is not possible or practical to type a report. We all have an idea of what an offense or accident report looks like—you can view various formats from different agencies online.

Investigative Case Files

Our focus is on the investigative **case file**, which contains all the documentation compiled by investigators who are examining every aspect of the event to determine the truth—what happened and who is responsible for that activity. Was a crime committed? What activities will be necessary to properly evaluate the circumstances and determine whether or not to proceed with a full investigation?

In this technologically advanced era of computers, digital images, and cloud storage, it is becoming more and more difficult to envision an investigative case file. Yet it is essential

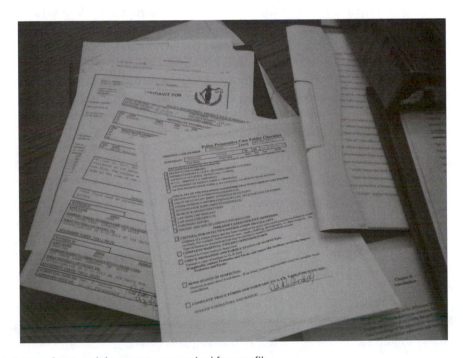

FIGURE 1-1 Many forms and documents are required for case files.

that all activities are documented so that any authorized individual reviewing the associated records will arrive at an informed decision regarding the investigation.

Terminology Used Throughout the Book

What is the definition of a report? **Reports** are permanent records of all important facts in a case. We need to examine this statement. Just what exactly is a fact? Look around the room now, examine an object, and then state a fact related to that object. For example, the highlighter I use when I am studying is yellow. Would you agree? How would you know this is a fact? The definition of a **fact** is simple: it is a statement that can be proven. When you read that statement, a picture formed in your mind of a yellow highlighter. Would you call that a preconceived notion because you are familiar with yellow highlighters? How do you know whether my highlighter has the diameter of a pen or a magic marker? How do you visualize yellow? Was it fluorescent or banana yellow? Was the cap chewed on? Why does it matter?

This exercise demonstrates the limited knowledge of an individual who was not at the scene and does not have first-hand knowledge with the events contained in the police report. The activities and observations recorded in an official report must be accurate and all information must be reported. Although it seems entirely petty to record such detail as the brand and style of the highlighter, at some point that type of precise information could become vital in creating a **linkage** or association among a victim, the crime scene, and a perpetrator. If you gain the skill of accurately conveying the totality of the information in every instance, your work will survive the scrutiny of a defense attorney in the courtroom.

You have no doubt completed many courses in criminal justice, from the historical beginnings to current-day Homeland Security issues. As students, you can probably list the steps that should be taken by an officer who observes criminal activity or who is dispatched to the scene of an event requiring police assistance. Can you clearly define an **investigation**? It is a systematic and detailed inquiry to determine the truth and let the facts prove or disprove allegations. It also involves seeking to identify those responsible for the events and to eliminate the innocent from suspicion. Finally, if a *corpus delicti* is established (evidence that a crime has been committed), a complete investigative file will present the best case possible for prosecution.

An investigator must establish **elements** of the crime, which are specific legal aspects of a criminal offense that must be proven. If a suspect is charged with the offense, all elements must be established beyond a reasonable doubt or there can be no finding of guilt. Determining the truth is more important than obtaining a conviction or closing a case. State statutes vary regarding the specific elements of offenses, but in every criminal proceeding, each specific condition must be identified for an act to be called a specific crime.

This case studies book consists of carefully structured learning experiences that place you in the role of an investigator who is conducting an investigation and completing the paperwork necessary to build a criminal case file. Although this book is by no means comprehensive, it will provide you with a guide as you gain knowledge and skills in the "art" of writing. Remember, good writers can write about anything. A good investigator will establish **credibility** by remaining unbiased and impartial, and those traits will be reflected in your written work. Credibility is hard to establish and easy to lose.

Not all crimes are solvable. Many cases have insufficient evidence, no witnesses, and no informants to provide leads. In many instances, the responding officer will complete the initial report and an investigator will examine that report and determine the **solvability factors**—statements that are crucial to solving crimes and in prioritizing caseloads. The data are used for compiling statistics, and the victim (if insured) will provide a copy of the report for claim reimbursement; then the case is removed from active investigation.

The **narrative** section of the report is where the story is told. A well-structured narrative focuses on content and factual statements. Although incident and offense reports vary considerably in format, there is always a section where the officers record personal observations, document actions, and "tell the story." There is never any room for your opinion in this type of report. Always use the first-person, past tense, active voice, and present the events in chronological order. Use short, clear, concise, and concrete words to explain the situation. **Jargon**, which consists of words, expressions, or phrases specific to a profession or occupation, can create confusion and cause delays or dismissals of criminal charges and should therefore not appear in the reports.

Detailed notes can make or break a case. Take notes on every step taken in every investigation. Ensure the information you record provides a complete and accurate depiction of the scene, the victims, the witnesses, the physical evidence, and the results of all analyses. You should always carry a personal notebook to write down complete, accurate, specific, and factual information. Remember, your opinion has no place in the reports. **Opinions** are beliefs that may not be accurate and may not be provable, whereas facts are tangible things used to make solid decisions and that can be proven. Your job is to provide case files that are **objective**—that is, the documents and statements display no bias, are non-opinionated, fair, and impartial.

As an investigator, you will establish a timeline—or sequence of the events. This timeline will assist you as you complete all of the paperwork following the **chronological order** of the incident. The importance and accuracy of the sequence can be used to establish the whereabouts of suspects, witnesses, weapons, and subsequent activities in relation to the victim. In fact, to proceed with an investigation, one of the primary responsibilities of law enforcement officers is to establish the ***corpus delicti***, or "the body of the crime." This does not literally mean that a body must be discovered, but it must be proven that someone has committed an offense. For example, if a purse with identification and personal items is found discarded alongside a highway, would you agree that it is the *corpus delicti*? With the discovery of the purse, it has not been proven that a crime occurred, so the answer is no. What does it take to make the purse the *corpus delicti*? First, it has to be proven that the property has been stolen and that a person is criminally responsible for this activity. If it cannot be established that the purse was stolen, then no crime has occurred.

CHRONOLOGICAL TIMELINE	
0735	Call received at 911
0735	Call dispatched to patrol officer
0741	First officer arrived on scene (Duncan)
0742	Fire department on scene
0743	Backup officer arrives on scene
0744	Perimeter established
0746	Supervisors notified
0748	Investigator dispatched to scene (Humphrey)
0750	Crime scene investigator (CSI) dispatched to scene (Reeves)
0814	CSI arrives on scene
0820	Investigator and CSI conduct scene walkthrough
0850	Coroner arrives on scene (Rhodes)
0900	Photographs completed and sketches started
0903	Patrol supervisor arrives on scene (Potter)
0911	Backup officer begins neighborhood canvas to locate potential witnesses
1110	CSI completes diagram, photos, evidence collection
1115	Witness list provided to investigator; canvas is completed
1210	Coroner releases body to be removed from scene
1320	Patrol and CSI debrief with investigator
1330	Patrol and CSI clear scene
1405	CSI checks physical evidence in to Evidence/Property Unit
1415	Investigator begins interviewing neighborhood witnesses
1600	CSI reports to morgue to brief medical examiner and witness autopsy

To be continued throughout the investigation.

The Purpose of This Book

Each chapter of this book involves a different type of criminal offense. After reading the opening section of the case, you will assume the role of investigator. Read the case narrative and then identify the steps you will take to conduct the investigation (your investigative strategy) and the accompanying documentation that must be completed. What criminal offenses have occurred? What are the elements of the crime? As you review the narrative, create a timeline. You will find this extremely useful as events unfold throughout the investigation and you are the primary person responsible for making sure every step is identified and examined throughout the case.

PRIMARY GOALS OF AN INVESTIGATION

The primary goals of an investigation are to discover the truth by determining whether or not a crime was committed, identifying those responsible, eliminating the innocent from suspicion, legally obtaining information, and compiling the best possible information for prosecutorial purposes. An investigator must be able to interview and write reports and must be thoroughly familiar with crimes and their elements. Although state and federal statutes vary, each crime has elements that must be established throughout the investigation.

Important Information for Every Investigation

No two cases are alike. Even if you identify a serial offender who continually commits the same offense, the circumstances always vary. For example, a burglar who always targets households in the daytime and enters through the backdoor has established a ***modus operandi***, a method of operation, but every house is different, and each victim deserves an investigation. Who are the victims? **Victims** can be individuals, groups of people, or corporations. They can be young, elderly, physically or mentally challenged, or you.

Do you know anyone who has been the victim of a crime? Think back on the incident; now that you know there must be a *corpus delicti* for a crime to have occurred, did a criminal offense really take place? What factors were present that meet the parameters for the event to be classified as a crime? Were the perpetrators identified? Were criminal charges placed against them? How do you know whose actions constituted the commission of a crime—or the identity of the perpetrator? Did witnesses identify the subjects? A **complainant** is the person who reports an incident to the law enforcement agency responsible for responding to that specific jurisdiction. The complainant may or may not be a victim of a crime. Think of an example where a complainant is not a victim of the criminal offense that has been committed. A common occurrence would be a robbery of a bank or business during the daytime hours. In these circumstances, the complainant may be someone who drives by a store, observes a robbery taking place, then calls the police on a cell phone. This complainant is not a victim. In this situation, there may be multiple victims, including the store employee who is being robbed as well as any customers who are in the store at the time.

Look closely at the definition of a crime in your specific state statutes. Actions that are in violation of local ordinances, state statutes, and federal laws are criminal acts. How do you define the elements of a criminal offense? They are clearly identified in the state statutes. Will the prosecutor check your work to ensure you have established the *corpus delicti*? Absolutely, so material evidence and objective proof must clearly be included in the reports and statements contained within the case file.

DESCRIPTOR INFORMATION FOR EVERY SUSPECT	
Collect as much data as possible, including the following:	
Name	Complexion
Alias	Speech/voice
Address	Abnormalities
Sex	Mustache or other facial hair
Race	Chin
Hair	Hands
Eyes	Posture
Height	Type of clothing
Weight	Scars/marks/tattoos
Age	Teeth
Build	

What makes a person a **suspect**? First, you must know what constitutes a crime and how to establish it in writing. Proof that a crime has occurred must be established as the first step. A conviction is one of the final steps and cannot occur if reports are faulty or there is no investigative strategy that culminates in an arrest. Your investigation should identify a person or persons who appear to be directly or indirectly connected with the crime. Not everyone you encounter in the investigation will be a suspect, so remain unbiased and nonjudgmental.

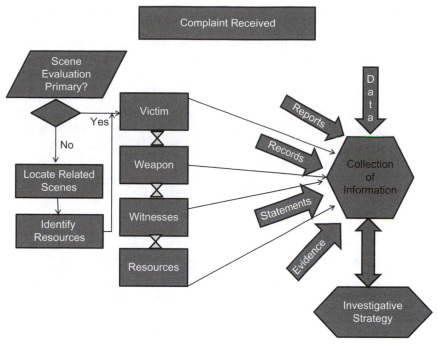

FIGURE 1-2 Investigative decision tree.

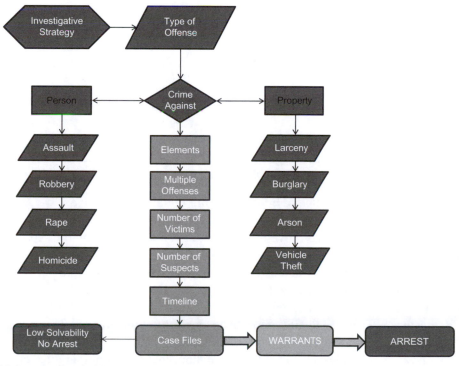

FIGURE 1-3 Investigative decision tree.

Review of Basic Crime Scene Investigation

Edmond **Locard's exchange principle** makes criminal investigation a reality. Locard's theory basically states that every contact leaves a trace. Therefore, when a perpetrator enters a crime scene or interacts with a victim, the perpetrator leaves something at the scene and takes something away—that is, there is an exchange of physical evidence. As you become familiar with the case files, you should be able to identify types of physical evidence that must be documented, collected, and preserved. Investigators must work closely with crime scene investigators (CSIs) as they process the crime scene or the victim. The case files will contain some lists of evidence and show reports of scientific analyses that were performed on the items. But are all the items documented, collected, and sent to the proper facilities for processing?

Moving Forward into the Case Files

ELEMENTS OF A CASE FILE

- Incident or offense report
- Supplemental report(s)
- Victim or witness statement(s)
- Entry/exit log
- Photo log
- Crime scene rough sketch
- Crime scene final sketch
- Evidence/property sheet
- Chain of custody log
- Investigative strategy
- Timeline
- Miranda rights waiver
- Field interview card
- Affidavit for search warrant

- Search warrant
- Affidavit for arrest warrant
- Arrest warrant
- Suspect statement
- Consent to search waiver
- Request for crime laboratory examination
- Crime laboratory analysis report
- Polygraph examination report
- Autopsy report
- Arson investigation report
- Photo lineup form
- Vehicle inventory/tow sheet
- Arrest report
- Booking sheet

Now that you have completed your briefing for the content of this book, we are ready to move forward. The book contains case files of commonly encountered types of crimes. Accompanying each case is a narrative that will assist you as you review the seemingly endless array of police reports that must be completed for every investigation. As you read the case, documentation will be provided so that you can see how witness statements and investigations are intertwined and become part of a case file. This collection of documents begins with the first responding officer and concludes with a court trial if it is established that a crime occurred and that the suspect identified probably committed the alleged offenses. The cases you are reviewing were developed by a group of graduate students studying criminal justice at Charleston Southern University. The documentation, including photographs, crime scene sketches, statements, search warrants, lineups, and so on, were identified as necessary in order to build a case file that could be presented to the prosecutor's office to press charges on behalf of the state.

After you have carefully reviewed a narrative and the case file, you will be asked to answer questions pertaining to the investigation. Again, this is the time when constructing a timeline of events will help to determine if additional steps are necessary or if documents are missing that need to be evaluated in order to close the investigation.

When you have completed each of the chapters, it becomes your turn. The final chapter will set up a case for you and provide the necessary information. You will have to establish a strategy for managing the case as well as determining which of the forms are necessary for your case file. The blank forms are provided for you to download and complete based on the information you have learned from this course. It is also your responsibility to generate a case narrative and a timeline to ensure you have identified all the steps necessary to take this investigation from the crime scene to the courtroom.

■ ■ ■ ━━━━━━━━━━━━━━━━━━━━━━━━━━━━━━━━━

Sample Case
Critical Questions and Activities

1. Review the case narrative, and construct a timeline.
2. Familiarize yourself with the forms and reports contained within the case file.
3. List the elements of each of the crimes contained in the case file.
4. It is possible that not all physical evidence was collected/processed. Create a list of additional physical evidence you believe should have been collected and what type of scientific testing you would request from the crime lab.
5. Explain the key investigative strategies, and describe how you as the case investigator would address those problem areas in this case file.

CSI Officer Roberts was called to respond to a street address adjacent to a location where fire-fighters were extinguishing a house fire. The reporting officer, Lonnie Downs, had spotted a pool of blood in the street in front of the residence; the residence was on fire, but no victims had been located. The amount of blood in the street indicated a victim should be found suffering from a severe loss of blood. While Officer Downs began canvassing the neighborhood and knocking on doors, CSI Officer Roberts took photographs and created a crime scene diagram. Having just completed bloodstain pattern analysis training last month, Officer Downs knew how to use string to map out the path of the blood droplets and determine where the indicators converge. This might identify whether the victim was standing or sitting as the blood droplets were falling. The measurements indicated that the point of impact was the front bumper of the fire engine. Officer Downs questioned the fire truck engineer, who stated he had not seen anyone around the area when they arrived on the scene in response to the fire call. The entire squad deployed immediately and did not treat any patients. Both a fire supervisor and a police supervisor were summoned to the scene.

Already, several reports must be completed. Which ones have you identified, and who will be completing those reports?

When the fire trucks were ready to clear the scene, the lead fire truck was pulled back to depart. A body was discovered underneath the truck. So now it is a good thing the CSI had already completed his initial investigation by taking photos and mapping the blood spatter.

Apparently the victim was struck by the lead fire truck and had crawled back under the vehicle where he later expired. This is an excellent example of well-trained officers beginning to document actions before it is ever determined that a crime was committed. CSI Roberts had photographs, a sketch, and a stringing diagram of the crime scene. Officer Downs had already begun to complete the preliminary investigation report and had identified all the first responders on the scene. It was, however, impossible to get a statement from anyone else. They were too busy laughing. The victim was an opossum.

Not all investigations are going to lead to criminal prosecutions. This is a good example; however, keep in mind that you may not know the outcome of an event or incident for many years. That doesn't mean that shortcuts are taken or required paperwork is not completed because in your opinion, no crime has occurred. Police officers encounter unexpected outcomes throughout their careers. What appears to be a clear-cut suicide may actually be a well-staged homicide. There is no room for second guessing or taking shortcuts when conducting an investigation and building a case file.

What are the positive outcomes of this scenario? Was due diligence undertaken until a resolution occurred? Sometimes you will discover no crime was committed; however, every investigation demands that protocols and standard operational procedures be completed.

■ ■ ■

And Finally

Many famous instructors and detectives know the key to success is to allow the evidence to speak for itself. An investigator does a thorough and ethical investigation and then hands that case file over to the prosecutorial branch of the American criminal justice system. Criminalist Paul Kirk penned these words back in 1953, and they are still so relevant today:

> However careful a criminal may be to avoid being seen or heard, he will inevitably defeat his purpose unless he can also control his every act and movement so as to prevent mutual contamination with his environment, which may serve to identify him. . . . Wherever he steps, whatever he touches, whatever he leaves—even unconsciously—will serve as silent evidence against him. Not only his fingerprints and his shoeprints, but also his hair, the fibers from this clothes, the glass he breaks, the tool mark he leaves, the paint he scratches, the blood or semen that he deposits or collects—all these and more bear mute witness against him. . . . Physical evidence cannot be wrong; it cannot perjure itself; it cannot be wholly absent. Only in its interpretation can there be error. Only human failure to find, study, and understand it can diminish its value.

Kirk P. (1953), Crime investigation. New York: Interscience.

Discussion Questions

1. List four people outside the law enforcement agency who may review police reports.
2. What are three differences between facts and opinions? Why do you need to be able to provide this explanation?
3. Where are the elements of each specific crime identified? Why is it important to document the elements of a crime in the case file?
4. Why is it necessary to develop a timeline for every investigation?
5. Criminalist Paul Kirk tells us that physical evidence cannot be wrong, but the interpretation of that evidence can leave room for error. Why is that statement important to criminal investigators?

2

Burglary and Kidnapping

OBJECTIVE

Distinguishing among the criminal offenses and establishing timelines and the sequential events yield valuable information that will increase the probability of case closure through efficient and effective investigation. This chapter incorporates the logical thought process throughout various interviews and interrogations, and utilization of these skills yields a positive outcome for the victims and the detective. The case presented in this chapter involves a group of young teens who set out to steal electronics and end up terrorizing an elderly woman.

KEY TERMS

accident reports

actus reus

affidavit

arrest warrants

burglary

confession

crime

crime analysis

follow-up investigation

incident reports

larceny-theft

mens rea

modus operandi

motor vehicle theft

offense reports

preliminary investigation

recanting

robbery

search warrants

solvability factors

supplemental reports

traffic citations

Uniform Crime Report

What You Will Learn

LEARNING OUTCOMES

- Demonstrate knowledge of the difference between burglary and robbery
- Analyze case facts to determine elements for various crimes
- Explain the process of reviewing the preliminary report for solvability factors
- Gain knowledge of the information necessary to obtain a search warrant
- Compare and contrast statements and confessions

CRITICAL THINKING

- Elements of the crime
- Types of physical evidence
- Establishing the timeline
- Why determining the sequential events is critical
- Key investigative strategies

Introduction

This publication contains a series of case studies designed to introduce the various methods of investigation, demonstrate how to create and maintain case files that can be submitted for successful prosecution, and provide insight into recognizing the various elements of crime. Is there a specific definition for crime? Explanations revolve around two central themes: **crime** is an act or omission that is illegal, which results in injury to the public. Penalties can range from minor fines to a lifetime in prison or even a death sentence. Prosecutors also seek answers to other concerns that must be proven in court beyond a reasonable doubt. First, was there a design or purpose to commit a crime—also known as *mens rea* or "guilty mind"? Second, was a prohibited act or *actus reus* committed? Finally, there must be a timely relationship established between the intent and the act. To charge an individual with a criminal offense, the facts developed during the investigation and the physical evidence, statements from victims, witnesses, and other sources must combine to show the alleged perpetrator had the capability and intent and that a crime did occur.

How We Track Crime

There are two major categories in which serious crimes are classified: crimes against property and crimes against persons. What offenses fall into each of these categories? The most serious crimes are those committed against people. The Federal Bureau of Investigation collects crime data using the **Uniform Crime Report** (UCR), which consists of information reported on a monthly basis by more than 16,000 law enforcement agencies in the United States. Part I offenses are the following crime classifications:

- Criminal homicide
- Forcible rape
- Robbery
- Aggravated assault
- Burglary
- Larceny-theft (except motor vehicle theft)
- Motor vehicle theft
- Arson

It is important for students and police officers to be familiar with all the Part I offenses because you must classify the crime properly in order to identify the elements and assure that a criminal offense has occurred. This chapter focuses on a multiple-offense situation—that is, several crimes are committed at one time by a group of people. Every criminal violation must be accurately identified to ensure the prosecution team proceeds correctly with charges and sentence recommendations against specific individuals involved in the crimes.

DEFINITIONS OF PART I OFFENSES

FEDERAL BUREAU OF INVESTIGATION (FBI) UNIFORM CRIME REPORTING HANDBOOK

Criminal Homicide—Murder and Nonnegligent Manslaughter (1a)
The willful (nonnegligent) killing of one human being by another.

Justifiable Homicide
Certain willful killings must be classified as justifiable or excusable. In UCR, justifiable homicide is defined as and limited to the killing of a felon by a peace officer in the line of duty or the killing of a felon, during the commission of a felony, by a private citizen.

Criminal Homicide—Manslaughter by Negligence (1b)
As a general rule, any death caused by the gross negligence of another is classified as criminal homicide—manslaughter by negligence (1b).

Forcible Rape—Rape by Force (2a)
The carnal knowledge of a female forcibly and against her will.

Robbery (3)
The taking or attempting to take anything of value from the care, custody, or control of a person or persons by force or threat of force or violence or by putting the victim in fear.

Assault (4)
An unlawful attack by one person upon another.

Burglary—Breaking or Entering (5)
The unlawful entry of a structure to commit a felony or theft.

Larceny-Theft (6)
The unlawful taking, carrying, leading, or riding away of property from the possession or constructive possession of another.

Motor Vehicle Theft (7)
The theft or attempted theft of a motor vehicle.

Arson (8)
Any willful or malicious burning or attempt to burn, with or without intent to defraud, a dwelling house, public building, motor vehicle or aircraft, personal property of another, and so on.

The full UCR Handbook can be viewed online at www.fbi.gov/about-us/cjis/ucr/additional-ucr-publications/ucr_handbook.pdf.

Crime Statistics

The annual crime statistics are published in a comprehensive analysis, *Crime in the U.S.*, which can be viewed online at www.fbi.gov/stats-services/crimestats. This chapter provides the UCR definition of several offenses. The case file presented includes several criminal offenses. Become familiar with the UCR definitions, and then use this new knowledge to determine what offenses have been committed by the perpetrators in each of the case files.

Case Narrative

Consider the following situation: You are dispatched to a residence where the victim states, "I've been robbed." To you, an officer preparing to conduct a preliminary investigation, the victim's comments convey there was a direct confrontation with a threat of physical violence involved during the commission of the crime. As you check to make sure there are no physically injured victims and then begin asking for a description of the perpetrator, the victim then tells you, "I didn't see anyone. I came home and found my house had been broken into. They took my computer and my jewelry." Do these statements change the type of investigation, the classification of the crime, and the questions you will be asking during your conversation with the victim?

Terminology Used Throughout the Book

This is one of the most prevalent misconceptions among the public. The crime of **robbery** is defined by *Merriam-Webster's Dictionary of Law* as "the unlawful taking away of personal property from a person by violence or by threat of violence that causes fear: larceny from the person or immediate presence of another by violence or threat of violence and with intent to steal" (1996). As you reread the definition, identify the elements of this crime. Compare this definition with the UCR commentary: "Robbery is a vicious type of theft in that it is committed in the presence of the victim" (FBI, 2004). When no theft of property in the presence of the victim and no violence or threat of violence occurs, then no robbery took place. The classification of this criminal offense has now been changed to burglary. The UCR defines **burglary**, or breaking and entering, as the unlawful entry of a structure to commit a felony or theft.

THE DIFFERENCE BETWEEN BURGLARY AND ROBBERY

Burglary and robbery are both felony offenses in most states; however, they are not interchangeable terms. The elements that compose the crimes are very different. Robbery involves the taking of property from a person by another with the intention, knowing, or reckless causing of bodily injury *or* the threat of imminent bodily injury or death. Aggravated robbery involves the use or exhibition of a deadly weapon or places another person in imminent bodily injury or death. Strong-arm robbery involves the use of physical force or the threat of the use of force. Armed robbery involves the use of a deadly weapon and it does not have to be a firearm.

Burglary requires an unlawful entry or remaining on the premises of another without effective consent of the owner for the purpose of committing a felony or theft. Residential burglaries are the most common; however, commercial burglaries present less risk of encountering victims. A burglary can end up as a robbery when victims are encountered. A crime escalates to a residential robbery or home invasion when force is used in dealing with the residents and items are taken from the victims.

The dynamics of this criminal investigation have just been altered dramatically. Now your focus will be on locating any physical evidence left at the scene rather than immediately broadcasting a description of a potentially dangerous individual who just committed a robbery. This is just one example of why the definitions of criminal offenses as well as the elements that compose those crimes are carefully studied and why it is important that you are able to determine the clear distinctions between various offenses as you begin your investigations.

The **preliminary investigation** begins when the first officer arrives on the scene. It consists of rendering aid to the injured, making the initial inquiry to establish whether a criminal offense has occurred, arresting any suspects who may be present, securing the crime scene, and identifying and interviewing witnesses. Every response to a call for service is different, and the responding officer must ensure quality work during every preliminary investigation. Many times the case will be solved during the preliminary work. There is not a need for a follow-up investigation. However, in the case of most burglaries, the investigation moves on to the detective division for further analysis. At this point, the case is examined and ranked according to the potential for bringing about a successful conclusion. **Solvability factors** are issues and circumstances that are evaluated to determine whether or not further resources will be assigned to the case.

SOLVABILITY FACTORS

What are solvability factors? Information and identification leads that are most likely to result in the successful conclusion of the criminal investigation are considered significant factors when determining whether or not to assign additional resources to a case. This information is generated through the preliminary investigation, which is conducted by the first officer to arrive at the scene of a crime. After determining that a criminal offense has occurred, the responding officer will begin to gather information that includes the following:

1. Witness identification and the availability of witnesses
2. The name(s) of the suspect
3. Knowledge regarding the location of the suspect
4. Information about the description of the suspect
5. Validity of the identification of the suspect
6. Information regarding a suspect vehicle and movements of the vehicle
7. Identifiable characteristics, marks, or numbers (traceable) property
8. Significant *modus operandi*
9. Discovery of useful physical evidence
10. Input from responding officers concluding that no one else could have committed the offense
11. Determining if enough information is available and if a reasonable investigation will solve the crime.

Whether or not the criminal offenses rank high or low on the solvability scale, they are still crimes committed against others. Many times, the data containing the circumstances of the crime are recorded and the reports are filed. If there is a low solvability factor, detectives must focus on other offenses. **Follow-up investigation** efforts do not duplicate the steps already completed by the responding officers and are designed to allocate resources to those crimes that have a chance to be solved. The statements of the victims and witnesses will be analyzed to pinpoint commonalities and discrepancies. Suspect statements are also weighed for their value as detectives seek to determine a productive investigative strategy for each case.

Many times investigators will recognize the ***modus operandi*** (method of operation) from reports of the same type of crime being committed in the same manner or circumstances. For example, a string of car burglaries has been reported over the past two weeks. The crimes occur between 2 a.m. and 6 a.m. at car dealerships. The thieves are taking catalytic converters from the underside of the cars and the airbags from the passenger side of the dashboard. At least twice a week, the detectives are responding to calls from area car dealerships. What are the elements of this crime? Are the dealerships being robbed? What seems to be a sound investigative strategy for this series of criminal offenses?

In this type of crime, it is important for law enforcement agencies to coordinate their efforts and information. Investigators should survey possible outlets where the catalytic converters and airbags are being sold illegally, use a mapping system to gain an idea of when and where the victim dealerships are located to determine if a pattern emerges, talk with managers to discuss whether they have disgruntled employees or former employees, and work with patrol supervisors to establish special emphasis patrols of car lots by uniformed and plainclothes personnel. There are various ways to integrate information and share resources in an effort to prevent further crimes from occurring and identifying those guilty of the offenses.

Integrating this information onto a geographic mapping system will result in a more unified effort by establishing factors surrounding the common events—or **crime analysis**. Location, time of day, the day(s) of the week, partial suspect information gleaned from witnesses or victims, and other aspects of the cases can be linked to provide investigative leads. When a crime analyst creates a computer summary of the auto part larcenies, similarities are collated, which may provide a more succinct picture of the offenses.

Using crime analysis information provides law enforcement agencies with a tool that establishes a pattern and can help forecast when and where crimes may be committed. With these types of data, police agencies can plan stakeouts or directed patrols when the pattern indicates the next locations and probable days for the thieves to attempt to steal these valuable car parts. There are various ways to integrate information and share resources in an effort to prevent further crimes from occurring and identifying those guilty of the offenses. Crime analysis is not restricted to large agencies. Using this investigative strategy can benefit even the smallest law enforcement agencies, and it can be utilized for any type of criminal offense.

This type of offense would be classified by the UCR as **larceny-theft**, which is the unlawful taking, carrying, leading, or riding away of property from the possession or constructive possession of another. **Motor vehicle theft** is the theft or attempted theft of a motor vehicle—one that is self-propelled and runs on land surface and not on rails. Construction equipment, boats, airplanes, and farm equipment are excluded from this category.

With every investigation there is the paperwork that builds the foundation of the case file. The responding officer will file a report—whether it is an incident, offense, accident, or other type of report varies among jurisdictions and, of course, depends on the situation. For example, **accident reports** are generally used by insurance adjusters to determine who is at fault and whether or not civil actions need to be pursued. The reports document details of motor vehicle crashes and establish the facts that led to the incident. **Traffic citations** are issued by police officers who observe traffic infractions that are violations and create hazardous conditions for motorists or pedestrians. Generally traffic citations are adjudicated through municipal courts and can result in fines and judicial orders for the offenders to attend a driving school. There are criminal charges that can arise from a motor vehicle crash, including impaired driving, and there can be stolen vehicles, police pursuits, and hostage situations—but each of these events would be accompanied by additional reports.

Incident reports are often used to document events when no further investigation is warranted: there may not have been any criminal intent by the actions that occurred, or property may have been found and reported to the police. **Offense reports** are filed for crimes, even where there is no physical evidence or witnesses. For example, if a construction company reports twelve orange barrels are missing from a site with no witnesses and no real time frame for investigation, an incident report would be filed to document the loss. However, if the construction area is under video surveillance and a review of the recording shows the barrels being taken by perpetrators, an offense report would be completed to document the theft of the property.

Once an investigation is under way, there are plenty of additional forms to complete. Detectives who are conducting follow-up investigations will take statements from witnesses, victims, and suspects. Reports documenting activity on the case (visiting locations, following up on leads, corroborating information) as well as narratives, transcripts of interviews, time-lines, and case progress reports consume valuable time but provide immense value to the overall investigation. Case files are built and maintained so that all activities are chronicled. It may be months or even years before a case is solved, and the case file must be adequately maintained so that the facts can be accurately presented in the courtroom. It is just as important to document inaccurate information or leads that turn out to be useless. These actions all reflect an investment of time and valuable resources. If another investigator reviews a case file, it should clearly identify all actions taken to eliminate duplication of effort. **Supplemental reports** document these additional activities in the case file.

Warrants cannot be issued until an **affidavit**, which is a sworn statement containing all the facts necessary to establish probable cause, has been presented to a judicial authority. The same is true whether the investigator is seeking an **arrest warrant** or a **search warrant**; a judge or magistrate must sign the affidavit, and then it becomes a court order to any lawful police officer in the jurisdiction. These processes require substantial paperwork to maintain the credibility of the investigation, assure that any physical evidence located during the execution of a search warrant is admissible, and ensure that a suspect was legally arrested.

Many types of statements are gathered during the course of an investigation. Victims, witnesses, and people who may have general knowledge of the conditions surrounding an incident (such as medical professionals or subject matter experts) all become contributors to the case file. For the detective, this is how a case is built, how the facts are determined, and how an investigative strategy is developed. Many new avenues of potential information can be revealed through the use of effective interview techniques. Skilled investigators can quickly determine the value of information provided by witnesses and redirect the focus of the questions when the responses do not yield useful answers.

For every interview and interrogation, a Miranda rights waiver must be read and signed, statements written, and accurate records maintained so that no allegations of threats or coercion can be leveled against the investigators. Statements must be given voluntarily. If a suspect chooses to invoke the right to remain silent, the detective must honor that request and terminate the interview. With video or audio recordings of interviews becoming more prevalent in this age of technology innovation, it is much easier to demonstrate the conditions during the interview. Transcripts of these conversations are also placed in the case file and can play a major role in the detection of discrepancies among witnesses, victims, and alleged perpetrators.

MIRANDA RIGHTS AND WAIVER

1. You have the right to remain silent.
2. Anything you say can and will be used against you in a court of law.
3. You have the right to an attorney and to have that attorney present during questioning.
4. If you cannot afford an attorney, one will be appointed for you.
5. Do you understand each of these rights?
6. Understanding each of these rights, do you wish to speak to me without a lawyer being present?

When a suspect provides a confession, additional statements and documentation must accompany that effort. The **confession** is a disclosure of one's actions and may be given orally or in writing. The suspect should be asked to provide a written statement in addition to the audio/video recording. For agencies where audio/video recording equipment is not available, the handwritten statement becomes invaluable, even though suspects can later withdraw or repudiate a former statement, which is known as **recanting**. It is important to remember that suspects can provide information in their confessions that implicate others; and investigators must focus on obtaining complete information including last names, dates, locations, and other data to substantiate the claims made during a confession.

Prosecutors rely heavily on the accuracy and totality of the documentation in the case files when considering which charges to pursue against specific defendants, so intense scrutiny is focused on the accuracy of the statements contained in the files. Remember that when people provide statements, they may not always be truthful; in some instances they may have volunteered to come in and give you a statement in an attempt to divert investigation from themselves and on to others.

SAMPLE CRIMINAL CODES

SAMPLE CRIMINAL CODE FOR BURGLARY

A. A person is guilty of burglary in the second degree if the person enters a dwelling without consent and with intent to commit a crime therein.

B. A person is guilty of burglary in the second degree if the person enters a building without consent and with intent to commit a crime therein, and either:

1. When, in effecting entry or while in the building or in immediate flight there from, he or another participant in the crime:
   a. Is armed with a deadly weapon or explosive; or
   b. Causes physical injury to any person who is not a participant in the crime; or
   c. Uses or threatens the use of a dangerous instrument; or
   d. Displays what is or appears to be a knife, pistol, revolver, rifle, shotgun, machine gun, or other firearm; or
2. The burglary is committed by a person with a prior record of two or more convictions for burglary or housebreaking or a combination of both; or
3. The entering or remaining occurs in the nighttime.

C.

1. Burglary in the second degree pursuant to subsection (A) is a felony punishable by imprisonment for not more than ten years.
2. Burglary in the second degree pursuant to subsection (B) is a felony punishable by imprisonment for not more than fifteen years, provided that no person convicted of burglary in the second degree pursuant to subsection (B) shall be eligible for parole except upon service of not less than one third of the term of the sentence.

SAMPLE CODE FOR POSSESSION OF BURGLARY TOOLS

Making, mending or possessing tools or other implements capable of being used in a crime.

It is unlawful for a person to make or mend, cause to be made or mended, or have in his possession any engine, machine, tool, false key, picklock, bit, nippers, nitroglycerine, dynamite cap, coil or fuse, steel wedge, drill, tap-pin, or other implement or thing adapted, designed, or commonly used for the commission of burglary, larceny, safecracking, or other crime, under circumstances evincing an intent to use, employ, or allow the same to be used or employed in the commission of a crime, or knowing that the same are intended to be so used.

A person who violates the provisions of this section is guilty of a felony and, upon conviction, must be fined in the discretion of the court or imprisoned for not more than five years, or both.

SAMPLE CODE FOR KIDNAPPING

Whoever shall unlawfully seize, confine, inveigle, decoy, kidnap, abduct or carry away any other person by any means whatsoever without authority of law, except when a minor is seized or taken by his parent, is guilty of a felony and, upon conviction, must be imprisoned for a period not to exceed thirty years unless sentenced for murder as provided in Section 16-3-20.

Witnesses may not remember details—the events to which they were subjected may have been traumatic, emotional, or too immense for them to accurately recount in an initial statement. Sometimes people are interviewed numerous times, and each interview will have the ancillary paperwork to substantiate the discussion. It is extremely useful for the detective to establish a strong working relationship with the prosecutor's office so that complicated cases can be discussed and reviewed while the investigation is continuing. The insight of the prosecutor charged with overseeing the case can be very beneficial in the overall development of the investigative strategy. Do not wait until the investigation is complete to seek the advice of the prosecutor's office.

Crime scene investigation adds a plethora of documentation, photographs and sketches, chain-of-custody forms, logs, video recordings, fingerprint cards, and final reports from crime lab analyses of physical evidence. Each facet of the investigation relies on the coordination of activities and paperwork in order to sustain the integrity of all physical evidence involved in the investigation.

The ability to construct complete case files matures over time. By developing a chronological timeline as you read the documents of a new investigation, you will be creating a picture of what happened, when, where, and who was involved; a review of the case progress thus far may even reveal an answer as to why this crime occurred.

■ ■ ■ ━━━━━━━━━━━━━━━━━━━━━━━━━━━━━━━━

Case File: Terrorizing an Elderly Woman

Case File Elements

- Incident/offense report
- Supplemental reports
- Victim/witness statements
- Miranda warnings
- Suspect statements
- Follow-up
- Additional keys to solving the investigation
- Photo lineups
- Search warrants and returns
- Property/evidence–chain-of-custody forms
- Crime scene logs

Critical Questions and Activities

As you move into the case file, reflect on the various aspects of paperwork that lead to substantiation of the facts. Determine how the case begins and builds on each new fact that is uncovered throughout the investigation. Remember to identify the elements of the crimes as you study the various forms and reports that compose this case. It is possible you may identify additional steps that could have positively affected the progress of this investigation. Look for any discrepancies among statements, paperwork, and the ultimate outcome of the investigation. What types of physical evidence did you note? Was it accurately identified and documented?

You are now assuming the role of the defense attorney. Review the case as if you are representing one of the defendants. Did you detect any deficiencies that might result in a different outcome for your client? What steps were taken that led to the resolution of this investigation? What investigative strategies did the detective use?

Call to the Scene

12:49 p.m.—Friday, 17 December 2010

Detective Sergeant Meador was in the office talking to a patrol officer about what would be a good gift to buy his son for Christmas. The two were joking about past presents and comparing gifts their children had made for them in school when Detective Meador's cell phone began to ring.

"Detective Meador?" a voice asked through the line. "It's Sergeant Johnson from patrol. I'm calling to let you know about a home invasion and possibly a kidnapping or maybe a wrongful imprisonment involving an elderly lady."

"Good afternoon to you too, Sergeant," Meador replied wryly as he got out his notebook. "What's the situation?"

"One of my officers is at a scene where an elderly woman was forced into her bedroom and her home robbed. She's pretty shaken up about the whole thing."

"Was she harmed during the break-in?" Meador asked, scribbling notes on the pad of paper.

"No, although the Emergency Service Technicians (EMTs) are on the scene because she is very shaken up. The address is 401 Thirteenth Street. Your victim's name is Marian Fletcher."

"On my way," the detective replied.

Residence of Marian Fletcher

Detective Meador arrived at the scene at 1:15 p.m. and saw the EMS squad talking to a visibly upset elderly woman. After a brief conversation with the responding officer, Meador headed over to the crying woman and nodded to the EMS crew as they backed away to allow him to conduct his initial interview.

"Good afternoon, ma'am. My name is Detective Sergeant Meador. I am sorry you had to experience that ordeal; and I promise to do all that I can to find those responsible. Do you think you could answer a few questions?"

"S-s-sure," she stammered, visibly shaking, "I'll try." She stated that it all happened so fast. As she began to tell her story, it became apparent that she was too emotional to give a full accounting of the events, but Detective Meador decided to attempt to gain some minor but useful details and would save the full narrative for a time when she was more composed.

"Did you get a good look at who did this to you?" he asked.

"Only one of them. Before he pushed me back I saw his face. He was a regular looking fellow to me."

"One of them? There were multiple people?" the detective asked.

"Y-y-yes. I didn't see the other two boys' faces, but one of them had a jacket like my grandson, James Jones; but he goes by J.J."

"So the people who did this were all male?" Meador asked. She nodded and dabbed newly forming tears from her eyes.

When Detective Meador asked her if she could describe the jacket, she said that if it was like her grandson's, it would have to be a purple letter jacket from East Ashley High School where J.J. attended school.

Mrs. Fletcher began to cry again, and Detective Meador decided it was time to wrap it up until she had regained her composure. "One last question for now," he said, "How old do you think the people who did this to you are?"

She said, "They were in their teens, no older than my grandson who is 18."

The detective handed her his business card and told her to call if she thought of anything else that might be helpful. He advised her that he would contact her later for more information, and she thanked him between sobs. Mrs. Fletcher was transported to the hospital by the EMS squad at 1:40 p.m.

Detective Sergeant Meador's Statement
Initial Summary of Events on Scene

I met with first responding officer Amanda Barrett upon arriving at the scene at 1:15 p.m. She explained that she arrived at approximately 12:35 p.m. after receiving a call about a home invasion. Marian Fletcher, the victim, was "hysterical" when she arrived. Mrs. Fletcher is a resident of the home and was in her bedroom when the burglars entered. Mrs. Fletcher is a white female, approximately 75 years old. Officer Barrett called for EMS at the request of Mrs. Fletcher, who was feeling weak and complained of chest pain. The officer also requested a CSI to process the scene. While waiting for EMS to arrive, Officer Barrett tried to calm Mrs. Fletcher down and obtain some basic information about the alleged crime.

A second responding officer, Julie McCoy, arrived on the scene at 12:45 p.m. and immediately began to search the house for possible suspects. Upon finding the home empty, she began to tape off the area and tried to locate potential witnesses outside. EMS arrived at 12:47 p.m. and entered the residence only as far as the foyer. Officer Barrett quickly asked them to please take Mrs. Fletcher outside to the ambulance so the officers could begin to secure the scene. One of the EMTs shared with me that they would be transporting Mrs. Fletcher to Runnymead Hospital for further evaluation.

The officers told me they found a muddy shoeprint on the back porch.

FIGURE 2-1 Screen porch on rear of house where entry was made.

They said it appeared that the back door was pried open.

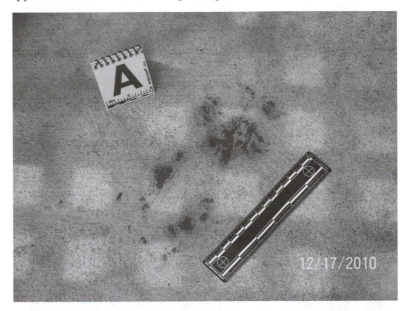

FIGURE 2-2 Muddy shoeprint on back porch at entry point.

FIGURE 2-3 An overall view of the living room area from the dining room.

The only room that seemed to be in disarray was the living room. It was littered with wrapping paper and Christmas gifts.

They explained that Mrs. Fletcher was not able to provide much information because she was in her room when she heard the burglars. When she opened the door and called out, someone shoved her backward and quickly closed the door.

FIGURE 2-4 View of front door on left and the doorway to Marian Fletcher's bedroom on right.

FIGURE 2-5 Door from living room to victim's bedroom.

She stated she was unable to open the door while they were in the home. The responding officers offered to walk me through the home and share what they viewed as potential evidence. Just about that time, CSI Perry arrived to begin his processing of the scene. It was approximately 1:30 p.m.

Officer's Walkthrough of the Scene

The four of us left the disheveled living room to examine the rest of the home. Officer Barrett led me through the dining room into the kitchen to view what appeared to be the point of entry, the muddy print and the back door. The officers stated they would be outside writing their reports if I needed anything. We established the front door area to be our point of entry to avoid contaminating the crime scene.

CSI Perry's Statement

Crime Scene Inspection

I arrived at 401 Thirteenth Street, Misola, Alabama, at 1:30 p.m. on Friday, December 17, 2010. I immediately got out my camera and began photographing the scene. I donned a primary and secondary set of gloves and began at the back door where it is obvious that the perpetrators gained entrance. I noticed there was some minor damage to the doorjamb. It appeared to have been made by a small tool, such as a screwdriver or crowbar. I photographed the damage and asked Officer McCoy if she saw any tools in the home lying in a conspicuous place. She told me no, so I asked her to search the perimeter of the home for any tools. At the back door I noticed a set of shoeprint impressions on the patio with a Nike logo visible.

Knowing the importance of transient evidence, I took several pictures of the shoeprint and immediately lifted the impression using a gel lifter to preserve the shoeprint. I continued into the home on my hands and knees with a flashlight looking for more shoeprints. However, it appeared that the trail stopped at the patio and the mat at the back door appeared to have been used to wipe off the muddy shoes. Another possibility is that the perpetrators may have removed their shoes at this point. I took a scraping from the mat and sealed it in an evidence container. The kitchen appeared to be untouched. There was one plate in the sink, a possible source for DNA. I noted it and continued my walkthrough. There were two entrances into the living area. It is not clear which entrance the perpetrators went through to get into the living room. I chose to enter the area through the dining room. I examined the dining room table, using the alternate light source (ALS) and noticed there were a few fingerprints on the tabletop. I noted the prints and returned to process them once the crime scene sketch and photographs were completed.

I entered the living room and found Christmas wrapping paper scattered everywhere. There were ripped-open boxes and clothing strewn about also. It appeared that all of the gifts were opened, but some contents were obviously missing. I knew from Mrs. Fletcher's statement to Officer Barrett that the burglars did not enter the back three rooms because she was locked in that part of the house. I continued down the hallway and into the back bedroom. The bedroom door was shut. When I opened it everything appeared to be in perfect order. The bed was made and the room looked very clean with no dust on the dressers.

On the way to my vehicle to get more supplies, I encountered Mr. Robert Jones, the homeowner. He was anxious to go into the home and do his own searching, but I told him the area must be processed and evidence collected before he could gain access. He reluctantly agreed to take a quick glance around to help me determine what might be out of place.

We started again at the back door. He immediately noticed the muddy shoeprint and stated it was not there in the morning when he let the cat out. He looked at the back door and was visibly upset at the damage. He looked around the kitchen and stated that everything was like he left it, except for the plate in the sink, which he stated was probably his mother-in-law's, Marian Fletcher. We went through the dining room and entered the living room and Mr. Jones gasped. He knew immediately what gifts were missing—they are all for James, his son. A Sony PlayStation 3, a Nintendo Wii, and a Nintendo DSi XL—all video gaming devices—were missing. He stated that they all had the same kind of wrapping paper. This, he said, was a trick he uses so that everyone knows which gifts are theirs. Mr. Jones did not touch anything. He advised he did have all the receipts for the gaming devices and that he would provide those to Detective Meador because they would have the serial numbers needed to identify the property should it be located.

I asked him about the bedroom, and we walked to the back of the house. He asked if the door was closed to the back bedroom. I told me it was. He told me they do that to keep the cat out of the room.

Officer McCoy came into the home and informed me that although she did not find any tools, they did find a cigarette butt in the backyard near the patio.

FIGURE 2-6 Cigarette butt found outside the back porch area.

FIGURE 2-7 Close-up of cigarette butt with evidence marker.

Mr. Jones stated that none of the residents or usual visitors are smokers. Officer McCoy showed me where the cigarette butt was located, outside the door beside the patio. I placed a protective covering over the cigarette butt and returned inside to continue my analysis of the crime scene.

James Jones (J.J.) pulled into the driveway and spoke to his father briefly. It was approximately 1:55 p.m. Officer Barrett talked with him and advised him that he could not enter the house until the CSI had finished processing the scene. J.J. stated that he did not know who might have broken into the house. Both father and son were fingerprinted for elimination purposes at 2:10 p.m., and they left together to go to the hospital to see Mrs. Fletcher. I reentered the home to finish documenting, collecting, and preserving of the physical evidence. I lifted several latent fingerprints from the tabletop in the dining room and from the door of the bedroom where Mrs. Fletcher was imprisoned.

FIGURE 2-8 Victim's door processed for latent fingerprints.

FIGURE 2-9 Multiple fingerprints now visible from application of fingerprint powder.

FIGURE 2-10 Photo shows ridge detail in latent fingerprints on victim's door.

On the outside of the house, there was a lot of damage on the wooden doorjamb done with the sharp tool the perpetrators used to gain entrance to the house.

FIGURE 2-11 Tool mark at the entry point.

I photographed the area and then used a silicone casting agent to make copies of the impressions left in the wood by the tool. I collected one cigarette butt lying in the grass beside the concrete patio near the entrance to the house. I also collected the plate from the sink for processing as well. Detective Meador had requested that I collect a soil sample from the doormat, which I gathered in a paper box.

A full list of all evidence was completed and added to the case file. I cleared the scene at 4 p.m. The residence was secured and turned over to Detective Meador.

Neighborhood Interviews—Detective Sergeant Meador

Detective Sergeant Meador released Officers McCoy and Barrett from the scene at approximately 2:15 p.m. CSI Perry secured the scene and was processing inside the house. The detective decided that he would canvass the neighborhood for witnesses while he waited for Perry to finish.

The residence was on a corner with a cul-de-sac behind it. There were five homes in the cul-de-sac. The neighborhood is a middle- to upper-middle-class area and appeared to consist of largely two-income families, as no one had attempted to approach the scene at the sight of police cars and an ambulance nearby. The detective decided to try each surrounding house to see if anyone was home.

Detective Meador tried the home directly behind the scene, 786 Holiday Road, to no avail. The house next door, 788 Holiday Road, was inhabited. As Detective Meador knocked on the door, a woman answered.

"Good afternoon, ma'am," Meador said, "My name is Detective Meador and I was hoping that I could ask you a few questions about an incident that occurred next door."

The woman introduced herself as Ms. Murphy and invited the detective in. As they sat in the kitchen sipping coffee that she had insisted upon serving, Detective Meador learned that yes, Ms. Murphy was home at the time of the incident.

"I saw three boys in their backyard around noon," Ms. Murphy said, "But I didn't think anything of it because it looked like one of the boys was J.J. in his purple letter jacket." When pressed, though, Ms. Murphy could not say for certain that the boy she had seen was definitely James Jones. "Like I said, I just didn't think too much of it, so I didn't pay that close of attention. I'm sorry, Officer."

"Did you hear anything unusual during this time period? Loud noises? People yelling? Things breaking or crashing perhaps?" Detective Meador asked.

"No, no, not that I can recall. My goodness, what has happened?"

"When you saw the three boys in the backyard," Meador began, "you said it was about noon. How certain are you about that time frame?"

"Absolutely positive," she replied, "Bob Barker reruns start every day at noon on the Game Show Channel, and I haven't gone a day without seeing Bob in almost twenty years!" She said with a chuckle. "Do tell me what has happened!"

"Marian Fletcher's house was broken into today, and some of the Christmas gifts were taken. I'm trying to determine who might be responsible for those crimes. Thank you, ma'am, for your assistance. Here's my card. If you can think of anything else, please give me a call."

"Absolutely, Officer, and if any of your boys out there would like some coffee or tea, let them know they are welcome here. Thanks to all of you for the good work you do."

"Thank you, ma'am. I'll be sure to pass the word along," Meador said with a smile as he pulled the front door closed behind him.

Meador continued canvassing the area. The next two homes, 790 and 792 Holiday, were vacant also; however, a Mr. Jack answered the door at 794 Holiday.

"Yeah, I was home around noon. Make my lunch while watching the *Noonday Show* every day." When plied with questions about the incident, Mr. Jack reported that he did hear a loud noise in the Jones's backyard, but when he looked outside and saw three boys at the back door. He went back inside.

"It's not unusual for the neighbor boy to come home for lunch with his friends," Mr. Jack said.

"Are you certain one of the boys you saw was James Jones, or J.J.?" Meador asked.

"Certain? Nah, I didn't look that closely. I just assumed. I mean, who else could it be?" Mr. Jack paused and looked thoughtful for a moment, "Well, except burglars, I guess. Sorry, Detective." Detective Meador thanked the man and continued his canvass.

The last home in the cul-de-sac at 796 Holiday Road was vacant as well. Detective Meador then headed to the home next to the Jones's at 403 Thirteenth Street and found no one home. At 405 Thirteenth Street, a Mr. Karl Neal answered the door. Detective Meador introduced himself and apprised Mr. Neal of the situation. Mr. Neal informed the detective that he worked third shift (11 p.m. until 7 a.m.) at the Robert Bosch plant.

"I was sleeping until around noon when I got woke up by some kind of home repairs, it sounded like hammering or something. I looked out my bedroom window but saw nothing special." Mr. Neal said that his wife was also home at the time of the incident but was gone to pick up the kids from school. Detective Meador gave Mr. Neal his business card and told him to contact him if he or his wife had further information.

The detective headed over to the final house in the area at 402 Thirteenth Street, across from the crime scene. A retired naval officer named Jayson Edwards answered the door.

"My family and I were getting ready to take a trip up to Pennsylvania. I was loading the RV around noon."

"Did you see or hear anything unusual?" Meador asked.

"No, no sorry, sir. I was too involved in my work. I'll tell you what though," Mr. Edwards said, "I'm pretty active in the Neighborhood Crime Watch Committee. I'll check around with anyone else on the committee to see if anyone knows anything. Do you have a way I can get in touch with you if I find out anything?" Detective Meador gave him his card. "I'll let you know if I hear about anything. And hey, when this is all said and done, do you think you could give us the full score on this thing so that we can be more prepared in the future?"

"Sure thing," Detective Meador said, thanking Mr. Edwards as he left.

Detective Meador's Statement, continued
Monday, 20 December 2010

At 9 a.m. I called the victim, Mrs. Marian Fletcher, to see if I could visit with her for a follow-up interview. She agreed, and I arrived at the home at 9:30 a.m. Mrs. Fletcher is a 76-year-old white female and resides in the home with her son and grandson. She was still visibly shaken and emotional. I received permission from Mrs. Fletcher to record our interview after I explained it would be easier to listen to her and take notes later. I asked her to tell the whole story in her own words. (A copy of the transcript of this interview has been placed in the case file.) Mrs. Fletcher stated she was in her bedroom at around 12 p.m., at which time she heard a noise at the back door. She described the noise as sounding like a hammer hitting wood. It startled her, so she looked out her bedroom door. Mrs. Fletcher saw three white teenage boys entering the house through the back door. She stated the young men appeared startled when they saw her. Immediately, the tallest young man grabbed her by the shoulders, pushed her back into the bedroom, and pulled the door shut. Mrs. Fletcher said she heard a lot of noise in the living room. She stated she was afraid to come out of the bedroom because one of the boys had what looked like a screwdriver in his hand.

Mrs. Fletcher told me she waited approximately 15 minutes and then looked out the bedroom door. She stated that there had been no noise for approximately 10 minutes. She observed a very messy living room. There was Christmas wrapping paper scattered on the living room floor. She looked at the clock to see what time it was and remembered that it was 12:18 p.m. She stated she was concerned because those boys made a big mess in the 5 minutes they were in the house.

I asked her if she could possibly identify any of the boys. She was sure, if she was given a photo lineup, she could pick out the one who pushed her. She stated that he was approximately 5'10", just like her grandson. He had short, dirty blond hair and a mild case of acne. She further stated that all three boys were white, but that was really all she remembered about the other boys. I then finger-printed her so that I would have her prints on file for elimination purposes and told her that if she remembered anything else to please call me.

I headed back to my office with the recorded interview and began working on my options to solve this case. From the interview, I decided to go to East Ashley High School and speak to the school resource officer (SRO). I arrived at 1 p.m. in hopes of discovering more information about the jacket that one of the suspects was wearing. Surprisingly, the staff was excited about helping me and told me they would give me whatever information was needed. They felt like the person responsible for committing this crime against an elderly person needed to be apprehended. I asked the secretary, Jasmine Sowell, for the roster of students that either missed school or were present for classes before lunch but didn't show up to any classes after lunch on Friday. Ms. Sowell was able to provide a printout of students who met those criteria.

She stated that the person we were looking for was Raymond Lewis. I asked her why she thought Mr. Lewis was involved, and she stated he had been suspended from school for various behavioral offenses. His last suspension was the result of getting into a fistfight at school. Having a high level of aggression put him at the top of my suspect list. The list had seven students on it: Raymond Lewis (senior), Crystal Miller (sophomore), Cathy Washington (junior), Mark Lockhart (senior), Derrick Clark (senior), Joe Smith (senior), and Ron Johnson (junior). The two females were eliminated immediately because the attackers had been all males. When asked whether the remaining names on the list had an excuse or reason to be out of school, Ms. Sowell said that Mr. Lockhart brought in a doctor's excuse for Friday; he had a stomach virus. I asked about the remaining three boys' history at school. She told me they all were on the honor roll and never had been in any disciplinary trouble. They all played on a sports team at some point in school. I asked for the addresses of the suspects, but she stated that it was school policy to not give out that type of information without a warrant. I left the high school at 1:45 p.m..

Once I returned to my office, I ran the list of names through the Alabama Department of Motor Vehicle records and retrieved the addresses of the students on the list given to me by Ms. Sowell at East Ashley High School. Mr. Lewis's address was conveniently the closest one to the station. I decided to pay him a visit once school was out for the day. Of the four possible suspects he fit the profile of a person that would be involved in a home invasion.

4:14 p.m.—Monday, 20 December 2010: Residence of Raymond Lewis

Detective Meador arrived at the home of Raymond Lewis in time for school to have let out. The home was located in a middle-income suburban neighborhood. It was a two-story brick house, and the yard looked well maintained.

The detective knocked on the door and a 6' tall young man with brownish blond hair, presumably Raymond Lewis, answered.

"Can I help you?" the boy asked.

"Raymond, I take it?" Meador began, "My name is Detective Meador."

"What can we do for you?" a gruff, older-sounding voice asked. An older man joined Raymond at the door.

"Seymour Lewis, I presume?" Meador asked. "Raymond's father?"

"Yeah, what about it?" the older man replied harshly. Sensing they were none-too-friendly toward his intrusion, Meador decided to take a different tactic to the interview by not mentioning the robbery.

"Sir," Meador said, addressing the father, "your son didn't go to school Friday, and I'm checking to see why he missed school that day."

"It was my girlfriend's birthday," Raymond blurted out. "We spent the whole day together. She's a freshman at Hemming University, so I drove up to Jackson to surprise her."

"Do you have any proof that's where you were?" Meador asked.

"Now wait a minute…," the father began.

"No, Dad, it's cool. Be right back." Raymond went back into the house and returned a few moments later with a purple parking garage ticket that read "Hemming University Central Parking." The pass was stamped with the words "free 12-17-2010. 9 a.m.–5 p.m."

Meador pondered. The university was almost an hour away, but this ticket alone only proved he was at the university that day, not that he wasn't also at the Fletcher residence. "What'd you have for lunch while you were up there?" Meador asked, "Take her out to a nice meal for her birthday?"

"Yeah," Raymond replied, "Went to one of those Japanese steakhouses where they cook the food right in front of you. Here, take a look."

Raymond pulled out a smart phone with a video recorder and showed the detective a video of the staff of a Japanese hibachi restaurant singing "Happy Birthday" to a young lady. The video turned to show Raymond holding the camera facing himself singing along with the group. Meador noted the timestamp on the video as 1:28 p.m.

"Are we done here?" the father asked in an impatient voice.

"Yeah, yeah, we're done. Thank you both for your time."

The door slammed in Meador's face before he could finish his sentence.

Detective Meador's Statement, continued
Tuesday, 21 December 2010

At approximately 11 a.m. I returned to East Ashley High School in response to a call I had received from John Marques, the tool shop instructor at the school. Mr. Marques informed me he had read the police blotter in the *East Ashley Journal Scene* concerning a breaking and entering complaint from a residence that is in close proximity to the high school.

Mr. Marques said once he read about the crime he decided to do an inventory of his tool crib to ascertain if anything was missing or out of place. Mr. Marques stated that a large, Kobalt brand flat-head screwdriver was missing from the tool crib.

I asked if the screwdriver was checked out, perhaps, from the tool crib, but he stated he had taken full inventory that morning and the tool was in place. A microscopic comparison to determine consistency or inconsistency could be completed if the screwdriver could be located. CSI Perry had collected a silicone impression of the tool mark on the door and had taken several photographs of the damage that had been done to the doorjamb.

Before I left the school I stopped by the school resource officer's (SRO) office. I was given four yearbooks so that I could create photo lineups for Mrs. Fletcher to view. When I returned to the office, I began immediately putting together three different lineups, one containing each suspect. Mrs. Fletcher was contacted and agreed to view the lineups the next day.

Wednesday, 22 December 2010

At 9 a.m. I arrived at the Jones's house to meet with Marian Fletcher. I explained to her the rules of the photo lineup. I asked her if she was nervous. She did tell me she felt pressure to pick out the boy that pushed her. I told her not to let her anxiety affect her decision. We sat at her kitchen table and I displayed the first set of pictures, with Ron Johnson's picture included. She stared for about a minute and told me, sounding very upset, that she did not recognize any of them with certainty. The next group had Derrick Clark's picture included. She looked and stated none of them looked familiar either. I brought out the final group of photos, this one contained Joe Smith's photo. Mrs. Fletcher almost immediately recognized Joe Smith, exclaiming "It's him!" I asked her to please make sure that he was indeed the man who pushed her into the room and pulled the door closed. She noted the hair was the same and so was the complexion. I flipped the lineup photo over and had her sign it, indicating that she positively identified Joe Smith. I shared his name with her to see if the name sounded familiar. It did not, but she stated she would be sure to have her son call me later to try to establish a relationship or even a motive.

At 9:45 a.m. I headed back to my office to secure a search warrant. I had obtained the serial numbers for each of the three gaming devices from sales receipts provided by Mr. Jones. The following items were listed on the search warrant affidavit: one Nintendo DSi XL, one Nintendo Wii, and one Sony PlayStation 3 with serial numbers included, plus a pair of Nike tennis shoes. I prepared my affidavit and headed to the courthouse next door to secure the warrants.

Affidavit and Search Warrant

State Judge Brian Fielding reviewed the application for a search warrant. He signed it and approved the search warrant, which provided my agency with a legal order to search both the residence and the person of Joe Smith, located at 707 Richter Drive, Misola, Alabama.

STATE OF ALABAMA
COUNTY OF JASPER

APPLICATION FOR SEARCH WARRANT

Applicant: Det. J. Meador   Agency: Misola Police Department
Badge: 1488   Date of Application: Dec. 22, 2010
Date of Offense: 17 Dec. 2010   Case No. 20101217453301
Location of Premises to be searched: 707 Richter Drive, Misola, AL 64000

Affiant Statement:

The Affiant, Det. James Meador has been employed by the Misola Police Department as a police officer for 14 years. I have served as a patrol officer (8 years) and currently work as a Detective Sergeant in the Investigative Section. During my career I have investigated approximately 743 property crimes involving burglary; and have completed more than 250 hours of specialized training on property crime investigation.

This case involves a home invasion which began with the breaking and entering into 401 Thirteenth Street, Misola, AL, 64000, the home of Robert Jones at approximately 12:00 p.m. It further involves the theft of several pieces of property, including three electronic video games (DSIXL, a Wii, and a Sony Playstation 3) and subsequent kidnapping, though temporary, of Ms. Marian Fletcher. Ms. Fletcher is also a resident of 401 Thirteenth Street, Misola, AL, 64000. The victim reported three young white males were involved in the crimes.

The home did yield some trace evidence, including a shoe print, a cigarette butt, latent fingerprints, and soil samples. This evidence is currently being analyzed by the Misola Police Department Criminalistics Unit, and the State Law Enforcement Division's Crime Laboratory.

The home is situated behind East Ashley High School and the victim identified the suspects as teenagers. The investigation is focusing on the possibility the perpetrators attend East Ashley High School. I obtained a list of students reported absent from school on the day the crimes were committed and compiled photo lineups from the yearbooks. Marian Fletcher identified one of the perpetrators as Joseph Smith – the subject who pushed her into the bedroom and locked her in the room preventing her from fleeing the scene of the criminal activity.

Joseph Smith resides at 707 Richter Drive, Misola, AL, 64000 with his mother, Patricia Smith. This address was verified through the Alabama State Driver's License Bureau. This Search Warrant is to search the premises to locate and recover the items taken from 401 Thirteenth Street, Misola, AL.

_____
Affiant's Signature

FIGURE 2-12 Affidavit for search warrant.

STATE OF ALABAMA   )

)   **SEARCH WARRANT**

COUNTY OF JASPER   )   _____803959_____

TO THE SHERIFF OR BONDED LAW ENFORCEMENT OFFICE OF THIS STATE OR COUNTY OR THE <u>MUNICIPALITY OF MISSOULA:</u>

It appearing from the attached affidavit that there are reasonable grounds to believe that certain property subject to seizure under provisions of Title 15 § 5-5 (1975) of the Code of Alabama, as amended, is located on the following Premises:

**DESCRIPTION OF PREMISES (PERSON OR THING)
TO BE SEARCHED**

<u>Dwelling: 707 Richter Drive
Missoula, Alabama 64000</u>

Now, therefore, you are hereby authorized to search the subject premises for the property listed below and to seize such property if found:

DESCRIPTION OF PROPERTY

Item #1	DSIXL
Item #2	Wii
Item #3	PS3

This Search Warrant shall not be valid for more than ten days from the date of issuance.

A written inventory of all property seized pursuant to this Search Warrant to

<u>Missoula Police Department Property Control & Disposition Officer in Charge</u>

Within ten days from the date of this warrant, such inventory to be signed by the officer executing this warrant, and a copy of such inventory shall be furnished to the person whose premises are searched if demand for such copy is made.

A copy of this Search Warrant shall be delivered to the person in charge of the premises searched at the time of such search if practicable, and, if not, to such person as soon thereafter as is practicable; in the event the identity of the person in charge is not known or if such person cannot be found after reasonable diligence in attempting to locate the person; a copy shall be attached to a prominent place on such premises.

MISSOULA, Alabama   *Judge Brian Fielding*
     Dated: 12/23/2010   Signature of Judge

FIGURE 2-13 Search warrant.

RETURN

I received the attached Search Warrant 803959 on December 22, 2010, and have executed it as follows:

On ___12/22___, 20_10_ at __2:45__ o'clock _P_.m. I searched the premises at:

_____707 Richter Deive , Misola , Ac_____

I left a copy of the warrant with: _____Mrs. Pat Smith_____

(name of person at the place of search)

together with a receipt for the items seized pursuant to the warrant.

The following is an inventory of property taken pursuant to the warrant:

_____No property taken_____

This inventory was made in the presence of _____Pat Smith_____.

I swear that the inventory is a true and detailed account of all the property taken by me on the warrant.

Sworn to and Subscribed before me
This __22__ day of __Dec__, 2010

_____Judge Brian Fielding_____
Signature of Judge

_____James Meador_____
(Signature of Officer Executing Warrant)

FIGURE 2-14 Completed search warrant return.

Wednesday, 22 December 2010: Search of Joseph Smith's Residence

Detective Meador notified central dispatch of the warrants, and CSI Perry along with two additional patrol units were assigned to aid in serving the warrant. At approximately 2:45 p.m. the four arrived at the residence of Joseph Smith, 707 Richter Drive. The two patrol officers covered the back of the house, and CSI Perry and Detective Meador knocked on the door.

A white female answered the door. "Yes, can I help you?"

"Ma'am, my name is Detective Meador and this is CSI Perry. We have a warrant to search these premises."

"What's going on here? What do you mean? What happened?" the woman babbled.

Detective Meador read the search warrant to the woman, who identified herself as Sophia Smith, the mother of Joseph Smith. After reading the warrant, he motioned for her and her son, who had joined her at the door, to follow him outside while CSI Perry and the other officers entered the house to conduct the search. Meador explained the crime and the known facts of the case up to this point and added that her son had been identified as one of the perpetrators.

After an hour of thoroughly searching the house, neither the gaming devices nor the Nike tennis shoes were located. The home was small and there were not many hiding spaces.

"Joe, you've been identified as a suspect in a crime. I need you to come down to the station and make a formal statement. This is your chance to set the record straight before things get any worse." Joe Smith nodded demurely, and his mother stated they would meet him there.

Transcribed Interview with Joseph Smith, Conducted by Detective Sergeant Meador
Wednesday, 22 December 2010

BE ADVISED: In accordance with all federal, state, and local regulations, all formal interviews conducted by police officials are digitally recorded.

Detective Meador: "Interview 29432 A Detective Sergeant Meador interviewing Joseph Smith, white male, eighteen years of age. It is 5:45 p.m. on Wednesday, December 22, 2010. [brief pause] Mr. Smith, can you please verify that you have been informed of your rights, that you do not have to speak to me if you do not want to, and that you have the right to have an attorney present at this interview.

Joseph Smith: "Yes, sir, I've been, uh…so advised."

Detective Meador: "And it is your intention to waive these rights today, is that correct?"

Joseph Smith: "Yes, sir. I signed the form."

Detective Meador: "As we have discussed, you have been identified as a suspect in a criminal burglary and unlawful imprisonment case involving Mrs. Marian Fletcher. Could you please tell me, in your own words, why you have been implicated in these events?

Joseph Smith: "Yes, sir. Look, I want to tell my side of the story and put this situation behind me! This whole thing was a way to teach that jerk J.J. a lesson and get some good gifts; but the whole thing, it just went too far! In class J.J. was bragging about all the gifts he was going to get this year for Christmas. His grandma and his parents had all got him the gifts that he had asked for. That's so not fair! Why should he get more gifts? His parents are divorced for God's sake. Do you always get your kids everything they want?"

Detective Meador: "This is not about me, Mr. Smith. Just tell me about your involvement."

Joseph Smith: "It's all J.J.'s fault. Ron and J.J. have third period math and J.J. was bragging about all his gifts, so Ron developed a plan to steal them. Ron said J.J. mentioned that he helped pick out his gifts and he already had a PS3, Wii, and a Nintendo DX under his tree. I was looking forward to keeping the Wii for myself. I really enjoy the bowling game. Do you play?"

Detective Meador: "Please tell me full names. J.J. is?"

Joseph Smith: "J.J. is James Jones, but he always goes by J.J. Derrick's last name is Clark, and Ronald Johnson is the other one."

Detective Meador: "What was the exact plan?"

Joseph Smith: "Derrick played football with J.J. and had been to his house several times so he knew his way around the house. Ron knew that Derrick was mad at J.J. because J.J. beat him for the starting quarterback job in the fall. Ron asked Derrick to tell him the layout of J.J. grandma's house. Ron told Derrick that he would pay him $20 for the information, but Derrick insisted that he go with us."

Detective Meador: "Then what happened?"

Joseph Smith: "When we got there the house wasn't empty like we had planned. It was planned to happen on a Friday because J.J. always ate lunch at the YMCA on Monday, Wednesday, and Friday. Ron knew the house didn't have an alarm and stole a screwdriver from his shop class to open the door. After lunch, we would walk to the house and steal the gifts, then go back to school so we could have an alibi. We were going through the gifts when we heard the old lady. I flipped out and pushed her down! I can get real anxious at times. She freaked me out so I grabbed some gifts and ran. Once we were outside the house, Ron took all of the gifts and said that he would pawn them and give us the money later. Everything was taken to his home. [long pause] Can I still get my money?"

Detective Meador: "Where does Ron live?"

Joseph Smith: "948 Horseshoe Road."

Detective Meador: "I need all of that in writing."

Joseph Smith: "I want to make sure that I get a good deal before I put this in writing."

Detective Meador: "The DA does all the plea bargaining, but I will tell them that you helped us. We are now going down to the station so that you can give me all the information, and I have paperwork to complete. You are under arrest for burglary. I need to read you your Miranda rights."

Joseph Smith: "But I am willing to help you! Why would you arrest me?"

Detective Meador: "You have told me you were involved in a burglary at James Jones' house. There may be additional charges, so by going with us and providing a statement voluntarily, you will be placing yourself in a better situation when the DA's office reviews the case file. Mrs. Smith, you may want to contact a lawyer. Later this evening you can come down to the station to check on your son's status."

(End of transcript)

Detective Meador's Statement, continued

I summoned a patrol unit to transport Joseph Smith to the station and once again read him the Miranda rights. Joe Smith signed the waiver and composed a written statement detailing the plan, naming his co-conspirators, and identifying the items taken from the house. He was taken to the jail to await booking. I prepared my affidavit for an arrest warrant for Joseph Smith for burglary and a second search warrant for Ron Johnson's house. I also completed the return for the search warrant on Joe Smith's residence at 707 Richter Drive, noting that I did not recover any of the items specified in the search warrant.

Thursday, 23 December 2010: Second Affidavit and Search Warrant

State Court Judge Fielding reviewed my search warrant application and Joseph Smith's signed confession. He signed the new application and issued a search warrant for 948 Horseshoe Road, Misola, Alabama. The same four items were again listed on the search warrant, including three gaming devices and one pair of Nike tennis shoes.

STATE OF ALABAMA
COUNTY OF JASPER

APPLICATION FOR SEARCH WARRANT

Applicant: Det. J. Meador   Agency: Misola Police Department
Badge: 1488   Date of Application: Dec. 23, 2010
Date of Offense: 17 Dec. 2010   Case No. 20101217453301
Location of Premises to be searched: 948 Horsehoe Road, Misola, AL 64000

Affiant Statement:

The Affiant, Det. James Meador has been employed by the Misola Police Department as a police officer for 14 years. I have served as a patrol officer (8 years) and currently work as a Detective Sergeant in the Investigative Section. During my career I have investigated approximately 743 property crimes involving burglary; and have completed more than 250 hours of specialized training on property crime investigation.

This case involves a home invasion which began with the breaking and entering into 401 Thirteenth Street, Misola, AL, 64000, the home of Robert Jones at approximately 12:00 p.m./ It further involves the theft of several pieces of property, including three electronic video games (DSIXL, a Wii, and a Sony Playstation 3) and subsequent kidnapping, though temporary, of Ms. Marian Fletcher. Ms. Fletcher is also a resident of 401 Thirteenth Street, Misola, AL, 64000. The victim reported three young white males were involved in the crimes.

The home did yield some trace evidence, including a shoe print, a cigarette butt, latent fingerprints, and soil samples. This evidence is currently being analyzed by the Misola Police Department Criminalistics Unit, and the State Law Enforcement Division's Crime Laboratory.

The home is situated behind East Ashley High School and the victim identified the suspects as teenagers. The investigation is focusing on the possibility the perpetrators attend East Ashley High School. I obtained a list of students reported absent from school on the day the crimes were committed and compiled photo lineups from the yearbooks. Marian Fletcher identified one of the perpetrators as Joseph Smith – the subject who pushed her into the bedroom and locked her in the room preventing her from fleeing the scene of the criminal activity.

A Search Warrant was secured for Joseph Smith. Upon execution of that warrant, no evidence was discovered; however Mr. Joseph Smith confessed to his involvement in the criminal activities and stated the electronic video games are located at Ronald Johnson's home at 948 Horsehoe Road, Misola, AL, 64000. Ronald Johnson was absent from East Ashley High School at the time the crimes occurred on December 17, 2010. The affiant has verified the address of Ronald Johnson through his Department of Motor Vehicle Operators License.

_____
Affiant's Signature

FIGURE 2-15 Affidavit for search warrant for 948 Horseshoe Road.

STATE OF ALABAMA)

) **SEARCH WARRANT**

COUNTY OF JASPER) _803962_

TO THE SHERIFF OR BONDED LAW ENFORCEMENT OFFICE OF THIS STATE OR COUNTY OR THE <u>MUNICIPALITY OF MISOLA</u>:

It appearing from the attached affidavit that there are reasonable grounds to believe that certain property subject to seizure under provisions of Title 15 § 5-5 (1975) of the Code of Alabama, as amended, is located on the following Premises:

DESCRIPTION OF PREMISES (PERSON OR THING)
TO BE SEARCHED

<u>Dwelling: 948 Horseshoe Road</u>
<u>Misola, Alabama 64000</u>

Now, therefore, you are hereby authorized to search the subject premises for the property listed below and to seize such property if found:

DESCRIPTION OF PROPERTY

<u>Item #1</u>   <u>DSIXL</u>
<u>Item #2</u>   <u>Wii</u>
<u>Item #3</u>   <u>PS3</u>

This Search Warrant shall not be valid for more than ten days from the date of issuance.

A written inventory of all property seized pursuant to this Search Warrant to

<u>Misola Police Department Property Control & Disposition Officer in Charge</u>

Within ten days from the date of this warrant, such inventory to be signed by the officer executing this warrant, and a copy of such inventory shall be furnished to the person whose premises are searched if demand for such copy is made.

A copy of this Search Warrant shall be delivered to the person in charge of the premises searched at the time of such search if practicable, and, if not, to such person as soon thereafter as is practicable; in the event the identity of the person in charge is not known or if such person cannot be found after reasonable diligence in attempting to locate the person; a copy shall be attached to a prominent place on such premises.

MISOLA, Alabama
Dated: 12/23/2010

Judge Brian Fielding
Signature of Judge

FIGURE 2-16 Search warrant issued by judge for 948 Horseshoe Road.

RETURN

I received the attached Search Warrant 803962 on December 23, 2010, and have executed it as follows:

On ___12/24___, 20 _10_ at ___10___ o'clock _A_.m. I searched the premises at:

948 Horseshoe Rd, Misola Ac

I left a copy of the warrant with: _Mr. Alan Johnson_

(name of person at the place of search)

together with a receipt for the items seized pursuant to the warrant.

The following is an inventory of property taken pursuant to the warrant:

1) DSI XL SN# 05988656
2) Wii SN# 3000958960
3) PS3 SN# 4848113PR
4) white and blue, size 10 NIKE tennis shoes
5) red, clean and black huge Kobalt Flathead screwdriver)

This inventory was made in the presence of _Ron Johnson_ .

I swear that the inventory is a true and detailed account of all the property taken by me on the warrant.

Sworn to and Subscribed before me)
This _24_ day of _Dec_, _2010_)
)
Judge Brian Fielding)
Signature of Judge)   _Jamon Maador_
) (Signature of Officer Executing Warrant)
)

FIGURE 2-17 Search warrant return with inventory completed.

I also presented my affidavit to arrest Joseph Smith for burglary of the Jones's house at 401 Thirteenth Street, Misola, Alabama. A second warrant was issued for kidnapping Marian Fletcher. The warrants were delivered to the jail as I prepared to execute the search warrant on Ron Johnson's residence.

Attempted Search of Ron Johnson's Residence

Detective Meador notified dispatch of the new warrant, and CSI Perry and two patrol units were assigned to the warrant service. Arriving at Ron Johnson's home at 9:25 a.m. at Horseshoe Road, Detective Meador noticed that there were no cars in the driveway, although they could have been parked in the adjacent four-car garage. When Perry and Meador approached the front door and rang the bell, there was no response.

"Hey," a neighbor said as he walked by with his dog. "You lookin' for the Johnsons? They're gonna be gone all day. Visiting a relative, I think."

"Thank you, sir," Perry said, before turning to Meador. "Guess I'll be seeing you again tomorrow, eh?

Detective Meador's Statement, continued

We would indeed visit the Smith residence again the following day, but I still had another young man to interview. I found Derrick Clark at his home, 53 Trout Place. He seemed shocked to see a detective at his door asking about the burglary at the Jones's home. Derrick denied any knowledge of the events, so I then shared with him that Joe Smith was already in custody and was currently residing at the jail. Derrick's demeanor did not change. I called for a patrol unit to transport Derrick to the station.

Interview with Derrick Clark

Thursday, 23 December 2010: Misola Police Department Detective Office

Detective Meador: "Derrick, this interview is being recorded. I will read your Miranda rights to you, and we will continue our conversation from earlier today. The time is 11:30. It is Thursday, December 23, 2010, and this interview is being conducted in the detective office of the Misola Police Department by Detective Sergeant Meador. Derrick Clark is being interviewed regarding the home invasion that occurred on December 17, 2010, at 401 Thirteenth Street, Misola, Alabama."

As soon as I read the Miranda rights form to Derrick, he refused to waive his rights and demanded an attorney. Derrick Clark maintained he had no knowledge of the plan to steal Christmas presents from James Jones's house. He contacted his mother, Sheila Clark, and asked her to call Tony Stephens, his uncle and the family lawyer. I advised Derrick he was going to be transported to the jail and that I would be obtaining arrest warrants for burglary and kidnapping. He would not cooperate and did not want to put anything in writing until he talked to his attorney. When the two arrest warrants were secured, I served them on Derrick Clark at the jail. He steadfastly maintained his innocence and was still waiting for his attorney when I left to work on other cases.

Detective Meador's Statement, continued

Friday, 24 December 2010

I returned to the Johnson's home at 10:30 a.m. on Friday, December 24. I was greeted by a middle-aged woman who looked to be about 45. She told me her name was Dawn Johnson. I told her that the reason for my visit was that I needed to speak with her son and search their home. I showed her the warrant, and Mrs. Johnson immediately began to cry. She allowed me to enter the foyer and called out for her husband. The patrol officers, Sanderson and Winters, who met me at the residence were in place at the rear of the house.

Ron and his father, Jack Johnson, walked down the stairs. I explained to them I was investigating a burglary and that Ron had been implicated in the crime. I then showed them the search warrant and asked for their cooperation. In response to my inquiry concerning whether or not the house contained a mudroom where dirty shoes are kept, Dawn Johnson led me there and I observed several pairs of shoes. After donning gloves, I picked up a pair of boots. They were fairly clean on the bottom. I picked up a pair of white Nike tennis shoes, and they too were not very dirty. Mr. Johnson came into the room and told me that those were his shoes. He stated that Ron never takes his shoes off there. I asked him if I could see Ron's room, and we headed upstairs.

I opened Ron's door and was shocked at the bright pink walls.

FIGURE 2-18 The pink bedroom.

Mr. Johnson told me that they had just moved in and had not painted yet. I headed to the closet and next to the dresser there was a pair of Nike tennis shoes with a considerable amount of dirt on the outside. CSI Perry photographed the shoes, and then I asked Ron, "Are these your shoes?" He replied they were his shoes.

FIGURE 2-19 The shoes in the pink bedroom.

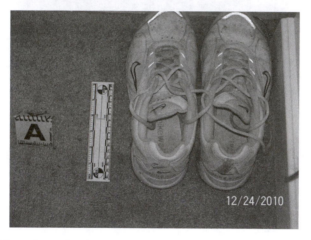

FIGURE 2-20 Shoes with marker and scale.

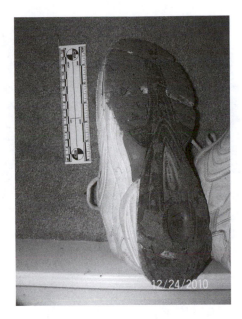

FIGURE 2-21 Close-up of shoe.

I told them that I needed to take them with me to test the dirt on the bottom and to allow the crime lab to compare the pattern on the bottom with shoeprints found at the scene. Ron stated that pair was his only set of tennis shoes.

I asked Ron once again to help me, so he can help himself. His mother pleaded for him to talk to me, but Ron just mumbled, "Open up my closet." Inside the closet, on the floor were the three missing gaming devices and a Kobalt screwdriver.

FIGURE 2-22 Games in the closet.

FIGURE 2-23 Screwdriver used to gain entry

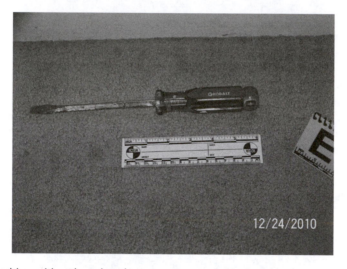

FIGURE 2-24 Screwdriver with scale and marker.

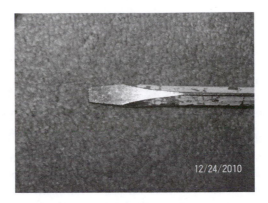

FIGURE 2-25 Close-up of the screwdriver.

CSI Perry photographed the closet and its contents. When I asked if these items belonged to Ron, Dawn Johnson replied they did not belong at her house. They had purchased a Wii for Ron's Christmas present, but it is wrapped and in her closet. I turned to Ron, advised him he was under arrest for burglary and possession of stolen goods, and began to read him his Miranda rights. CSI Perry took more photos and completed a sketch of the closet area. I notified the patrol officers to come inside the front door and take custody of Ron. Mr. Johnson was instructed that if he had an attorney, he should call him. Officer McCoy transported Ron Johnson to the station.

After CSI Perry had photographed each video gaming device separately and placed each item in large paper bags, we compared the serial numbers to the information provided by Mr. Jones. The numbers all matched those of the items we had just packaged. We also confiscated the pair of Nike tennis shoes. CSI Perry took custody of the items and left to take the evidence to the evidence/property room at the station. I will send a digital photo of the screwdriver to Mr. Marques so that he can identify it as the one missing from the tool shop. It is Christmas Eve, so I probably can't wrap up that part of the investigation until next week because schools are closed for the holidays.

Interoffice Case Update from Detective Sergeant Meador to Lieutenant Denning

On December 24, at 11:30 a.m., Ron Johnson was interviewed at the police station in an effort to substantiate his involvement in the crime. First he was read his Miranda rights again (11:40 a.m.) and was told the interview was being recorded. He waived his right to have an attorney present during questioning, and I used a narrative method in questioning at first, to allow Ron Johnson to tell his own version of the events of December 17 without any outside interruption.

Ron Johnson stated he left East Ashley High School around 11:45 a.m., which was corroborated by the school. Ron stated he did meet with Joe Smith and Derrick Clark for a while outside the school, but he left them and went home for lunch. I then informed Ron Johnson that we had unequivocal evidence, such as fingerprints and witness statements, that contradicted his statements. Ron Johnson then appeared agitated and stated he wasn't going to take the rap for Derrick Clark or Joseph Smith. Ron Johnson stated that it was Joseph Smith who pushed the old lady around. Ron Johnson stated that hurting the woman was not a part of the plan.

Ron said he wasn't a rat, but he wasn't going to take blame for what some of his friends did. I told him that we knew who was there at the time of the crime and he needed to come clean and be a standup guy. Ron Johnson then stated that he never wanted to hurt anybody but just wanted to rob the house and get some stuff and maybe some quick cash.

At this time I informed Ron Johnson that he needed to complete a defendant's statement. As he began writing the statement he stated, "I just want to go forward and put this whole mess behind me." After Ron Johnson completed his written statement, he was escorted to the jail holding area.

Detective Meador's Statement, continued

I was able to contact Mr. Marques, the shop teacher, and he stopped by the station to view the screwdriver. He quickly identified it as the one missing from his tool shop, and completed an affidavit stating the screwdriver found in Ron Johnson's closet belonged to East Ashley High School. He had forgotten to tell us that every tool was engraved with a specific identifier, "EAHS," on the handle. With this confirmation, I prepared arrest warrants for Ronald Johnson. Because it was Christmas Eve, I had to visit the on-call judge (Peter Barrier) at his residence to swear to the content of the warrant and obtain his signature. By 2:30 p.m. I arrived back at the jail and served the arrest warrants for burglary and possession of burglary tools on Ron Johnson.

At 3:30 p.m. I contacted my supervisor, Lieutenant Scott Denning, to update him on the progress of the case and the arrest of Ron Johnson. He granted me permission to return the video gaming devices to the Jones family. He agreed that we had more than enough evidence and because CSI Perry had documented the recovery of the items, it would be fine to return them. I arrived at the Jones's home at approximately 4:15 p.m. and rang the doorbell. There was Mrs. Fletcher, and when I walked in she immediately asked what was in the bag. J.J. and his father, Mr. Jones, came into the living room. I opened the bag and one at a time I returned the video gaming devices. I advised them the investigation was moving forward and that Ron Johnson had admitted to the crimes.

STATE OF ALABAMA
County of Jasper

Misola Police Department

GENERAL AFFIDAVIT FORM

Before the undersigned, an officer duly commissioned by the laws of Alabama, on this
24 day of Dec , 20 10 ,

Personally appeared ___JOHN MARQUES_____

Who having been first duly sworn depose and say:

I am employed at EAST Ashley HIGH SCHOOL. THE KOBALT SCREWDRIVER
IN tHE POSSESSION OF THE MISOLA POLICE DEPT. IS THE PROPERTY OF EAST
AsHLEy HIGH SCHOOL AND WAS MISSING ON DEC. 17, 2010. THE SCREWDRIVER
IS MARKED As PART OF OUR TOOLSET IN OUR WORKSHOP. THIS IS THE END
OF MY STATEMENT. JM.

                                                                John Marques

Case No. ___20101217453301___

Witness: ___James Meador___

Sworn and subscribed before me this 24 day of Dec A.D. 20 10

FIGURE 2-26 Screwdriver release form.

CHAIN OF CUSTODY SHEET

CASE NUMBER	EVIDENCE TAG #
2010 1217 453301	

CITY COURT DATE

Revised 12/05

PAGE #   3   OF 3

OFFICER NAME/BADGE #	DATE	TIME	PROPERTY CLASSIFICATION (Mark one box only)
0716198?	12·24·10	10:2	

DEFENDANT/OWNER NAME and ADDRESS		✓ GSC EVIDENCE
EAST Ashley High School		CITY COURT EVIDENCE
98 Wildcat Circle		FAMILY COURT EVIDENCE
Misola, Alabama, 64000.		FOUND PROPERTY
		✓ SAFEKEEPING (RETURN TO OWNER)

(ONLY PROPERTY THAT CANNOT BE PHOTOGRAPHED AND RETURNED TO THE OWNER SHALL BE TURNED IN)

ITEM #	DESCRIPTION (Caliber, brand, model, serial number, color - Currency Amount & Denominations, Etc.)
E	Kobalt screw driver, large, red black + clear

PROPERTY RECEIPT (OWNER/DEFENDANT SIGNATURE)

ITEM #	DATE	RELEASED BY	RECEIVED BY	PURPOSE: (Do Not Write In This Column)
E	12·24	NAME Bruce Perry ORGANIZATION mPD SIGN Bruce Perry	NAME John Maeues ORGANIZATION EAST Ashley H.S. SIGN John M....	
		NAME ORGANIZATION SIGN	NAME ORGANIZATION SIGN	
		NAME ORGANIZATION SIGN	NAME ORGANIZATION SIGN	
		NAME ORGANIZATION SIGN	NAME ORGANIZATION SIGN	

White Copy: Evidence   Green Copy: Case Disposition   Blue Copy: Case File/Officer   Pink Copy: Defendant/Owner

FIGURE 2-27 Screwdriver chain-of-custody form.

Wrapping Things Up

The case files were handed over to the prosecutor's office after the Christmas holiday. What started out as a plan to steal electronic games turned into a serious criminal investigation. The participants faced various felony charges. Although none of the conspirators had a prior history of arrests, they managed to rack up the charges with only one incident. It is up to the prosecutor's office to determine how to pursue the charges. It is the responsibility of the law enforcement agency to investigate crimes, identify perpetrators, collect and preserve physical evidence, and prepare the case for prosecutorial review.

Discussion Questions

1. Did you note any physical evidence the investigators missed? If so, name the items and explain why they may have been important to the investigation.
2. Develop the timeline for this case. Do you have all the documentation necessary to withstand the scrutiny of a defense attorney?
3. What information did you gather from the neighborhood survey?
4. What links did you establish between the suspects as you were reviewing the documentation and narrative for this investigation?
5. Why is it important to have the entry/exit log for the case file?
6. The crime scene investigator prepared a narrative of the actions he completed at the scene. Why should this be a standard operating procedure for major crime scenes?
7. List the information that Detective Meador had to provide to the court in order to obtain the search warrants in this case.
8. How do you explain the differences between robbery and burglary?

3

Criminal Sexual Misconduct, Kidnapping, and Human Trafficking

OBJECTIVE

Many times one's first impression when viewing a crime scene does not accurately portray the events that actually occurred. Investigators must maintain an open mind while gathering information. This chapter examines various aspects of evidence that will become part of a case file and lead the investigators to examine previously unsolved cases searching for links to the current scenario. The case examined in this chapter involves a rape and kidnapping.

KEY TERMS

associative evidence

chain of custody

circumstantial evidence

confession

conditional evidence

exculpatory evidence

jurisdiction

mens rea

modus operandi

motive

pattern evidence

probative evidence

transient evidence

venue

What You Will Learn

LEARNING OUTCOMES

- Classify varying types of evidence, and determine the value of the evidence to the investigative strategy

- Recognize the importance of motive to develop suspects

- Identify elements of crimes for prosecutorial purposes

- Compare and contrast various types of evidence

CRITICAL THINKING

- Elements of the crime

- Types of physical evidence

- Key investigative strategies

Introduction

CSI technicians are trained to identify, collect, and preserve physical evidence at the crime scene. Maintaining the **chain of custody** is particularly important, as this documentation identifies everyone who has taken custody of or had contact with a particular item of evidence. The chain-of-custody documentation begins when evidence is discovered and must be maintained throughout all court proceedings. A break in the chain of custody could mean physical evidence would be considered tainted and therefore excluded from any criminal proceedings. Every time a piece of evidence changes possession—for example, being transported from the property/evidence unit to a crime laboratory for examination—another entry must be added to the custody log and on the evidence packaging. This is one of the most litigated issues, and even the slightest deviation can disqualify the evidence for future consideration by a judicial officer. It is a good thing to remember that once physical evidence is "bagged and tagged," it must be accounted for every step of the way.

Types of Evidence

Transient evidence is physical or forensic evidence that may be easily lost or destroyed and must be collected immediately to preserve it for future examination. Transient evidence will be photographed and preserved before other evidence is processed in order to prevent loss or destruction.

Investigators must also learn to recognize other types of evidence that may prove to be valuable throughout the course of a criminal investigation. **Associative evidence** may link or associate a victim or a suspect to each other or to a particular scene. **Conditional evidence** includes observations and documentation of the situation at a crime scene. Some examples of conditional evidence are lighting conditions, whether or not the doors and windows were locked, the room temperature of a crime scene, or even or the precise location of specific pattern evidence located within the scene.

Pattern evidence ranges in variety from fingerprint impressions to fire burn patterns, furniture position patterns, trailers (paths where accelerants were poured), imprints, or striations. Many times this type of evidence is either obliterated by the first responders to an emergency scene or is overlooked by the improperly trained investigator. Burn patterns or trailers may not be discovered until hours or even days have passed in a residential or commercial fire. Both of these types of pattern evidence can yield valuable information in cases where arson is suspected.

Circumstantial evidence is also known as indirect evidence and tends to incriminate a person. Several items of circumstantial evidence may be used to corroborate an inference, but circumstantial evidence will not stand alone. **Exculpatory evidence** must also be introduced in the courtroom. This is any type of evidence that indicates the innocence of the accused. It is not ethical or legal for anyone to withhold exculpatory evidence during an investigation. An appropriate example of exculpatory evidence would be blood found at a scene that did not come from the suspect or the victim. Finally, **probative evidence** is used to weigh the value of evidence necessary for proving something during the trial process.

Where Was the Crime Committed?

Accurate crime scene reconstruction relies on the actions of the CSI technician and the investigator working collaboratively to properly document relevant evidence. Whether that evidence is physical, personal observations, or facts that are uncovered through witness and victim interviews, it is essential that the information is validated and entered into the case file. All individuals involved in an investigation must remain nonbiased and nonjudgmental, cooperate, and follow a logical systematic plan that may yield leads that result in solving the case. Many times multiple jurisdictions are working on cases at the same time. Criminal offenders do not respect the city limits or county lines when they are committing crimes. **Jurisdiction** is the statutorily granted authority of an agency to apply the law and a court to hear criminal charges within the boundaries of the geographical area of responsibility. It is important to double-check with central dispatch when recording case numbers to ensure the address is within the jurisdiction of the responding agencies. Urban areas have multiple streets and addresses, many of which are located in adjacent jurisdictions. Fortunately, this does not occur often, but it is a primary concern that you establish **venue**, the scene or locale of any action or event, to ensure the results of the investigation can be tried in the correct court of jurisdiction.

Defense Strategies

Criminal defense attorneys also devise strategies to overcome allegations against their clients. There are three basic foundations: impeach the evidence, impeach the police, or create confusion and delay, resulting in termination of the criminal proceedings. By recognizing these potential areas for attack, well-trained investigators can develop strategies that will enhance the credibility of the entire case. If you presume that every criminal investigation you conduct will end up in the courtroom, you will develop credible procedures that enhance the integrity of your efforts and the quality of the case file. Tainted evidence cannot be introduced during a trial. Cross contamination of evidence within the crime scene invalidates all the evidence, so extreme care must be taken when officers arrive on the scene and conduct the initial walkthrough with the detectives. Justice cannot be served when an inconsistent or discredited investigation results in the offender being released from charges as a result of human error.

It is not necessary for motive to be proven in the courtroom. The textbook definition of **motive** is establishing that a person could have a reason for committing a crime or explaining why it is possible that a suspect did have a basis for taking action. Many perpetrators will argue there is no reason to think they would have committed a crime because they did not have a motive for doing so. Motive is not to be confused with intent. Guilt is not dependent on motive. Intent or ***mens rea*** is Latin for "guilty mind." Prosecutors must prove the suspect intended to commit the crime, and this is incumbent on the defendant's state of mind at the time the crime was committed. Typically statutes require that a person acts knowingly, purposely, or recklessly in order to be found guilty of committing criminal offenses.

Even when a suspect provides a confession, the investigator must persist in concluding the case file. A **confession** is a statement that allows suspects to acknowledge personal responsibility for their actions, but many times a confession is obtained and the investigator moves on to the next case. It is not uncommon for an alleged perpetrator to change his or her story. Just because a confession is secured does not ensure the case has been closed. A confession can be written or oral. It is recommended that a confession be recorded on video and written by the perpetrator, but even these steps cannot ensure that the confession will not be recanted at a later date. You should always seek to have the suspect include details of the crime that only the perpetrator would know when conducting an interrogation that leads to a confession.

And Finally

Modus operandi (MO) is a familiar term to criminal justice students but is of particular interest to investigators. Establishing the method of operation creates patterns of behavior that serial violators will continue from crime scene to crime scene. This analysis is useful to investigators who work to build profiles of persistent offenders. When the MO is ascertained, the number of suspects in the pool may be narrowed down. It is also useful when linking multiple cases and associating the previous known behaviors of suspects to additional cases, thereby creating associative evidence. MO patterns can help crime analysts to predict future targets and can lead to the arrest and conviction of the serial offenders. Establishing the MO of the perpetrators in cases may connect previously unlinked cases, which can bring closure to cold cases as well as the families and victims of those cases.

■ ■ ■ ────────────────────────────

Case File: There's Been a Kidnapping and Rape
Case File Elements
- Incident/offense report
- Crime scene sketches
- Property/evidence reports
- Witness statements
- Supplemental reports
- Follow-up

Critical Questions and Activities

In the following case file, your assignment is to determine the timeline and ascertain what crimes have been committed. What is the *corpus delicti* in this case? National crime statistics over the years indicate that 66% to as much as 75% of all assault victims are acquainted with their attackers. Does this hold true for this case? What evidence substantiates your decision? Are there missing documents in the case file? Did you develop any questions that remain unanswered even after you reviewed the narrative and the documents in the case file?

Case Narrative: Saturday, 22 August 2010

At 11:30 a.m. I received a call from Patrol Sergeant Smith. "Detective, we have a possible sexual assault and kidnapping."

"What's going on?"

"All we know," said the sergeant, "is that the roommate of the victim returned to their apartment this morning and found blood and signs of a struggle throughout the apartment. The young women are both college students, but the missing one is a foreign exchange student. The roommate found some blood and a used condom in the apartment and called us."

"All right, I'm only about five minutes away. Will you call the crime scene unit for me?"

"I'm already on it. See you in a few minutes," the sergeant said.

My partner and I drove to Meeting Street, parked across from the apartment complex, and walked to the area sealed off by yellow police tape. Two officers and an evidence technician were standing by.

Sergeant Smith's Statement

The officers briefed my partner and me about whom they interviewed and what they had seen and done. They said that they arrived at 11 a.m. and met the roommate outside of the apartment. She directed them to the apartment and the missing young woman's bedroom. The officers explained that the victim appeared to have been attacked in the entrance of the apartment and assaulted in her bedroom. They added that her purse and cell phone were found on the living room floor in front of the couch. There was blood on the floor in front of the bedroom and a condom on the left side of the bed. There were also a few drops of blood on the floor on the right side of the bed.

The officers secured the perimeter of the scene. They also secured the area 500 feet from the entrance to the end of the street on both sides and across the street. Sergeant Smith stated that the two other police officers arrived at the scene and helped locate possible witnesses. The evidence technician arrived and began photographing and sketching the crime scene.

STATE OF _IOWA_

COUNTY OF _Centralia_

INCIDENT REPORT

DISPATCH NUMBER		ORIGINAL CASE NUMBER			NCIC ENTRY	INQ.	ENT.
0100000	08222010	2010543486	PAGE 1 OF PAGES 1				

EVENT

	INCIDENT TYPE	INCIDENT CODE	COMPLETED	FORCED ENTRY	PREMISE TYPE	UNITS ENTERED	TYPE VICTIM
1.	Criminal Sexual Assault	21	☑ YES ☐ NO	☑ YES ☐ NO	Apartment		☐ INDIVIDUAL ☐ BUSINESS ☐ FINANCIAL INST.
2.	Missing Person	16	☐ YES ☐ NO	☐ YES ☐ NO	Apartment		☑ GOVERNMENT ☐ RELIG. ORG ☐ SOC./PUB.
3.			☐ YES ☐ NO	☐ YES ☐ NO			☐ OTHER ☐ UKNOWN ☐ POLICE OFF.

INCIDENT LOCATION:	ZIP CODE	WEAPON TYPE				
411 Meeting Street Apt 201 New Columbus, IO	50515					

BEGINNING INCIDENT DATE	24 HR. CLOCK	ENDING INCIDENT DATE	24 HR. CLOCK	DISP. DATE	DISP. TIME	TIME ARRIVED	DEPART TIME	TRACT #
08-22-10	2022	ongoing				1130		

COMPLAINANT

NAME: (LAST, FIRST, MIDDLE)		RELATIONSHIP TO SUBJECT			RESIDENT	RACE	SEX	AGE	DOB	ETH
Adams, Samantha		#1 roommate #2 #3			Y	C	F	21	050289	

HEIGHT	WEIGHT	HAIR	EYES	FACIAL HAIR, SCARS, TATOOS, GLASSES, CLOTHING, PHYSICAL PECULIARITIES, ETC.	DRIVERS LIC / ID & STATE	SOCIAL SECURITY #
503	115	Bro	Bro	None	8790009645 NY	414-00-2311

ADDRESS #	STREET NAME	CITY	STATE	ZIP CODE	DAY PHONE	EVENING PHONE
411	Meeting St. Apt 201	New Columbus	IO	50515	712-478-5962	

OCCUPATION	EMPLOYER	ALIAS	NIC #
waitress	Karen's Cafe		

VICTIM #1

NAME: (LAST, FIRST, MIDDLE)		RELATIONSHIP TO SUBJECT			RESIDENT	RACE	SEX	AGE	DOB	ETH
Pantovich, Nadia		#1 roommate #2 #3			Y	C	F	21	071589	

HEIGHT	WEIGHT	HAIR	EYES	FACIAL HAIR, SCARS, TATOOS, GLASSES, CLOTHING, PHYSICAL PECULIARITIES, ETC.	DRIVERS LIC / ID & STATE	SOCIAL SECURITY #
501	101	Bln	Blu	Russian accent	unk Iowa	003-69-1022

ADDRESS #	STREET NAME	CITY	STATE	ZIP CODE	DAY PHONE	EVENING PHONE
411	Meeting Street Apt 201	New Columbus	OH	50515	244-863-8020	

☐ VISIBLE INJURY	COMPLAINT OF NON-VISIBLE INJURIES	USING ALCOHOL	☐ TWO-MAN VEHICLE ☐ DETECTIVE SPLASMT ☐ ALONE
☐ NO ☐ YES	☐ NO ☐ YES	☐ NO ☐ YES ☐ UNK	☐ TWO-MAN VEHICLE ☐ DETECTIVE SPLASMT ☐ ALONE
EXPLAIN Unk		DRUGS ☐ NO ☐ YES TYPE ☐ UNK	☐ ONE-MAN VEHICLE ☐ OTHER ☐ ASSISTED

OCCUPATION	EMPLOYER	ALIAS	NIC #
Student -	College of Columbus Bookstore		

SUBJ. I.D.

☐ COMPLAINANT ☐ VICTIM # ☒ SUSPECT # 1 ☐ SUBJECT # ☐ WITNESS # ☐ WANTED ☐ WARRANT ☐ ARREST ☐ RUNAWAY ☐ MISSING PERSON	NAME: (LAST, FIRST, MIDDLE)		RELATIONSHIP TO SUBJECT			RESIDENT	RACE	SEX	AGE	DOB	ETH
	Romonov Alexander		#1 NONE #2 #3			Y	C	M		112283	

HEIGHT	WEIGHT	HAIR	EYES	FACIAL HAIR, SCARS, TATOOS, GLASSES, CLOTHING, PHYSICAL PECULIARITIES, ETC.	DRIVERS LIC / ID & STATE	SOCIAL SECURITY #
602	240	Blk	Grn		SC R-451-333-5488	005-22-8484

ADDRESS #	STREET NAME	CITY	STATE	ZIP CODE	DAY PHONE	EVENING PHONE
315	Meeting St Apt 123	new Columbus	IO	50515	712-478-5962	

☐ VISIBLE INJURY	COMPLAINT OF NON-VISIBLE INJURIES	USING ALCOHOL	☐ TWO-MAN VEHICLE ☐ DETECTIVE SPLASMT ☐ ALONE
☐ NO ☐ YES	☐ NO ☐ YES	☐ NO ☐ YES ☐ UNK	☐ TWO-MAN VEHICLE ☐ DETECTIVE SPLASMT ☐ ALONE
EXPLAIN		DRUGS ☐ NO ☐ YES TYPE ☐ UNK	☐ ONE-MAN VEHICLE ☐ OTHER ☐ ASSISTED

OCCUPATION	EMPLOYER	ALIAS	NIC #
teacher's aide	College of Columbus		

ARREST

(A) CHARGE	(C) CHARGE
Sexual Assault -	
(B) CHARGE	(D) CHARGE
Kidnapping	

NARRATIVE

Complainant Samantha Adams returned home at approx. 1120 hrs on Sat. 08-22-2010. She entered the apartment looking for her roommate, Nadia Pantovich. Ms Adams found blood and signs of a struggle throughout the apartment and could not find Nadia, so she immediately called 911. She has not seen Ms. Pantovich since 08-21-10 at approx. 1700 hrs when Nadia, Samantha and two other friends met for an outing. Patrol officers arrived on the scene at 1136 hrs and searched the premises. Nadia Pantovich was not located. Due to the presence of blood, and overturned furniture, Homicide Detectives were summoned to the scene. Det. Greene and Daniels arrived at 1159 hrs and reporting officer cleared the scene.

PROPERTY EST.

TYPE (GROUP)						TOTAL VALUE	JURISDICTION OF THEFT LAW ENFORCEMENT AGENCY
STOLEN						Unk	
DAMAGED							
BURNED							JURISDICTION OF RECOVERY LAW ENFORCEMENT AGENCY
RECOVERED							
SEIZED							

ADMINISTRATIVE

SUBJECT IDENTIFIED ☐ YES ☐ NO	SUBJECT LOCATED ☐ YES ☐ NO	☐ ACTIVE ☐ UNFOUNDED	☐ ADM. CLOSED	☐ ARRESTED UNDER 18 ☐ ARRESTED 18 AND OVER	☐ EX-CLEAR UNDER 18 ☐ EX-CLEAR 18 AND OVER

REASON FOR EXCEPTIONAL CLEARANCE: 1. ☐ OFFENDER DEATH   2. ☐ NO PROSECUTION   3. ☐ EXTRADITION DENIED   4. ☐ VICTIM DECLINES COOPERATION   5. ☐ JUVENILE NO CUSTODY

REPORTING OFFICER(S)	DATE	BADGE NUMBER	APPROVING OFFICER	DATE	BADGE NUMBER
PO Ryan Golden	08-22-10	3712	Lt. D. Greeley	08-22-10	2500
			FOLLOW-UP INVESTIGATION ☐ YES ☐ NO OFFICER		

FIGURE 3-1 Offense report.

Witnesses

The officers briefed my partner and me as to witnesses' statements prior to our inspection of the crime scene in order to give us as much information as possible to help us to recover evidence. So far, the officers had interviewed four neighbors.

Janet Williams told officers that at about 3 a.m. she was returning home and saw a young woman walking on the opposite side of the street toward the complex. She stated that a man was walking not far behind the woman. She said he was wearing a lime green shirt, blue jeans, sneakers, and a baseball cap.

Brian Matilla stated that he was awakened by screams and loud banging sounds around 3:30 a.m. He said he walked out on his balcony on Meeting Street to see if anything was wrong but did not see anything. He then proceeded to look out of his door into the hallway but did not see anything or hear any more of a commotion.

Frederick Brown stated that he was awakened about 3:15 a.m. by a loud noise, but because his dog did not bark, he went back to sleep.

Shannon Smith stated that she was awakened about 4 a.m. by yelling or loud talking that was not in English, but because she knew that the college had multiple foreign-exchange students, she went back to sleep.

PAGE __1 of 1__   COMPLAINT NO. __20108 2212__

NEW COLUMBUS POLICE DEPARTMENT
WITNESS STATEMENT

STATEMENT OF __Brian Matilla__   DATE OF BIRTH __8/1/1987__ AGE __23__

HOME ADDRESS __409 Meeting St. Apt 104__   PHONE __712-863-1158__

EMPLOYER __NA__   BUSINESS PHONE __NA__

THIS STATEMENT IS IN REFERENCE TO __Criminal sexual misconduct / Kidnapping__

WHICH OCCURRED AT __411 Meeting St. Apt 201__   ON OR ABOUT __8-22-2010__

AT APPROXIMATELY __3:15__ AM PM, IN NEW COLUMBUS, IOWA.

THIS STATEMENT IS GIVEN BY __Brian Matilla__   (DATE) __8-22-20__ (TIME) __4:28pm__

__New Columbus Police Dept (Courtyards Investigation)__ (LOCATION)

I was awakened by screams and loud banging sounds about 3:30 A.M. I walked out on my balcony on Meeting Street to see if anything was wrong, but I did not see anything. I proceeded to look out the other door through the hallway, but there was no one out there and I didn't hear any more commotion. Since mostly college kids live here, we hear lots of noise — especially late at night. I did not see or hear anything else, so I went back to bed. End of Statement BM

I HAVE READ THE FOREGOING STATEMENT OR HAVE HAD IT READ TO ME AND IT IS TRUE AND CORRECT TO THE BEST OF MY KNOWLEDGE. I HAVE GIVEN THIS STATEMENT FREELY AND VOLUNTARILY AND HAVE BEEN PROVIDED A COPY OF MY STATEMENT.

WITNESS: _____

WITNESS: _____   SIGNATURE: __Brian Matilla__

FIGURE 3-2 Witness statement, page 1.

PAGE __1 of 1__   COMPLAINT NO. __201082212__

NEW COLUMBUS POLICE DEPARTMENT
WITNESS STATEMENT

STATEMENT OF __Frederick Brown__   DATE OF BIRTH __5-26-90__ AGE __20__

HOME ADDRESS __411 Meeting St. Apt 101__   PHONE __712-863-4011__

EMPLOYER __NA__   BUSINESS PHONE __NA__

THIS STATEMENT IS IN REFERENCE TO __Criminal sexual misconduct / Kidnapping__

WHICH OCCURRED AT __411 Meeting St Apt 201__ ON OR ABOUT __8-22-2010__

AT APPROXIMATELY __3:00__ AM PM, IN NEW COLUMBUS, IOWA.

THIS STATEMENT IS GIVEN BY __Frederick Brown__   (DATE) __8/22/10__ (TIME) __3:12 pm__
__New Columbus Police Dept. /Courtyards Investigation__ (LOCATION)

I was woke up around 3 or 3:15 AM this morning by a loud
noise, but since my dog did not bark, so I went back to sleep.
END OF STATEMENT FB

I HAVE READ THE FOREGOING STATEMENT OR HAVE HAD IT READ TO ME AND IT IS TRUE AND CORRECT TO THE BEST OF MY KNOWLEDGE. I HAVE GIVEN THIS STATEMENT FREELY AND VOLUNTARILY AND HAVE BEEN PROVIDED A COPY OF MY STATEMENT.

WITNESS: __Det Greene__

WITNESS: __BmD__

SIGNATURE: __Fed Brown__

FIGURE 3-3 Witness statement, page 2.

PAGE _l of l_   COMPLAINT NO. _201082212_

NEW COLUMBUS POLICE DEPARTMENT
WITNESS STATEMENT

STATEMENT OF _Shannon Smith_   DATE OF BIRTH _6-19-88_ AGE _22_

HOME ADDRESS _____NA_____   PHONE _712-863-9000_

EMPLOYER _____NA_____   BUSINESS PHONE _____NA_____

THIS STATEMENT IS IN REFERENCE TO _Criminal Sexual Misconduct / Kidnapping_

WHICH OCCURRED AT _411 Meeting St Apt 201_ ON OR ABOUT _8-22-2010_

AT APPROXIMATELY _3:30_ AM PM, IN NEW COLUMBUS, IOWA.

THIS STATEMENT IS GIVEN BY _Shannon Smith_ (DATE) _8-22-2010_ (TIME) _2:35pm_

New Columbus Police Dept / Courtyards Investigation (LOCATION)

I AM GUESSING BUT I THINK IT WAS ABOUT 3:30Am I heard some
SHOUTING AND YELLING IN A FOREIGN LANGUAGE. IT WOKE ME UP, BUT
THERE ARE LOTS OF FOREIGN STUDENTS HERE, SO I DID NOT PAY ANY
ATTENTION TO IT. I DON'T KNOW WHAT LANGUAGE IT WAS - BUT IT WAS
NOT SPANISH OR FRENCH. I WENT BACK TO SLEEP. END OF STATEMENT

I HAVE READ THE FOREGOING STATEMENT OR HAVE HAD IT READ TO ME AND IT IS TRUE AND CORRECT TO THE BEST
OF MY KNOWLEDGE. I HAVE GIVEN THIS STATEMENT FREELY AND VOLUNTARILY AND HAVE BEEN PROVIDED A COPY
OF MY STATEMENT.

WITNESS: _Nat Greene_

WITNESS: _____   SIGNATURE: _Shannon Smith_

FIGURE 3-4 Witness statement, page 3.

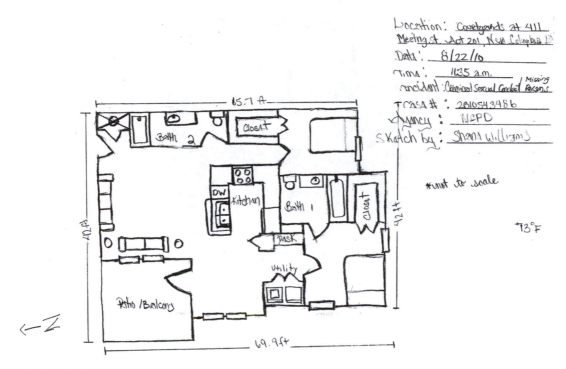

Location: Courtyards at 411
Meeting ct Apt 201, New Columbia D
Date: 8/22/10
Time: 1135 a.m.
Incident: Criminal Sexual Conduct / Missing Persons
Case #: 2010543486
Agency: NCPD
Sketch by: Shana Williams

*not to scale

73°F

65.7 ft.
69.9 ft.
40 ft.
42 ft.

←—N

Bath 2
Closet
Kitchen
DW
Bath 1
Closet
Pass.
Utility
Patio/Balcony

FIGURE 3-5 Crime scene sketch.

Officer Walkthrough

My partner and I went on a walkthrough of the crime scene. We observed where the struggle seemed to have taken place and where the sexual assault seemed to have occurred. We observed the blood patterns, a condom, and the other fluids in the bedroom.

We documented the scene in the living room and hallway, noting the location of the blood spatter pattern, cell phone, and purse.

FIGURE 3-6 Crime scene.

FIGURE 3-7 Blood found at the scene still appears fresh.

Crime Scene Inspection

I saw magazines thrown around the living room. There was blood on the bedroom door and on the floor in front of the bedroom. There was a used condom lying on the floor, slightly under the bed.

FIGURE 3-8 Evidence markers in the photograph indicate location of evidence.

FIGURE 3-9 Evidence markers indicate location of evidence.

FIGURE 3-10 Evidence item "T" was a used condom found at the scene.

There were scarves tied to the posts of the bed and blood on the sheet on the bed. The nightstand was tipped over.

My partner and I conducted a close inspection of the crime scene and found the following items:

1. Fingerprints on the bedpost

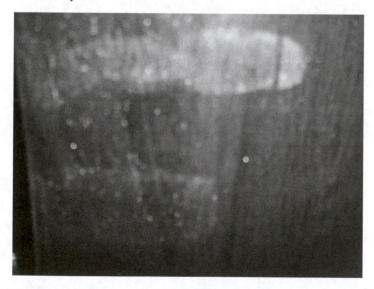

FIGURE 3-11 Latent fingerprints that were found on the bedpost.

2. Scarves on the bed
3. Blood on the sheet on the bed, and seven blood drops on the right side of the bed

FIGURE 3-12 Blood samples were taken from the bedsheet for lab analysis.

FIGURE 3-13 Example of blood drops on the sheets on the victim's bed.

4. Blood on the bedroom door

FIGURE 3-14 Fingerprint impressions left in blood on the door to the victim's bedroom.

5. Blood on the floor in front of the bedroom
6. Magazines scattered across the living room floor
7. The coffee table turned over with the cell phone and purse of the missing person close by

FIGURE 3-15 Victim's purse and cell phone marked with evidence markers "D" and "E."

PHOTOGRAPHIC LOG

Location: Apartment   Camera: #12
Date: 8/22/10   Type of Film and Rating: Kodak/400/24
Case Identifier: 2010543486   Remarks: Roll #1
Preparer/Assistants: Officer Cooper

PHOTO #	DESCRIPTION OF PHOTOGRAPHIC SUBJECT	USE OF SCALE	MISCELLANEOUS COMMENTS	SKETCH (IF APPLICABLE)
1.	Long shot-room (rt corner angle)		All photos from left side of living room	Location: 411 Meeting St. Apt 201, Charleston, SC
2.	Close shot- store bags		All photos from left side of living room	Date: 8/22/10
3.	Close shot- eye glass case		All photos from left side of living room	Case Identifier: 2010543486
4.	Close shot- magazines		All photos from left side of living room	Photographer: Officer Cooper
5.	Close shot- cell phone		All photos from left side of living room	Roll Number: 1 of 1
6.	Close shot- purse		All photos from left side of living room	
7.	Close shot- magazines		All photos from left side of living room	
8.	Long Shot- entrance into victims bedroom		photo from left side of entrance to bedroom	
9.	Close shot- finger/hand print		photo from right side of entrance to bedroom	
10.	Mid shot- door of victims bedroom		photo from left side of entrance to bedroom	
11.	Close shot- hand print of door		photo from left right of entrance to bedroom	
12.	Close shot- hand print on door knob		photo from left side of entrance to bedroom	
13.	Long shot- bedroom		photo from left side of entrance to bedroom	
14.	Close shot- scarf (left side of bed)		photo from left side of bedroom	
15.	Close shot- blood on sheets		Photo taken from left and right side of bedroom	

FIGURE 3-16 Photo log for Case 2010543486 Missing Person, page 1.

16.	Close shot-fingerprint on side of bed		Photo from right side bedroom	
17.	Close shot-comforter		Photo from left side bedroom	
18.	Close shot- scarf (rt side of bed)		Photo from right side bedroom	
19.	Close shot- end table		Photo from left side bedroom	
20.	Close shot-condom		Photo from left side bedroom	
21.	Close shot- blood on carpet		Photo from left side bedroom	

FIGURE 3-17 Photo log for Case 2010543486 Missing Person, page 2.

CRIME SCENE ENTRY LOG SHEET
ALL PERSONS ENTERING THE CRIME SCENE MUST SIGN THIS SHEET

AGENCY: New Columbia PD   INCIDENT #: 2010543486

SCENE LOCATION: 411 Meeting St Apt. 201 New Columbia, Iowa 50515

NOTE: Officers assigned to maintain scene security must also log in and out on this sheet and should state their reason as "Log Officer".   Weather Conditions: Sunny/ Clear Skies, 70°F

NAME & TITLE	INITIALS	AGENCY	IN DATE / TIME	OUT DATE / TIME	REASON FOR ENTERING
J. Smith -Sergeant	JD	NCPD	8/22/10 11:00am	8/22/10 12:00pm	911 Dispatched
T. Brown -Police Officer	TB	NCPD	8/22/10 10:45am	8/22/10 12:00pm	First responding officer Establish perimeter/secure scene
Ph. Taylor -Police Officer	PT	NCPD	8/22/10 10:45am	8/22/10 12:00pm	First responding officer Establish perimeter/secure scene
Q. Apple - CSI	QA	NCPD	8/22/10 11:00am	8/22/10 12:00pm	CSI
L. Oatn - CSI	LO	NCPD	8/22/10 11:00am	8/22/10 12:00pm	CSI
C. Johston Physical evidence technician	CJ	NCPD	8/22/10 11:45	8/22/10 12:00pm	Photography/sketching
Detective Daniels	DD	NCPD	8/22/10 11:45	8/22/10 11:45	Crime Scene Overview
Officer Cooper	SC	NCPD	8/22/10 11:45	8/22/10 11:45	Crime Scene Overview
			/	/	
			/	/	
			/	/	
			/	/	
			/	/	
			/	/	
			/	/	
			/	/	

Page ___1___ of ___1___

FIGURE 3-18 Entry and exit log.

PROPERTY REPORT

1. Original   2. Supplement   1

Agency Code: NCPD

Agency Report Number: 2,0,1,0,5,3,4,8,6

Date of Supplement: 0,8,2,2,2,0,1,0

Original Date Reported: 0,8,2,2,2,0,1,0

Primary Offense Description: Criminal Sexual Conduct/Missing Persons

Victim #1 Name: Nadia Pantovich

Type Theft: 00. N/A, 01. Burglary, 02. Robbery, 03. Shoplifting, 04. Pocket Picking, 05. Purse Snatching, 06. Embezzlement, 07. From Coin Oper. Machine, 08. From Public Access Bldg., 09. From Vehicle, 10. Extortion, 11. By Computer, 12. Fraud, 99. Other — 10.0

Person Code: V-Victim, S-Suspect, P-Proprietor, A-Arrestee, Z-Other

Status Code: 1. Stolen, 2. Recovered, 3. Stolen and Recovered, 4. Recovered for Other, 5. Lost, 6. Found, 7. Safekeeping, 8. Evidence/Seized, 9. Other

Damage Code: 0. N/A, 1. Arson, 2. Criminal Mischief, 3. During other Offense, 9. Other

Property Type: A. Auto Accessory/Parts, B. Bicycle, C. Camera/Photo Equipment, D. Drug, E. Equipment/Tool, F. Food/Liquor/Consumable, G. Gun, H. Household Appliance/Goods, I. Plant/Citrus, J. Jewelry/Precious Metal, K. Clothing/Fur, L. Livestock, M. Musical Instrument, N. Construction Machinery, O. Office Equipment, P. Art/Collection, Q. Computer Equipment, R. Radio/Stereo, S. Sports Equipment, T. TV/Video/VCR, U. Currency/Negotiable, V. Credit Card/Non-Negotiable, W. Boat Motor, X. Structure, Y. Farm Equipment, Z. Miscellaneous

Person Code #	Item #	Status	Damage	Property Type	Quantity	Name	Brand	Model Name/Number
V	1	0	2	1		eye glass case	NA	NA

Serial Number: N/A   Owner Applied Number: N/A   Description: Green   FCIC/NCIC: N/A
Value: 01.0.0   Value Recovered: 01.0.0   Date Recovered: 0,8,2,2,2,0,1,0

Person Code #	Item #	Status	Damage	Property Type	Quantity	Name	Brand	Model Name/Number
V	1	2	0	0	2	store bags	NA	N/A

Serial Number: N/A   Owner Applied Number: N/A   Description: small   FCIC/NCIC: N/A
Value: 01.0.0   Value Recovered: 01.0.0   Date Recovered: 0,8,2,2,2,0,1,0

Person Code #	Item #	Status	Damage	Property Type	Quantity	Name	Brand	Model Name/Number
V	1	3	9	0	10	Magazine	N/A	N/A

Serial Number: N/A   Owner Applied Number: N/A   Description: N/A   FCIC/NCIC: N/A
Value: 01.0.0   Value Recovered: 01.0.0   Date Recovered: 0,8,2,2,2,0,1,0

Person Code #	Item #	Status	Damage	Property Type	Quantity	Name	Brand	Model Name/Number
V	1	4	8	0	2	1 cell phone	iphone	A1331

Serial Number: 519B-E2380C   Owner Applied Number: Description: Black   FCIC/NCIC: N/A
Value: 01.0.0   Value Recovered: 01.0.0   Date Recovered: 0,8,2,2,2,0,1,0

Person Code #	Item #	Status	Damage	Property Type	Quantity	Name	Brand	Model Name/Number
V	1	5	8	0	2	3 Boxes	NA	N/A

Serial Number: N/A   Owner Applied Number: N/A   Description: Brown   FCIC/NCIC: N/A
Value: 01.0.0   Value Recovered: 01.0.0   Date Recovered: 0,8,2,2,2,0,1,0

Person Code #	Item #	Status	Damage	Property Type	Quantity	Name	Brand	Model Name/Number
	6	8	0	2	1	purse	N/A	N/A

Serial Number: N/A   Owner Applied Number: N/A   Description: gold   FCIC/NCIC: N/A
Value: 01.0.0   Value Recovered: 01.0.0   Date Recovered: 0,8,2,2,2,0,1,0

Property Stolen: $01.0.0   Change in Property Stolen Value: $9,0.0
Property Recovered: $01.0.0   Change in Property Recovered Value: $01.0.0

Activity: P. Possess, S. Sell, B. Buy, T. Traffic, R. Smuggle, D. Deliver, E. Use, K. Dispense/Distribute, M. Manufacture/Produce/Cultivate, Z. Other

Type: A. Amphetamine, B. Barbiturate, C. Cocaine, E. Heroin, H. Hallucinogen, M. Marijuana, O. Opium/Derivative, P. Paraphernalia/Equipment, S. Synthetic, Z. Other

Unit: U. Unknown, Z. Other, 1. Gram, 2. Milligram, 3. Kilogram, 4. Ounce, 5. Pound, 6. Ton, 7. Liter, 8. Milliliter, 9. Dose Unit/Item

Activity	Type	Description	Quantity	Unit	Estimated Street Value
		m			0 .00
		m			0 .00
		m			0 .00

"The above listed property (eye glasses case, magazines, cell phone boxes, purse, store bags) was taken on August 22, 2010 at 12:30 pm in reference to the above listed offense and turned over to evidence control for processing. This items were taken from Nadia's Pantovich's apartment by Officer Cooper

Officer(s) Reporting: Ryan Golden   ID. Number(s)/Locator Code: 3712   Unit: 7D   Date: 8/22/10

Officer Reviewing (if applicable):   ID. Number: Routed To: Evidence   Referred To: Raelnea Shine   Assigned To: Lance Sullivan   By: Date: 8/22/10

Page: Page:

FIGURE 3-20 Page 2 of property report.

Interviewing Witnesses

Sheryl Freeman (Friend and Coworker)

On August 22, 2010, at 2:30 p.m., my partner and I drove to the College of Columbus bookstore, where the victim worked, and met Sheryl Freeman, a coworker. She confirmed that she had worked with the missing woman, Nadia Pantovich, yesterday. She stated that Pantovich was in a good mood and that she was excited about it being Friday and going out with the girls that night. She stated that the day was busy because students were just arriving back and picking up their books for class, but nothing out of the ordinary occurred. Freeman made a point to mention "Gary," a guy who seemed to loiter around when Pantovich worked and even asked her out last year. She claimed she did not know Gary's last name but described him as being in his late 20s or early 30s, about 6' tall, and thin with glasses and brown hair. She recommended talking to him, and my partner handed her his card and asked her to call the next time she saw Gary. She assured him she would.

Billy Roach

After talking with Sheryl Freeman, my partner and I talked with another coworker who worked yesterday with Nadia Pantovich. He also admitted to seeing Gary but said he thought the guy was harmless if not just a little socially challenged. He did not remember anything out of the ordinary. He described Gary as approximately 28 to 32 years old, with brown nappy hair, about 6'1" tall and 210 pounds, with brown eyes.

Vicky Thompson

We then asked to speak with the manager who worked with Nadia Pantovich yesterday, Vicky Thompson. She claimed that nothing out of the ordinary occurred but did mention that Pantovich had complained last year about Gary hanging out and watching her. She had mentioned that Gary just happened to show up a lot wherever she was, and Pantovich felt like Gary was stalking her. In an incident that occurred around the middle of November of the previous year, another manager had actually kicked him out of the bookstore for loitering because Pantovich was uncomfortable with him there. She told us that Gary's last name is Daniels and that she remembered it because it was the name of her first boyfriend so it stuck out to her. My partner asked her if they had a record of the incident, and she promised to try to locate it for us.

INCIDENT REPORT FORM
(Incidents involving employees, students, visitors)

This is a confidential report and should not be made a part of an employee's personnel record. It is completed
to allow us to obtain advice from legal counsel and for the protection of the university and it's employees from potential liability.

******** PLEASE PRINT LEGIBLY *********

INFORMATION ABOUT THE PERSON INVOLVED IN THE INCIDENT:

Full Name: Nadya Pantovich   Social Sec.#: N/A

Home Address: 411 Meeting St. New Columbus, IC   Apt. 201   Gender: M (F)

Circle: Employee (Full-time, part-time, perm., temp.)   Student (SOM, SON, SOD, Other)   Visitor

Date of Birth: April 16, 1983   Home phone: (712) 313-0241   Campus Phone: (712) 325-4250

Campus address:

Job Title: Clerk   Supervisor: Julie Boleyn

INFORMATION ABOUT THE INCIDENT:

Date of Incident: August 15, 20   Time: 3:30 pm   Police notified: Yes (No) Case #:

Location of Incident: Book store

Describe what happened, how it happened, factors leading to the event, substances or objects involved. **Be as specific as
possible** (attach separate sheet if necessary): At approximatley 3:30 pm, Gary Daniels a visitor was loitering in the store. Mr. Daniels appeared to be paying extra attention to clerk Nadya Pantovich. He followed her around and continuously tried to start a conversation, and asked Ms. Pantovich on a date. She then notified me that she felt uncomfortable with his presence in the store. As manager I approached Mr. Daniels to leave, he became very loud and boisterous and two male employees came to assist me. At that time Mr. Daniels left the store.

Were there any witnesses to the incident? (Yes) No

If yes, attach separate sheet with names, addresses and phone numbers, or campus depts and phone.

Was the individual injured? If so, describe the injury (laceration, sprain, etc.), the part of body injured and any other
information known about the resulting injury(s): No

Was medical treatment provided?   Yes   (No)   Refused

If so, where (circle) :   Emerg. Rm.   The Workplace   Walk In Clinic   Other:

Will the employee miss time from work as a result of this incident? Yes (No) Unknown

REPORTER INFORMATION

Print Name of Reporter: Julie Boleyn

Reporter Signature: Julie Boleyn   Title: Manager

Date Report Completed: 8-15-09

V. April, 2002   EMPLOYEE REPORTS - Send to HRM in AB 360G.   VISITOR/STUDENT to Risk Management 500 Bldg
Suite 504.

FIGURE 3-21 Employer internal incident report.

Interview of Gary Daniels

At 4 p.m. my partner and I returned to the station and ran a National Crime Information Center (NCIC) report on Gary Daniels. We found that he had been arrested before on minor possession charges including a voyeurism charge when he was fifteen. We decided to interview Daniels and question him on his whereabouts last night and this morning.

My partner and I arrived at Gary Daniels' residence at approximately 5 p.m. We found him home and asked him if he would come down to the station to answer a few questions. He agreed, and at 5:30 p.m. we all sat down in the interrogation room:

Detective: "Before we start, I need to get some identification information. What is your full name?"

Daniels: "Gary Lee Daniels."

Detective: "Do you have any nicknames?"

Daniels: "No."

Detective: "Where were you born?"

Daniels: "New Columbus, Iowa."

Detective: "What is your birth date?"

Daniels "April 15, 1979."

Detective: "And what is your home address?"

Daniels: "Come on. Is this necessary? You know where I live. You picked me up!"

Detective: "Mr. Daniels, we just need a little background information for the official record just in case your information is useful. We do appreciate your patience and help."

Daniels: "Fine. I live at 2041 North Main Street, New Columbus, Iowa."

Detective: "And what is your occupation?"

Daniels: "I am a stocker at Bi-Lo."

Detective: "And how long have you been working there?"

Daniels: "Um, I don't really know. About five years."

Detective: "Have you held any other jobs?"

Daniels: "No."

Detective: "What about a wife? Are you married? Have any children?"

Daniels: "Nah, I'm not married yet, no kids."

Detective: "Yet? Are you and a certain someone serious?"

Daniels: "No, I just haven't met the right someone. She'll come along though."

Detective: "Yeah, been there myself. Just keep looking; that special someone will show up when the time is right. Can we get you anything to drink? Coffee, soda, or perhaps some water?"

Daniels: "Yeah, I'll take a Diet Coke."

Detective: "My partner will grab that for you. So tell me Mr. Daniels, where were you last night between 11:30 p.m. and 8:00 a.m. this morning?"

Daniels: "You gotta be kidding me, man. I got off work at 11 p.m. and went home. I like to watch Jay—he's a funny man, you know—then I went to bed. Didn't get up till damn near 11 o'clock this morning."

Detective: "You were working at Bi-Lo?"

Daniels: "Yeah."

Detective: "Do you know a Ms. Nadia Pantovich?"

Daniels: "Naddie? Yeah, I know her. What about her?"

Detective: "Well, we were just wondering, when was the last time you saw or talked to her?"

Daniels: "Man, I don't know. It's been a couple of months. Last time I saw her she had me kicked out of the school bookstore for nothing!"

Detective: "Yeah, we heard about that. Can you tell us what happened that day?"

Daniels: "Nothing happened! I was browsing the books—it is a bookstore—and she runs off and tells the manager that I have been harassing her and won't leave her alone. I only gave her a few compliments. I had asked her out a few days earlier and I just wanted to know if she had given it any more consideration."

Detective: "And had she?"

Daniels: "Yeah, and she made it very clear what her decision was, cause the next thing I know I have the manager coming over and all up in my face about how I need to leave and how I'm not welcome there. And she had this little punk stocker boy acting all big and tough like he could really take me on. It was laughable! Had I not been so taken off guard, I mean, come on, who would expect to get attacked just looking at some books?"

Detective: "Did you speak to her about this incident afterward?"

Daniels: "No. I received her message loud and clear. I try not to hang out with crazy chicks, and that one definitely proved to be mentally unstable."

Detective: "So, tell me again exactly the events of last night?"

Daniels: "I got off work at 11, went straight home, got there about 11:30, watched Jay Leno, and went to bed."

Detective: "Was anyone there with you?"

Daniels: "No. My roommate went home to visit his mom for the weekend."

Detective: "Is there anyone who can corroborate your story?"

Daniels: "No—look I thought you just needed my help? What is this about?"

Detective: "Ms. Pantovich is currently unaccounted for and we are just trying to find out where she may have gone. Do you have any idea where she may be?"

Daniels: "No, man. Wow, um, wow. I really didn't know her that well. I don't know where she might have gone."

Detectives: "Would you be willing to take a polygraph, attesting to the information you have given us?"

Daniels: "Yeah, man, whatever you guys need."

Detective: "Would you also submit to a quick examination by a nurse?"

Daniels: "What for?"

Detective: "She would look to see if you have any kind of wounds that could have been inflicted in a confrontation."

Daniels: "Yeah, sure, whatever."

We ended the interview at approximately 6:30 p.m. After walking Mr. Daniels to the waiting room, my partner called the polygraph examiner to set up an appointment for the polygraph, and we were in luck because she said she could be there in 40 minutes. I put on a clean pair of gloves and collected the Diet Coke can that Mr. Daniels was drinking from. I packaged the can and started an evidence log of it before carrying the can to the forensics lab for a quick comparison.

POLYGRAPH REPORT

To: MARK WILLIAMS

From: SANDRA WILSON   Polygraph Examiner SW

Subject: Polygraph Examination of: GARY DANIELS
            DOB: APRIL 15, 1979
            Race: CAUBASIAN
            Sex: MALE

Results: **NO DECEPTION INDICATED**

On (AUGUST 22, 2010) following consent to undergo polygraph examination, the subject was administered a specific polygraph examination. The main issue under consideration was whether or not the subject has any knowledge of, or personal involvement in a

During the test phase the subject was asked the following questions with responses as indicted:

DID YOU HAVE ANYTHING TO DO WITH THE DISAPPEARANCE OF NADIA PANTOVICH?

DID YOU HARM NADIA PANTOVICH IN ANY WAY?

DO YOU KNOW WHERE NADIA PANTOVICH IS NOW?

Upon completion of the examination, it was the opinion of the examiner that **NO DECEPTION** was indicated to the above relevant questions.

Respectfully submitted,

Sandra Wilson

Certified Polygraph Examiner

FIGURE 3-22 Polygraph results report.

The Preliminary Lab Report

I entered the forensic lab with Daniel's Diet Coke can in it and I was met by the excited and bubbly lab tech.

"I expect a nice juicy steak dinner for this fine scientific work," Amy Hepburn, the lab technician, stated, "Because you are about to looove me!"

I smiled at her indulgently and told her that if her latent fingerprinting skills were that good I would throw in an ice cream cone with a cherry on top. She laughed as she handed me a copy of her preliminary report. "I have a match for your fingerprints. One set belongs to Nadia Pantovich, but the other set is from a Mr. Alexander Romanov."

"That was quick. Do you have anything else processed for me?" I asked.

"As a matter of fact, I do." She stated, "I ran the DNA samples from the scene through CODIS, the Combined DNA Index System, to see if this guy has any priors, and I got a hit." The hit was from a case two years back with no arrests ever made, and the donor still unidentified.

"Anything else?" I asked her.

"Well, the fingerprints are the only thing really processed, but if you bring in Mr. Romanov's blood and semen sample, the DNA lab can run a comparison analysis and tell you if he matches the samples taken from the crime scene."

I thanked Amy and headed out to find the lead detective from the cold case, picking up my phone to let my partner know what I had just found out.

Cold Case

While my partner was running down some leads from witnesses, I made my way over to the desk of Detective Greene. I asked Greene about his cold case and any leads he might have had that might help us now. He claimed he wished he could help, but there wasn't much to go on. The girl, Audrey Taylor, went missing and was never found. Her apartment showed signs of a struggle and of sexual activity, which is why the semen was placed as evidence, but other than that there wasn't much to go on. The girl hadn't shown up for work for a couple of days and everyone assumed that she had gone home for spring break, so it wasn't until the next week that anyone even reported her missing. Detective Green offered to pull his file for me but said it probably wouldn't have anything of use in it. He said he would forward the file to me by the end of the day. I thanked him and went to meet up with my partner.

Sergeant Smith's Statement, continued
Maria Kostagonoas

At 4 p.m. I meet Maria Kostagonoas at the apartment complex across the street from the complex where our missing person resided. We walked to a nearby park and talked about the case. Kostagonoas is a graduate student at the college and is expected to graduate in December. She said she recognized the man following the female student as a graduate student who volunteers at Students Helping Students. She stated that the guy was very flirtatious and hands on. She also stated that a female friend of hers by the name of Jen Rosenberg had told her that last semester he seemed to follow her frequently. Rosenberg had said that when she went to the grocery store, gym, cafeteria, or for a run around the block, he would always appear. At first she thought it was just coincidence that he was always around, but then it started happening a lot more frequently and she became uncomfortable.

Kostagonoas said that she remembered the man helping Nadia Pantovich, as well as some other students, move in on August 13, 2010. After the students were moved in, she saw the young student and the man leave the building together. She said that they seemed to know each other and the girl seemed comfortable. Kostagonoas said that she was home all day and never left until she went out later that night around 9:30 p.m. She also said that Nadia Pantovich returned home approximately an hour after leaving with the young man. She said Pantovich was walking briskly but that she could not tell if she was upset or just in a hurry.

Maria Kostagonoas said that was all that she remembered about that night other than what she told police the previous night and that was at about 3 a.m. She was returning home and saw a young woman walking on the opposite side of the street toward the complex. She stated that a man was walking not far behind the woman. She said he was wearing a lime green shirt, blue jeans, sneakers, and a baseball cap.

Kostagonoas showed us a picture with the young graduate student in it. Although she did not remember seeing him at a party that night, he was wearing a white shirt, blue jeans, sneakers, and a baseball cap in the photo. The date on the photo was two weeks before the young student disappeared.

My partner and I decided to contact Jen Rosenberg. We asked Maria Kostagonoas about Rosenberg's whereabouts, and she directed us to an apartment in the same building where our missing student lived. She told us that since Rosenberg had been working at the campus bookstore and coffee shop, she had not seen much of her in the past few weeks.

The apartment was a few doors down from that of the missing student. Jen Rosenberg was home and agreed to speak with us. We asked her if she knew anything about the missing woman, and she said no. Rosenberg stated that she had been working a lot because it was the beginning of fall semester and she had not had time to get to know any of her neighbors.

We asked about the young man, and her body language and demeanor changed. Rosenberg stated that the young man was Alexander Romanov, a graduate student at the college. She said that Romanov was very friendly with the ladies and was always walking around. She said that he followed her one time but that she decided to confront Romanov and let him know that if he did not stop she would tell the police. She also informed him that her father was a police chief and would have no problem helping her get the man to leave her alone. Rosenberg said that after that confrontation he immediately stopped following her and she has not had a problem since.

My partner and I asked about the photo taken at a party two weeks before. She said that a group of students congregated at a bar on the weekends and that he was a regular at these parties. She said it was not uncommon for a person to shoot a picture and have random people jump into the photo. Rosenberg added that she believed Alexander Romanov lived on the top floor of the building, but she was not sure of the number.

My partner and I went back to the police station with the photo and tried to accurately identify our suspect. We identified the man in the photo as Alexander Romanov.

We pulled his information and found out he works for the biology department of College of Columbus, so my partner and I called down there to try to find out more about him. Because it was Saturday, the department was closed so we had to make a few more phone calls, but the work paid off because we spoke with his supervisor, Professor Malkivich, who informed us that Mr. Romanov was a polite, brilliant young man with a bright future ahead of him. He read off Romanov's list of achievements, and one in particular stood out—his volunteer work for Students Helping Students. As we inquired more about this program, Professor Malkivich informed us that the program is made up of students who spend their evenings walking students who have been in the bar too long back to their homes to ensure that they arrived safely. He informed us that Mr. Romanov was scheduled to work last night and offered to pull up the roster of students who volunteer. We exchanged information and he promised to fax us a copy of the roster and schedule, as well as a handbook of the program's rules and regulations.

Search Warrant

At 6:30 p.m. I began preparing a search warrant for Alexander Romanov's residence and vehicle. My partner returned to the complex to confirm Alexander Romanov's current address. I finished the search warrant and waited for my partner to return.

Nighttime Endorsement

We chose a nighttime endorsement because it seemed that Alexander Romanov tended to move about during the day. My partner confirmed Alexander's residence, and I walked to the courthouse and met the judge. He read my warrant, swore me in so that I could attest to my affidavit, and commanded that we search Alexander Romanov's residence at 938 Raymond Road, Apartment 30A, and his personal vehicle (a Nissan Sentra) in an effort to find the following items that may be linked to the commission of a felonious sexual assault or kidnapping:

1. Gun or weapon
2. Cell phone
3. Clothing and items belonging to potential victims

Miranda Rights Waiver

Place: ___New Columbus PS___

I, ___Alexander Romanov___ have been advised by

___Detective Daniels___ that I am suspected of

___a criminal sexual conduct and Kidnapping___

I have also been advised that:

(1) I have the right to remain silent and make no statement at all;

(2) Any statement I do make can be used against me in a court of law or other judicial or administrative proceeding;

(3) I have the right to consult with a lawyer prior to any questioning. This lawyer may be a civilian lawyer retained by me at no cost to the United States, or, if I cannot afford a lawyer, one will be appointed to represent me at no cost to me.

(4) I have the right to have my retained or appointed lawyer present during this interview; and,

(5) I may terminate this interview at any time, for any reason.

I understand my rights as related to me and as set forth above. With that understanding, I have decided that I do not desire to remain silent, consult with a retained or appointed lawyer, or have a lawyer present at this time. I make this decision freely and voluntarily. No threats or promises have been made to me.

Signature: ___Alexander Romanov___

Date and Time: ___8/22/10   9:00 pm___

Witnessed: ___David Daniels (detective)___

Date and Time: ___8/22/10   9:01___

At this time, I ___Alexander Romanov___ desire to make the following voluntary statement. This statement is made with an understanding of my rights as set forth above. It is made with no threats or promises having been extended to me.

FIGURE 3-23 Rights waiver signed by Alexander Romonov.

Search of Alexander Romanov's Car

Alexander Romanov's car was parked outside his apartment complex. We had it towed to the crime scene unit (CSU) processing garage. The car arrived for processing at 9:30 p.m. The interior of the car appeared to be freshly vacuumed and detailed. The exterior had the clean gleam of a newly washed and waxed vehicle.

The CSU technicians fingerprinted the entire exterior of the car but found no fingerprints. They also fingerprinted the interior of the car where fingerprints are always present and found only those belonging to the owner, Mr. Romanov.

During their search they examined the trunk and glove compartment, searching for any type of evidence that would help locate the missing person. In the glove compartment they found a gold cross necklace and collected it as evidence. The technicians also recovered a few hairs and a receipt from Mr. Bubbles Car Wash.

Reports

While the CSU technicians were processing the car, my partner and I went to Alexander Romanov's apartment and conducted the search authorized in the search warrant. We headed back to our desks to review the information and gather the reports from the lab on the evidence from the victim's apartment. Detective Greene came through, and the report from the cold case lacked any substantial evidence or leads and was quickly put to the side. We pulled up an NCIC criminal history report on Alexander Romanov; he came up without as much as a speeding ticket. As we were typing up the notes and writing our reports from the day, a young assistant delivered the report from the lab.

The evidence technicians found the following:

1. Latent fingerprints positively matched with Nadia Pantovich in various places and on the bedroom door in blood.
2. Latent fingerprints positively matched with Alexander Romanov on the front door, the bedroom doorknob, and the left and right top bedposts.
3. Semen tested positive on the sheets from the bed.
4. Blood tested positive from floor, bed, and door.
5. Human hair located on the bedroom floor to the left side of bed
6. A cell phone on the living room floor belonging to Nadia Pantovich

Interview with Alexander Romanov

Given the amount of evidence against Alexander Romanov, my partner and I decided it was time to begin formally questioning him about his involvement with the missing Nadia Pantovich. We took him into the interrogation room and read him his Miranda rights, which he waived. We then allowed him to sit in the room for about an hour by himself while we observed him for signs of nervousness and weaknesses.

SEARCH WARRANT AND AFFIDAVIT
(AFFIDAVIT)

_____ _Mark Williams_ _____ , being sworn, says that on the basis of the information contained within
(Name of Affiant)
this Search Warrant and Affidavit and the attached and incorporated **Statement of Probable Cause,** he/she has probable
cause to believe and does believe that the property described below is lawfully seizable pursuant to Penal Code Section 1524,
as indicated below, and is now located at the locations set forth below. Wherefore, affiant requests that this Search Warrant be
issued.

_____ _Mark Williams_ _____ , NIGHT SEARCH REQUESTED: YES [X] NO [   ]
(Signature of Affiant)

(SEARCH WARRANT)

THE PEOPLE OF THE STATE OF IOWA   TO ANY SHERIFF, POLICEMAN OR PEACE OFFICER IN THE COUNTY

OF Centralia   : proof by affidavit having been made before me by _____ _Mark Williams_ _____ ,
(Name of Affiant)

that there is probable cause to believe that the property described herein may be found at the locations set forth herein and that it
is lawfully seizable pursuant to Penal Code Section 1524 as indicated below by "x" (s) in that it:

_____ was stolen or embezzled

_X_ was used as the means of committing a felony

_XX_ is possessed by a person with the intent to use it as a means of committing a public offense or is possessed by another to whom he or she may have
delivered it for the purpose of concealing it or preventing its discovery,

_XX_ tends to show that a felony has been committed or that a particular person has committed a felony,

_____ tends to show that sexual exploitation of a child, in violation of P.C. Section 311.3, has occurred or is occurring;

YOU ARE THEREFORE COMMANDED TO SEARCH:

Alexander Romanov, 26 years old, DOB of Nov. 22, 1986, 6'2" 240 lbs
Green eyes, Brown Black hair.

Resides at 315 meeting Street. apt. 123.

FOR THE FOLLOWING PROPERTY:

Blood an Saliva samples for DNA Samples

Clothing from a female
Items belonging to a female
Cell phone
Gun or tools used for kidnapping or sexual assaults,

AND TO SEIZE IT IF FOUND and bring it forthwith before me, or this court, at the courthouse of this court. This Search Warrant
and incorporated Affidavit was sworn to and subscribed before me this _22_ day of _August_ , _2010_
at _8:00_ a.m./p.m. Wherefore, I find probable cause for the issuance of this Search Warrant and do issue it.

_____ _Peter Beck_ _____ , NIGHT SEARCH APPROVED: YES [X] NO [   ]
(Signature of Magistrate)

FIGURE 3-24 Search warrant and affidavit forms.

When we entered the interrogation room,, I began talking while my partner sat silently observing.

Detective: "Before we start, I will need to get some basic information. But first, can we offer you
something to drink?"

Romanov: "Water is fine." (My partner retrieved bottles of water for all of us.)

Detective: "What is your full name?"

Romanov: "Alexander Romanov."

Detective: "Do you have any nicknames?"

Romanov: "Yes, Alex and Zander."

Detective: "Where were you born?"

Romanov: "Kirov, Russia"

Detective: "How long have you been in the United States?"

Romanov: "Five years. I am here on a student visa working on my master's degree."

Detective: "What is your birth date?"

Romanov: "November 2, 1983."

Detective: "And what is your address here in the U.S.?"

Romanov: "It's 938 Raymond Road, Apartment 30A, New Columbus, Iowa 50515."

Detective: "What is your occupation?"

Romanov: "I am a full-time graduate student, and I am also a professor's aid. I work for Professor Malkivich over in the biology department."

Detective: "How do you know Nadia Pantovich?"

Romanov: "I don't know anyone by that name."

Detective: "Really? Because we have several witnesses placing you with her last night."

Romanov: "I am a volunteer for the school's program Students Helping Students. I help lots of people. I can't be expected to remember all of their names and faces."

Detective: "Do you remember anyone that you took home last night?"

Romanov: "No, I didn't know any of them. I only knew them as students from seeing them around campus."

Detective: "Well, do you remember the locations where you dropped these other students off? We would be more than happy to send out a couple of officers to talk with the residents."

Romanov: "No, I don't make it a practice to remember the homes of the students."

Detective: "Well, what time did you finish with your volunteering last night?"

Romanov: "About 3 a.m. The bars are closed at that time and people are generally done with finding food and ready to head home."

Detective: "Is there anyone that we can talk to who remembers seeing you after 12 o'clock?"

Romanov: "I am sure that there are plenty of people; I just can't tell you who."

Detective: "What about any other volunteers? Surely you must have run across them during the night?"

Romanov: "Sure. Ask around. I am sure one of them will remember talking to me."

Detective: "See, that's the funny thing. We did. They remember talking to you, but no one remembers seeing or talking to you after 12 o'clock. How do you explain that?"

Romanov: "Well, um. Fine, here it is. I accidentally fell sleep. I didn't want to say anything because I could get kicked out of the program, but I swear I didn't have anything to do with that girl getting kidnapped."

Detective: "You fell asleep? And where exactly did you do that?"

Romanov: "I fell asleep in my car. It was parked on the corner of Grove and Pine."

Detective: "Really? And what time did you wake up from your little nap?"

Romanov: "I must have woken up, I don't know, about 3:30 a.m."

Detective: "And what time did you decide to lie down and take that nap?"

Romanov: "About 11:30 that night I fell asleep."

Detective: "Interesting. We have a report here showing that your fingerprints were inside Nadia Pantovich's apartment. Can you explain this?"

Romanov: "Well, I would assume that I have probably walked her home before, if not last night, then some other night."

Detective: "So when you walk them home, you make it a habit of following them into their homes?"

Romanov: "Well, sometimes they get too inebriated to walk, and to prevent them from hurting themselves I sometimes take them inside so that they can lie down on the couch or whatever."

Detective: "And is this a normal operating standard?"

Romanov: "No, not really. They usually can manage to get into the house on their own, but there are the rare occasions."

Detective: "And when they are this drunk, you take them in the house by yourself, or do you have someone accompany you?"

Romanov: "We are not allowed to enter by ourselves. Someone has to be with us."

Detective: "So when is the last time you entered someone's apartment?"

Romanov: "I don't know for certain. It's not like I keep a journal of who I take home and where I take them."

Detective: "Okay, let's cut to the chase. We know you were the last one with Nadia. We have your fingerprints, we have your blood, and we have your semen at the scene. So where is she? You cooperate now and maybe the DA will cut you a deal. But make no mistake, we will find her and the longer it takes, the worse it's going to be for you."

Romanov: "You don't have anything, 'cause I didn't do anything!"

Detective: "Just like you didn't do anything to Audrey Taylor last year. Yeah, we know about her too."

Romanov: "I don't know what you're talking about."

Detective: "We have your semen from her apartment too. Are there are so many that you can't remember everyone you've killed? Come on, man. Where did you take her? We don't need their bodies; the jury will have no problem giving you the needle. I don't know how they do things in Russia, but here in the U.S. we don't look too kindly on predators who rape women and then kill 'em!"

Romanov: "I didn't kill nobody! You don't know what you are talking about!"

Detective: "No? Then why don't you enlighten us?"

Romanov: "I had been watching Nadia for a few weeks now. I had seen her at the bookstore when I went to pick up some books. The way she looked—so innocent, so full of life—just drew me in. So when I seen her come out of the club over on Bay Street, I don't remember which one, she appeared to have had too much to drink. I decided to approach her. She seen my shirt and recognized me as a Student Helping Students. She told me she was fine and that it had been a long day. She was planning to just go home and head to bed. I offered to walk her home. She told me she would be fine, that she only lived a few blocks away. I inquired about her roommate, and she let it out that her roommate was staying the night at her boyfriend's. I could tell Nadia was starting to get nervous and agitated that I was walking with her, so I fell back and followed her. When she got home she fumbled with her keys, so when she finally opened the door, that is when I came around the corner and up behind her.

She started to scream, so I pushed her back into the apartment and shut the door. She got up and tried to run into the bedroom. I ran after her, preventing her from shutting the door. She tried to climb over the bed and put distance between us. I grabbed her and pulled her back on the bed. She tried screaming again, so I slapped her and told her to be quiet. She continued to struggle and fight with me, so I grabbed one of the scarves she had on the end of her bed and began tying her up. I tied her to the bed and put another scarf across her mouth. Some of her clothes got ripped during the fight, so I just ripped the rest off of her. I keep a condom in my wallet just in case, you know, I get lucky, so I pulled it out. God only knows where this chick may have been. Little did I know that she turned out to be a virgin. Made a hell of a mess, but it was worth it. Meanwhile, she just sat there and cried, so I cleaned up a bit but realized that time had gotten away from me so I didn't clean up like I would have liked to. I figured I had her pretty well subdued so I untied her so we could go, and the little bitch hit me in the nose and I started bleeding. She got up and ran out of the room, and I chased her into the living room. I tripped as I came out of the bedroom, but I was still able to grab her ankle, causing her to lose her balance and run into some furniture. That slowed her down enough for me to get control of her again. She realized she had lost, so she became submissive again. I grabbed her and walked her into the kitchen where I grabbed a knife that was on the counter. I told her we were going to walk out to the car and if she made any noise I would kill her. She nodded that she understood. I grabbed a clean sheet and wrapped her up in it, and we walked across the street where I had parked my car. We drove to Hardeeville, South Carolina, where we met up with the transporters, and I passed her off. That is all I know. I don't kill them. I am only in charge of grabbing them."

Detective: "Wait a minute. You're telling us that you kidnap them for someone else?"

Romanov: "I am only the scout. I pick the women up and pass them to the transporters, who deliver them to the brokers. I don't know anything more than that. We only know our counterparts, to protect the brokers. I receive a call when they need a new girl along with a time to get her. Once I make the move, I notify them and we meet within two hours of my call to make the switch. They bring me $50,000, and I give them the girl. The phones are single use, and after we make the switch, they throw out the phone and will give me the number to the new one when they call with their next order."

Detective: "How many girls are we talking about?"

Romanov: "Eleven in the past two years."

Detective: "Where do you meet to exchange?"

Romanov: "The location changes, but this time we met at the Hess gas station in Hardeeville, off Highway 99.

Detective: "Is there anything else you would like to add at this time?"

Romanov: "No. That is everything I have. I did not kill the girls. They should all still be alive."

DATE/TIME OF ARREST	BOOKING REPORT	CASE NUMBER
8-22-10 10:00pm		2,0,1,0,5,4,3,4,8,6

PERSONAL DATA

DEFENDANT NAME (LAST, FIRST, MIDDLE): Romanov, Alexander | RACE: O | SEX: M | DATE OF BIRTH: 11-22-86 | DOCKET NUMBER:

AGE: | ETH.: | HEIGHT: 6'2 | WEIGHT: | HAIR: Black | EYES: Green | SOCIAL SECURITY NUMBER: | VISIBLE SCARS AND MARKS: none | NCIC: | I.D. NUMBER:

ADDRESS (NUMBER AND STREET): 315 Meeting St Apt 123 | CITY: New Columbus, ID | STATE: ID | ZIP CODE: 5055 | RESIDENT: J S (O) U | PHONE NUMBER:

ALIAS: | PLACE OF BIRTH: Kirov Romanov | DRIVERS LICENSE NUMBER: | STATE:

EMPLOYER OR OCCUPATION: | NEXT OF KIN: | ADDRESS (CITY AND STATE):

BOOKING OFFICER'S NAME: Ofc. Nicholas Grey | NUMBER: 4562 | ARRESTING OFFICER: Andre Perry | AGENCY: | NUMBER: 3257 |

ARRESTEE ARMED: ☐ YES ☒ NO   WEAPON TYPE: ☐ SEMI-AUTO ☐ FULL-AUTO   ☒ ON VIEW ARREST   ☐ SUMMONED   ☐ CUSTODY

JUVENILE DISPOSITION: 1. ☐ HANDLED, RELEASED 2. ☐ REFERRED TO OTHER AUTHORITY   * J — This Jurisdiction.   S — State.   O — Out of State.   U — Unknown

ADDITIONAL CASE NUMBERS   MORE IN REMARKS ☐

CHARGE / BOND

IF HOLDING FOR ANOTHER AGENCY, CIRCLE CHARGE - A, B, C

CHARGE I.D.	A	B	C
CHARGE	Kidnapping	Criminal Sexual Conduct 1st	
STATUTE	10-57-1473	32-16-3215	
BOND AMOUNT	N/A	N/A	
BOND TYPE			
RET. DATE			
DISPOSITION			

DISPOSITION

	DAYS	AMOUNT	DAYS	AMOUNT	DAYS	AMOUNT
SENTENCE						
TIME SERVED						
GOOD TIME						
BALANCE						
PAID						
RECEIPT NUMBER						

RELEASE DATE	TIME	RELEASING OFFICER		NUMBER	AGENCY RELEASED TO

SIGNATURE OF RECEIVING OFFICIAL X *Nicholas Grey*   LIST ANY REMARKS BELOW

REMARKS:

DEFENDANTS PERSONAL PROPERTY RECEIPT | TOTAL CASH AT TIME OF ARREST→ $ 76.32

QUANTITY	ITEM	QUANTITY	ITEM
1	pair Jeans		
1	gold ring		
1	pair sneakers		
1	T-shirt		

I HEREBY STATE THAT THE PROPERTY LISTED ABOVE CONSTITUTES ALL CLAIMS TO PROPERTY ON MY PERSON AT THE TIME OF MY ARREST.

X *Alexander Rom*   *Nicholas Grey*
DEFENDANT'S SIGNATURE AT TIME OF ARREST   OFFICER

I HEREBY STATE, ON THE DATE OF MY RELEASE, THAT THE ABOVE LISTED PROPERTY WAS RETURNED TO ME, IN SATISFACTION OF ALL CLAIMS TO PROPERTY ON MY PERSON AT THE TIME OF MY ARREST.

X _____

FIGURE 3-25 Alexander Romanov's booking report.

Sergeant Smith's Statement, continued

My partner and I left the interrogation in a bit of shock, stunned at what we just stumbled across. We decided to follow up on Romanov's claim of transferring the girl, so we called down to the police department in Hardeeville and asked them to follow up on the lead at the gas station. They called back 40 minutes later to inform us that the station had handed over the tape to them and they would review it for us. There was nothing left for my partner to do, and we had been working nonstop. We had Romanov booked and decided to call it a night and restart in the morning with a fresh outlook.

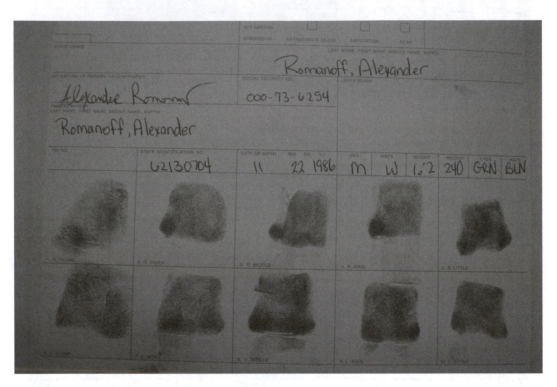

FIGURE 3-26 Alexander Romanov's fingerprint card.

COMPLAINT #<u>201082212</u>

NEW COLUMBUS POLICE DEPARTMENT

DEFENDANT STATEMENT

STATEMENT OF <u>Alexander Romanov</u>

HOME ADDRESS <u>315 Meeting Street. Apt. 123</u>

EMPLOYER <u>Cofc (Teacher's Aid)</u>   BUSINESS ADDRESS   <u>NA</u>

BUSINESS PHONE <u>NA</u>

THIS STATEMENT IS GIVEN   <u>8/22/10</u>   (DATE) AT   <u>9:15PM</u> (TIME)

New Columbus Police Department   (LOCATION)

I have been watching Nadia for a few weeks now, I had seen her at the bookstore when I went to pick up some books. The way she looked....so innocent, so full of life just drew me in. So when I seen her come out of the club over on Bay St., I don't remember which one, she appeared to have had too much to drink, I decided to approach her. She seen my shirt and recognized me as a Student Helping Students (SHS). She told me she was fine and that it had been a long day, she was planning on just going home and heading to bed. I offered to walk her home, she told me she would be fine she only lived a few blocks away. I inquired about her roommate and she let it out that her roommate was staying the night at her boyfriends. I could tell Nadia was starting to get nervous and agitated that I was walking with her so I fell back and followed her. When she got home she fumbled with her keys, so, when she finally opened the door that is when I came around the corner and up behind her. She started to scream so I pushed her back into the apartment and shut the door. She got up and tried to run into the bedroom. I ran after her preventing her from shutting the door. She tried to climb over the bed and put distance between us. I grabbed her and pulled her back on the bed. She tried screaming again so I slapped her and told her to be quiet. She continued to struggle and fight with me so I grabbed one of the scarfs she had on the end of her bed and began tying her up. I tied her up to the bed and put another scarf across her mouth. Some of her clothes got ripped during the fight so I just ripped the rest off of her. I keep a condom in my wallet just in case, you know I get lucky, so I pulled it out god only knows where this chic may have been. Well little to my knowledge but to my great pleasure she had turned out to be a virgin. Made a hell of a mess but it was worth it. Meanwhile she just sat their and cried, so I cleaned up a bit and realized that time had gotten away from me so I didn't clean up like I would have liked too. I figured I had her pretty well subdued so I untied her so we could go, and the little bitch hit me in the nose, which is how my blood got mixed into the scene. She got up and ran out of the room and I chased her into the living room, I tripped as I came out of the bedroom but I was still able to grab her ankle causing her to lose her balance but not enough that she didn't recover but it did cause her to run into some furniture causing her to slow down enough for me to get control of her again. So, once I regained control and she realized she had lost she became submissive again, I grabbed her and walked her into the kitchen where I grabbed a knife she had laying out, I told her we were going to walk out to the car and if she made any noise I would kill her. She nodded she understood I grabbed a clean sheet and wrapped her up in it and we walked across the street where I had my car parked. We drove to Hardeeville, S.C, where we met up with the transporters, and I passed her off. That is all I know. I don't kill them I am only in charge of grabbing them.

I am only the Scout, I pick the women up and pass them to the transporters, who deliver them to the brokers. I don't know anything more than that. We only know our counterparts to protect the brokers. I receive a call when they need a new girl along with a time to get her. Once I make the move, I notify them and we meet within two hours of my call to make the switch. They bring me $50,000 and I give them the girl. The phones are single use and after we make the switch they throw out the phone and will give me the number to the new one when they call with their next order.

I HAVE RAD THE FOREGOING STATEMENT OR HAVE HAD TO EAD TO ME AND IT TRUE AND CORRECT TO THE BEST OF MY KNOWLEDGE. I HAVE GIVEN THIS STATEMENT FREELY AND VOLUNTARILY AND HAVE BEEN PROVIDED A COPY OF MY STATEMENT.

WITNESS: Alexander Romanov
WITNESS: Detective

SIGNATURE: *Alexander Romanov*
Alexander Romanov

FIGURE 3-27 Defendant statement.

The next morning my partner and I returned to the station and began finishing the paperwork, and about 10 o'clock we received a digital recording of the video from the gas station in Hardeeville. We watched the video, which confirmed Romanov's claim to only pick up the girls and hand them to a transporter. We decided that in order to pursue this to the end, we were going to need far more resources than our department has to offer. We headed to the chief's office. We informed him of the turn in events, and he agreed that with this crossing borders aspect it would be best to hand this over to the Federal Bureau of Investigation. Human trafficking is a large and complex organizational crime that requires years of work and dedication with a great amount of resources not available to an agency of our size. However, we made a major break toward protecting young women in our city.

■ ■ ■

Discussion Questions

1. Review the case narrative and all the documentation. What (if any) inconsistencies did you note in the case file?
2. Explain the motive for the perpetrator to commit this crime.
3. What is the most significant physical evidence in this case?
4. Identify any problems with the fact that a victim was not located during this investigation. Could this have been a staged crime scene? Why or why not?

5. Are you familiar with the crimes that are committed on a daily basis in the United States that are linked to human trafficking? As you reviewed the case file, what evidence might have pointed to the victim, Nadia Pantovich, being abducted for the purposes of human trafficking?
6. What consistencies did you discover among the various witness statements?
7. How did DNA evidence factor into the investigation of Nadia Pantovich's disappearance?
8. Why was it necessary to read Alexander Romanov his Miranda rights?
9. Based on the investigation, what do you think happened?
10. Construct the timeline, and identify the investigative strategies implemented in this case.

Vehicular Homicide: Accidental or Intentional

OBJECTIVE

As we move further into studying various criminal offenses, the student will learn to differentiate between types of crimes, establish that a crime has occurred, and understand how the public can assist law enforcement investigative efforts. This case involves a hit and run, resulting in a murder charge.

KEY TERMS

affiant

affidavit

arrest warrant

complainant

corpus delicti

deductive reasoning

incident report

inductive reasoning

interrogation

interview

Miranda rights

offense report

probable cause

property/evidence form

report

return

search warrant

supplemental report

touch DNA

victim

waiver

witnesses

What You Will Learn

LEARNING OUTCOMES

- Fully comprehend the importance of conducting a thorough initial investigation
- Examine the critical aspects of sparse information and no witnesses to a crime
- Develop leads and a successful investigation to determine the truth
- Identify the underlying essentials to completing a thorough investigation
- Explain how perseverance contributes to solving criminal investigations

CRITICAL THINKING

- Elements of the crime
- Types of physical evidence
- Key investigative strategies

Introduction

Citizens report crimes to the police—that is the way it works, for the most part. The police cannot be all things to all people at all times. Sir Robert Peel, who was credited with the creation of the "bobbies" in England, said, "the police are the people and the people are the police" [1]. Therefore, it is necessary for members of the public to understand they have the responsibility and the right to report crime. They must be the eyes and ears of the police and provide the most accurate information possible to assist in the investigations. Police officers and investigators are trained to **interview** people to obtain information, verify that information, seek details, and question people who are not suspects but know something about the crime—all in an effort to determine if a criminal offense has occurred. Many crimes occur with no witnesses present; remember, however, that **witnesses** are not always *eyewitnesses*; they are simply people who have some key information that can be compiled by a competent detective. These data can be compiled to create the sequence of events that preceded criminal activity or that occurred after the event took place.

Most Common Types of Reports

Police officers create an incident report, an offense report, or some other type of event **report** to document the events that have been reported. A completed **incident report** covers a wide spectrum of activities, many of which do not involve a criminal activity. Incident reports are created when citizens suspect something has happened, but proof of the event cannot be established at that time. For example, after eating lunch at a deli in New York City, a tourist discovers her wallet is missing from her jacket pocket. She goes to a nearby police precinct to file a report. While answering the police officer's questions, she realizes that the wallet could have fallen out of her pocket in the taxi or she could be the victim of a pickpocket. At this point it cannot be determined that a crime did occur, and she cannot provide information that definitely indicates a crime has occurred. Without this ***corpus delicti*** evidence, which establishes that a crime has been committed and supports the elements of the crime, there is insufficient data for a crime or offense report. When an officer completes an **offense report**, it has been determined that all the elements of the criminal offense are present—meaning that a crime has occurred.

The officer files an incident report to document that the tourist reported her wallet missing, and a report number is generated. The tourist will need this number and a copy of the report to file an insurance claim and perhaps even to board the plane home if she does not have other personal identification when trying to enter the secure area of the airport. If a crime report was completed and later the wallet was found, then statistics on the type and frequency of crime occurring would be skewed as police agencies are required to report all offenses for the annual *FBI Uniform Crime Report* (UCR). Incidents reports, which do not compile criminal activity, are not included in the UCR.

Probable Cause

What information does the reporting officer in the preceding paragraph need to differentiate whether to file an incident or an offense report? When facts and circumstances are combined in a way that would lead a reasonable person to believe that a crime has occurred and that a specified individual committed that crime, **probable cause** has been established. What elements of this definition were missing in the lost wallet story? As the police officer interviewed the tourist, deductive reasoning was employed. **Deductive reasoning** is a reconstructive process one uses to draw conclusions based on reconstructing specific facts. For example, it was a fact that the tourist did not have her wallet. However, she could not state for certain that the wallet had been stolen from her pocket, only that the wallet was not in her pocket when she went to retrieve it to pay for her lunch. If the tourist had been able to affirmatively state she saw or felt someone remove the wallet from her jacket pocket, what criminal offense would have been investigated? In Chapter 2 you learned the elements of the crime of larceny or theft. Had those elements been present in this example, the officer would have completed an offense report, as it had been established a crime had occurred. Can the *corpus delicti*, the body of the crime, be definitively established? Was the complainant able to state the wallet had been taken from her to establish that a crime did in fact occur?

The tourist is the **complainant**—a person who requests that some action be taken. Regardless of whether a street thief picked her pocket or she lost the wallet in a taxi, the tourist would have been listed as the complainant on either an incident or an offense report. Using **inductive reasoning**, the practice of making a generalization and establishing it by gathering specific facts, the tourist created a theory that her wallet had been stolen. She could not prove that a crime occurred, and she would have been inducing the universal from the particular—that is, because her wallet was missing, it was stolen. In this case, the complainant is the **victim**—a person injured by a crime—only if she can prove she did not lose the wallet but that it was stolen.

Analyzing the Situation

Based on what you have read in this chapter, answer the following question: Every time a police officer completes an offense report, does that mean a crime has occurred? You will recall the definition for a crime is an act or omission that is illegal and results in injury to the public, and that in an offense report, all elements of a criminal offense must be identified. Now, take this discussion even further. If the victim is notified later in the day her missing credit cards are being used in stores all over New York City, is it correct to assume the wallet was stolen? There are new crimes being committed through the fraudulent use of a credit card, but this still does not prove the wallet was intentionally taken from the victim's pocket. The perpetrator using the credit cards could have found the wallet, either in a taxicab or on the street. Be sure in all incidents that every potential offense is identified, but you must go further and conduct an analysis of the facts to determine which actions constitute criminal activity and meet the minimum requirements for the particular crimes.

When the complainant/victim contacts the police with this new information, an offense report will be completed documenting the activities reported by the credit card company. Subsequent investigation will be handled by a specialized unit within the detective division requiring **supplemental reports**, which are continual documentation of the actions taken by the investigator to follow up and identify the perpetrator. Retail stores often videotape all customer transactions; the investigator may contact the stores where fraudulent activities were reported to obtain photos of the suspects. There is a strong possibility the credit card numbers will be used to purchase goods via the Internet, and consequently no suspects will be identified.

All the information gathered by the detective will be distributed among officers and is also available to the security divisions of retail stores. Although the stolen credit cards will be deactivated, the goods purchased with those cards often readily appear in pawnshops, yard sales, and other black-market outlets. Supplemental reports will detail the ongoing investigation. In the event some of the items purchased on the cards are identified and retrieved, this activity would be recorded on **property/evidence forms**, which begin the chain-of-custody process. These forms provide a description of the property or evidence, including the assignment of an item number and the signature of the person taking the property or evidence into custody. When the property is returned to the rightful owner, signatures are obtained that document the entire process. Property/evidence forms are maintained for every piece of physical evidence from the crime scene to the courtroom, and they ensure continuity and integrity of the evidence as well as provide the necessary paper trail that leads to courtroom acceptance.

The Effective Detective

Once the solvability factors indicate the potential for additional information and leads are identified, the detective begins the investigation. Establishing the timeline and an investigational strategy will assist in identifying individuals to be interviewed and locations where other information may be obtained during the follow-up. Effective detectives are talented talkers. They are attempting to glean information from witnesses, victims, concerned citizens, potential suspects, and disinterested third parties. A review of the data gathered from these interviews should begin to fill in the unknown portions of the timeline and sequence of events. Depending on the information that the detective obtains during interviews, additional people may be identified and placed into the investigative strategy for this case. Many interviews do not lead to useful information but must be documented in the case file. The detective must also verify all information provided throughout the interviews, and everything must be corroborated or disproved as the case advances. Again, the effective detective does not assume all information is truthful, and many times individuals must be interviewed more than one time to establish the credibility of the statements made to the detective.

No Witnesses?

If no witnesses are identified in the preliminary report, the detective will pursue leads provided through physical evidence analysis, video recordings from surrounding locations where the events occurred, and by relying on citizen input programs such as Crime Stoppers. Many people want to report information but do not want to "get involved." Crime Stoppers and similar programs provide outlets for people to offer information anonymously to law enforcement agencies.

There are many other reasons why citizens who possess information relating to a crime may not be willing to come forward and speak with the police. Cultural differences, threats, intimidation, language barriers, or distrust of the police are some of the obstacles detectives must overcome when seeking to identify potential witnesses.

Communities with active citizen-reporting programs often find these services to be extremely beneficial, as detectives are provided with information that may lead to the successful completion of a criminal investigation. Many offer some type of monetary reward upon conviction of the offender for the crimes under investigation. Internet access to these services has greatly enhanced the input provided by the community.

Physical evidence analysis may yield other paths of questioning for the detectives and may enhance their determination that additional physical evidence exists and the perpetrator can be identified through that evidence. The use of DNA profile databases is growing annually. Although this technology is still limited to investigations of serious crimes, more states are enacting legislation that requires arrestees to provide a DNA sample to be entered into the CODIS database. Perpetrators are identified through DNA that is deposited through skin cells when they come into contact with items—this process is known as **touch DNA**. If the *modus operandi* (MO) is identified and the perpetrator has an established pattern of touching specific areas in the residence or business, the detectives will recognize that the area needs to be swabbed to detect DNA left by the suspect. Once again, in a case where no witnesses have been identified, the physical evidence can provide the lead the detective needs to solve the case.

Miranda Rights

The case file grows as the detective documents investigative activities. These reports reflect the investigator's thorough knowledge of the elements of the crimes, the sequence of investigation, constitutional protections, and case law. When suspects are identified and placed into a custodial interrogation, they are always read their **Miranda rights** to protect their Fifth Amendment right against self-incrimination and the Sixth Amendment right to counsel. Made popular by television shows, most people can recite Miranda:

> *You have the right to remain silent. Anything you say can and will be used against you in a court of law. You have the right to speak to an attorney. If you cannot afford an attorney, one will be appointed for you. Do you understand these rights as I have explained them to you? Having these rights in mind, do you wish to talk to us now?*
>
> *Miranda v. Arizona* (1966)

Agencies and states require the detective to provide notification the subject can decide to stop answering questions and request an attorney at any time throughout the **interrogation** or questioning of a person who is the focus of an investigation.

As you read earlier, the suspect signs a Miranda rights **waiver** if he or she agrees to answer the questions presented during the detective's interrogation. The waiver must be articulated and voluntary and includes the signature of the suspect.

Court Documents

When enough information to establish probable cause has been compiled, the detective will complete statements presented to the court. At this time the detective is placed under oath and becomes the **affiant** who presents the facts and seeks either a search warrant or an arrest warrant (depending on the individual situation). A **search warrant** is a court order issued by a magistrate or judge, which commands the officer to proceed to a particular place and conduct a search for a specific item. If the item is found, it must be brought back to the court and documented in a **return**, or written inventory of the property seized, including the date and time when the search took place. A copy of the search warrant and the inventory must also be left at the place where the search was conducted.

An **arrest warrant** is a court order that commands police officers to take a person into custody and bring that person to the judge to answer to the allegations set forth by the affiant in the warrant. Contained in both types of warrants is a sworn **affidavit**, which is a statement of all facts leading to the establishment of probable cause that the crime was committed and the person under investigation committed the offenses. An arrest warrant also contains a return documenting the day, date, and time that the defendant named in the warrant was arrested.

An Arrest Does Not End the Investigation

The original documents are returned to the issuing court; however, copies of all documents pertaining to the search or arrest procedures are placed in the case file. Property/evidence forms are completed, which signifies the beginning of the chain of custody for evidentiary items pertinent to the criminal investigation.

The involvement of the detective does not end when an arrest takes place. The prosecutor's office must evaluate the validity of the case file and determine if there are additional avenues of investigation or even other perpetrators who may have been implicated by evidence obtained or through interrogations of the suspect. Open communication and ongoing collaboration are required as the case progresses to the courtroom. If physical evidence requires additional scientific examination, the detective must complete lab submittal forms and ensure the property/evidence unit is informed of the need for the evidence to be submitted and transported to the crime lab.

Crime lab analysis reports completed by the examining agency also become part of the case file. The evidence must be securely transported back to the property/evidence unit for storage until the court date. The chain of custody forms must document every movement of the physical evidence, including the name of the individual transporting the evidence to the lab, time and date of submittal, examiner's information, time and date, and then the same information for the return of the evidence to the property/evidence unit. This is a complicated, yet critical component of the case file, and if there is any break in the continuity of the record, the physical evidence may not be admissible in court. Detectives are aware of the considerable amount of time necessary for physical evidence to be transported, examined, and returned to the agency. Local, state, and federal crime laboratories are always faced with personnel shortages, reduced budgets, and a tremendous backlog of evidence submitted for analysis. No shortcuts or time reductions are available to ensure justice for everyone—including the suspect who has been arrested and may be residing in jail awaiting trial for several months.

■ ■ ■ ▬▬▬▬▬▬▬▬▬▬▬▬▬▬▬▬▬▬▬▬▬▬▬▬▬▬▬▬▬▬▬▬▬▬▬▬▬▬▬

Case File: Hit and Run

Case File Elements

- Offense report
- Supplemental reports
- Witness statements
- Follow-up
- Additional keys to solving the Investigation

Critical Questions and Activities

1. As you review the following case file, you must create the timeline for this case. Do you have all the documentation necessary to establish that timeline in the courtroom? If not, what is missing? How would you create that documentation?
2. What pieces of information link the suspect to the scene? How do you link the information so that a jury will accept the conclusions of your investigation?
3. What is the most significant information that led you to the suspect?

North Collins Police Department

CASE FILE: 2011CNCFH0005

VICTIM: Jose Ricardo Gonzales   SUSPECT: Dean J. Sanford

FIGURE 4-1 Opening page of case file.

Statement of Detective Robert A. Storey
17 January 2011

Approximately 0730: I (Detective Robert A. Storey, Badge #242) was detailed to the scene of a hit-and-run accident that occurred in the city of North Collins, Kentucky. The victim was a 37-year-old Hispanic male, later identified as Jose Ricardo Gonzales, address unknown. The victim was discovered on Ashley Phosphate Road lying in the grassy area in front of Norton Car Stereo. The victim was found clothed, with extensive wounds to his head, which was lying at an awkward angle. A damaged black Mt. Fury Roadmaster bicycle was found several feet from the body. This department launched an intensive investigation to determine the manner and cause of the victim's death.

0820: I interviewed the complainant, Linda L. Johnson, who discovered the body. She informed me that she was on her way to work when she saw the man. She walked within approximately 5 feet of the body but turned back when she saw the blood and called 911.

Incident Report

Approximately 0830: I dispatched responding Officer Jamie Harrell to canvas area businesses for potential eyewitnesses. His efforts resulted in nothing significant to the investigation.

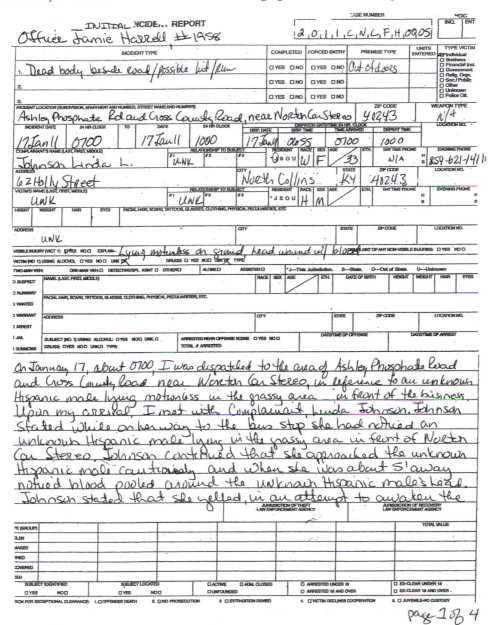

FIGURE 4-2 First page of initial incident report.

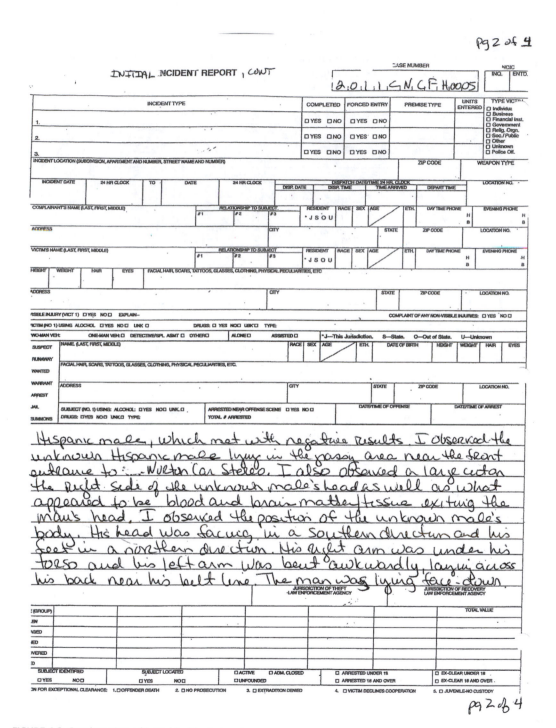

Pg 2 of 4

INITIAL INCIDENT REPORT, CONT

CASE NUMBER: 2011GNCFH0005

NCIC: INQ. ENTD.

INCIDENT TYPE 1. 2. 3. — COMPLETED ☐ YES ☐ NO — FORCED ENTRY ☐ YES ☐ NO — PREMISE TYPE — UNITS ENTERED — TYPE VICTIM: ☐ Individual ☐ Business ☐ Financial Inst. ☐ Government ☐ Relig. Orgn. ☐ Soc./Public ☐ Other ☐ Unknown ☐ Police Off.

INCIDENT LOCATION (SUBDIVISION, APARTMENT AND NUMBER, STREET NAME AND NUMBER) — ZIP CODE — WEAPON TYPE

INCIDENT DATE — 24 HR CLOCK — TO — DATE — 24 HR CLOCK — DISPATCH DATE/TIME 24 HR. CLOCK: DISP. DATE, DISP. TIME, TIME ARRIVED, DEPART TIME — LOCATION NO.

COMPLAINANT'S NAME (LAST, FIRST, MIDDLE) — RELATIONSHIP TO SUBJECT #1 #2 #3 — RESIDENT J S O U — RACE — SEX — AGE — ETH. — DAY TIME PHONE H B — EVENING PHONE H B

ADDRESS — CITY — STATE — ZIP CODE — LOCATION NO.

VICTIM'S NAME (LAST, FIRST, MIDDLE) — RELATIONSHIP TO SUBJECT #1 #2 #3 — RESIDENT J S O U — RACE — SEX — AGE — ETH. — DAY TIME PHONE H B — EVENING PHONE H B

HEIGHT — WEIGHT — HAIR — EYES — FACIAL HAIR, SCARS, TATTOOS, GLASSES, CLOTHING, PHYSICAL PECULIARITIES, ETC

ADDRESS — CITY — STATE — ZIP CODE — LOCATION NO.

VISIBLE INJURY (VICT 1) ☐ YES NO ☐ EXPLAIN— — COMPLAINT OF ANY NON-VISIBLE INJURIES: ☐ YES NO ☐

VICTIM (NO 1) USING ALCOHOL ☐ YES NO ☐ UNK ☐ — DRUGS: ☐ YES NO ☐ UNK ☐ TYPE:

TWO-MAN VEH: — ONE-MAN VEH: ☐ DETECTIVE/SPL. ASMT ☐ OTHER ☐ — ALONE ☐ — ASSISTED ☐ — *J—This Jurisdiction. S—State. O—Out of State. U—Unknown

SUSPECT / RUNAWAY / WANTED / WARRANT / ARREST / JAIL / SUMMONS — NAME (LAST, FIRST, MIDDLE) — RACE — SEX — AGE — ETH. — DATE OF BIRTH — HEIGHT — WEIGHT — HAIR — EYES

FACIAL HAIR, SCARS, TATTOOS, GLASSES, CLOTHING, PHYSICAL PECULIARITIES, ETC.

ADDRESS — CITY — STATE — ZIP CODE — LOCATION NO.

SUBJECT (NO. 1) USING: ALCOHOL: ☐ YES NO ☐ UNK. ☐ DRUGS: ☐ YES NO ☐ UNK ☐ TYPE: — ARRESTED NEAR OFFENSE SCENE ☐ YES NO ☐ TOTAL # ARRESTED — DATE/TIME OF OFFENSE — DATE/TIME OF ARREST

Hispanic male, which met with negative results. I observed the unknown Hispanic male lying in the grassy area near the front entrance to ... Wurton Car Stereo. I also observed a large cut on the right side of the unknown male's head as well as what appeared to be blood and brain matter/tissue exiting the man's head. I observed the position of the unknown male's body. His head was facing in a southern direction and his feet in a northern direction. His right arm was under his torso and his left arm was bent awkwardly, laying across his back near his belt line. The man was lying face-down.

JURISDICTION OF THEFT LAW ENFORCEMENT AGENCY — JURISDICTION OF RECOVERY LAW ENFORCEMENT AGENCY

(GROUP) / EN / AGED / ED / VERED / D — TOTAL VALUE

SUBJECT IDENTIFIED ☐ YES NO ☐ — SUBJECT LOCATED ☐ YES NO ☐ — ☐ ACTIVE ☐ ADM. CLOSED ☐ UNFOUNDED — ☐ ARRESTED UNDER 18 ☐ ARRESTED 18 AND OVER — ☐ EX-CLEAR UNDER 18 ☐ EX-CLEAR 18 AND OVER

REASON FOR EXCEPTIONAL CLEARANCE: 1. ☐ OFFENDER DEATH 2. ☐ NO PROSECUTION 3. ☐ EXTRADITION DENIED 4. ☐ VICTIM DECLINES COOPERATION 5. ☐ JUVENILE-NO CUSTODY

pg 2 of 4

FIGURE 4-3 Continuation of initial incident report.

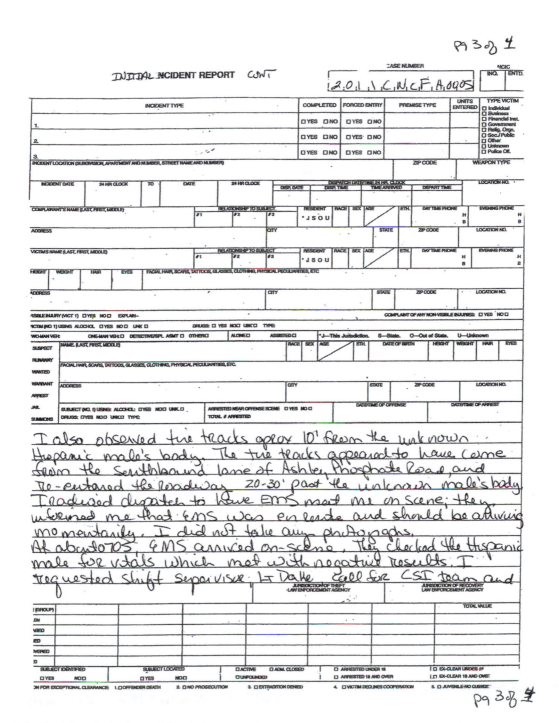

pg 3 of 4

INITIAL INCIDENT REPORT CONT

I also observed tire tracks aprox 10' from the unknown Hispanic male's body. The tire tracks appeared to have come from the southbound lane of Ashley Phosphate Road, and re-entered the roadway 20-30' past the unknown male's body. I radioed dispatch to have EMS meet me on scene; they informed me that EMS was en route and should be arriving momentarily. I did not take any photographs. At about 0705, EMS arrived on-scene. They checked the Hispanic male for vitals which met with negative results. I requested shift supervisor Lt Dake call for CSI team and

pg 3 of 4

FIGURE 4-4 Page 3 of a 4-page initial incident report.

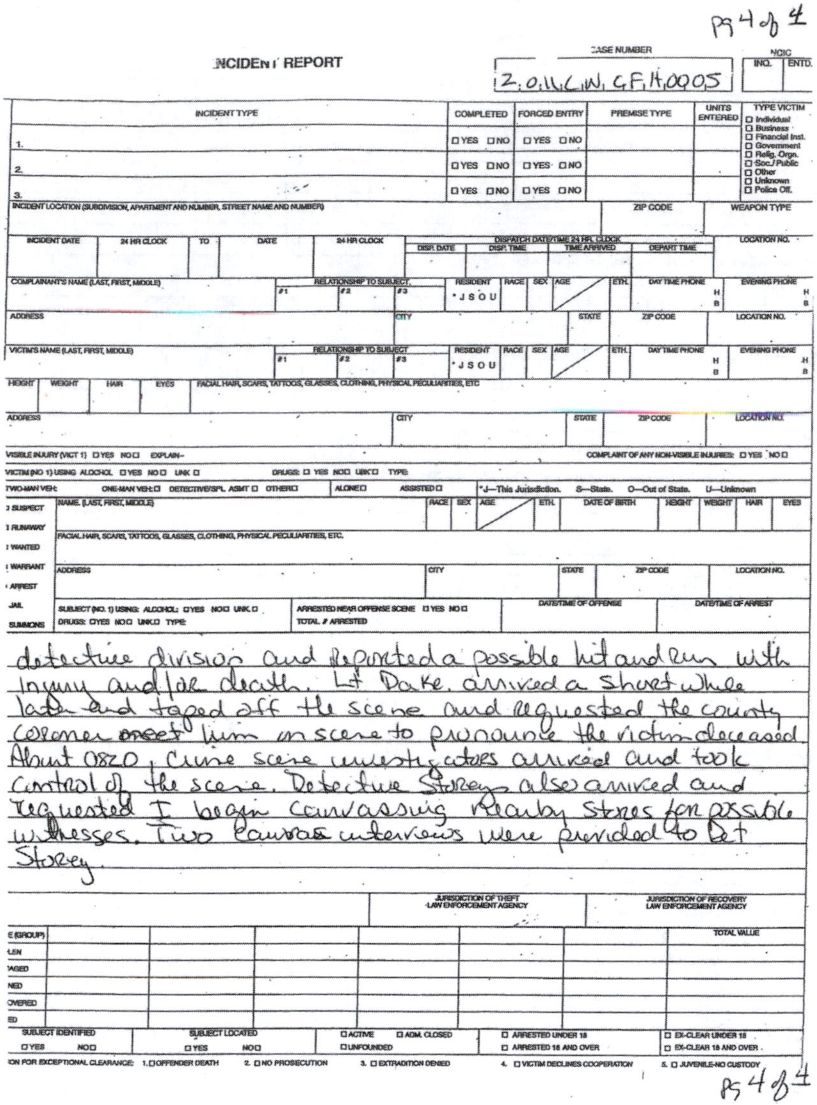

FIGURE 4-5 Incident reports may contain numerous pages.

Crime Scene Sketches

0840: Sergeant Bill Fulmer, crime scene investigator, arrived on scene to perform the crime scene investigation. His initial findings led him to believe the victim was hit by a vehicle and died on the scene.

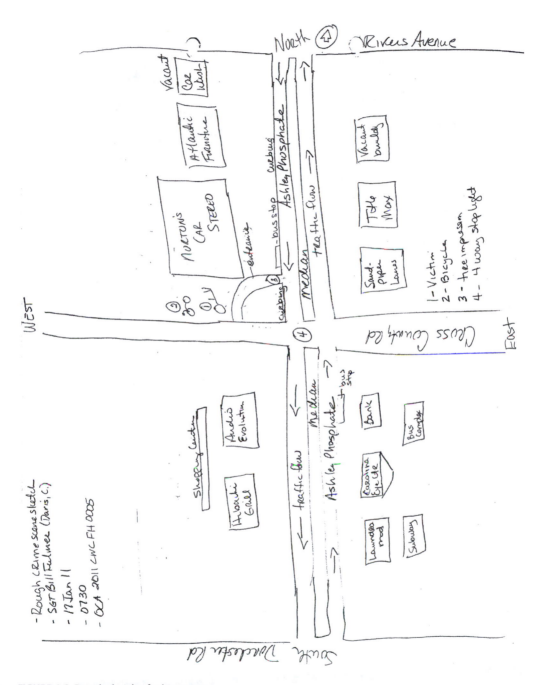

FIGURE 4-6 Rough sketch of crime scene.

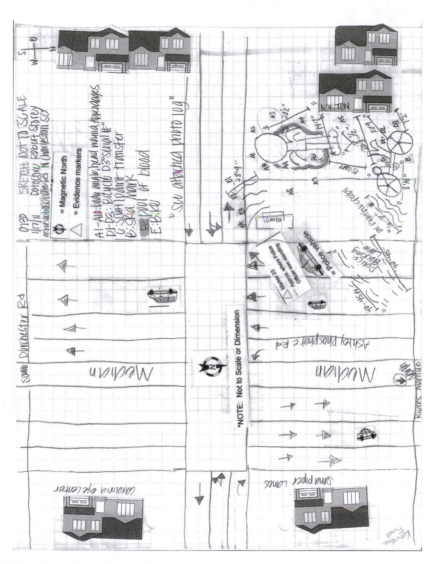

FIGURE 4-7 Detailed evidence sketch of scene.

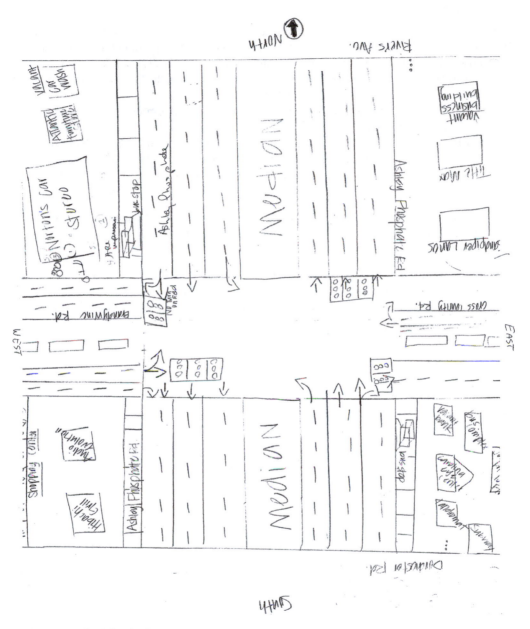

FIGURE 4-8 Finished sketch of scene.

Statement of Detective Robert A. Storey, continued

1000: I called the North Collins Police Department (NCPD) dispatch to see if the 911 tapes from 0700, January 16, 2011, to 0700, January 17, 2011, could yield anything pertinent to the investigation. Amy Houser, chief of dispatch, indicated she would review them and call me back.

1432: Amy Houser called reporting some possible information on the 911 tapes from January 16. I advised her I would be over soon to listen to them.

1700: I reviewed the 911 tape Amy Houser had discovered and determined that one segment may be of value to this investigation.

1900: I interviewed the 911 caller, Jose M. Hernandez, who reported that he had observed a Mercedes SUV crossing over into the southbound lane in front of him numerous times around 2030 on January 16, 2011. He thought the driver might be drunk, so he called 911 to report the driver.

18 January 2011

0830: I completed a Crime Stoppers ad detailing the hit and run and requested that the local news and radio stations run it for the next two weeks, as frequently as possible.

Autopsy

1115: I attended the autopsy of the victim. At the end of the autopsy, the medical examiner reported that the victim had died of blunt force trauma injuries sustained from being hit by a vehicle moving at a high rate of speed. Based on the pattern injuries on the victim, the vehicle was large and traveling upward of 60 miles per hour.

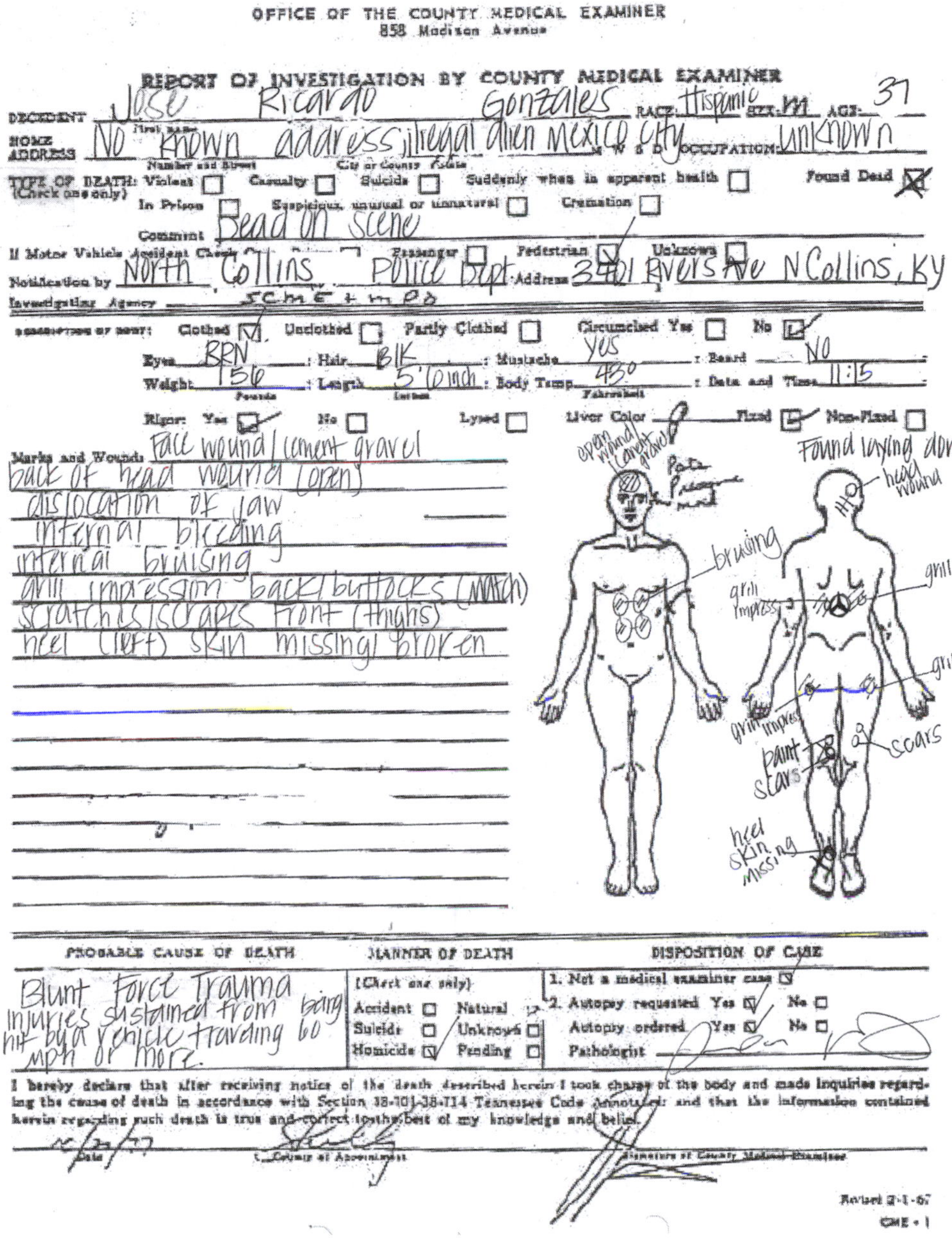

OFFICE OF THE COUNTY MEDICAL EXAMINER
858 Madison Avenue

REPORT OF INVESTIGATION BY COUNTY MEDICAL EXAMINER

DECEDENT: Jose (First name) Ricardo Gonzales RACE: Hispanic SEX: M AGE: 37

HOME ADDRESS: No known address, illegal alien Mexico City (Number and Street / City or County / State) OCCUPATION: unknown

TYPE OF DEATH: (Check one only) Violent ☐ Casualty ☐ Suicide ☐ Suddenly when in apparent health ☐ Found Dead ☒
In Prison ☐ Suspicious, unusual or unnatural ☐ Cremation ☐

Comment: Dead on scene

If Motor Vehicle Accident Check: Driver ☐ Passenger ☐ Pedestrian ☒ Unknown ☐

Notification by: North Collins Police Dept Address: 3401 Rivers Ave N Collins, KY

Investigating Agency: SCME+MPD

DESCRIPTION OF BODY: Clothed ☒ Unclothed ☐ Partly Clothed ☐ Circumcised Yes ☐ No ☒

Eyes: BRN ; Hair: BlK ; Mustache: yes ; Beard: NO

Weight: 156 (Pounds) ; Length: 5'10 inch (Inches) ; Body Temp: 430 (Fahrenheit) ; Date and Time: 11:15

Rigor: Yes ☒ No ☐ Lysed ☐ Liver Color: P Fixed ☒ Non-Fixed ☐

Marks and Wounds: Face wound/cement gravel
back of head wound (open)
dislocation of jaw
internal bleeding
internal bruising
grill impression back/buttocks (match)
scratches/scrapes front (thighs)
heel (left) skin missing/broken

PROBABLE CAUSE OF DEATH	MANNER OF DEATH	DISPOSITION OF CASE
Blunt Force Trauma injuries sustained from being hit by a vehicle traveling 60 mph or more.	(Check one only) Accident ☐ Natural ☐ Suicide ☐ Unknown ☐ Homicide ☒ Pending ☐	1. Not a medical examiner case ☒ 2. Autopsy requested Yes ☒ No ☐ Autopsy ordered Yes ☒ No ☐ Pathologist ______

I hereby declare that after receiving notice of the death described herein I took charge of the body and made inquiries regarding the cause of death in accordance with Section 38-701-38-714 Tennessee Code Annotated: and that the information contained herein regarding such death is true and correct to the best of my knowledge and belief.

12/24/77 (Date) ______ County of Appointment ______ Signature of County Medical Examiner

Revised 2-1-67
CME - 1

FIGURE 4-9 Autopsy diagram #1.

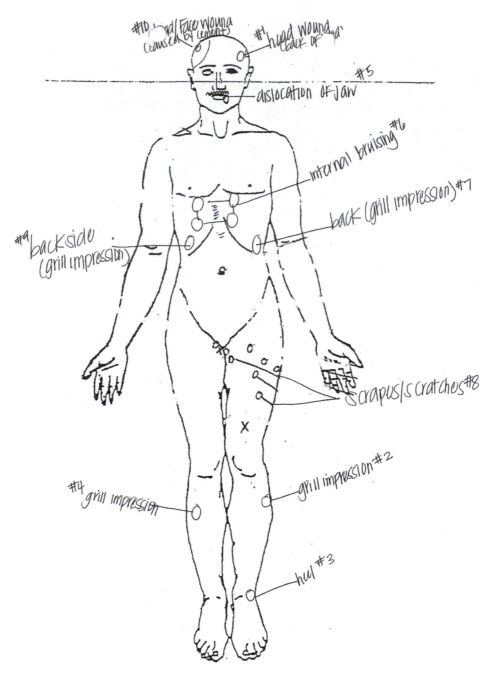

FIGURE 4-10 Autopsy diagram #2.

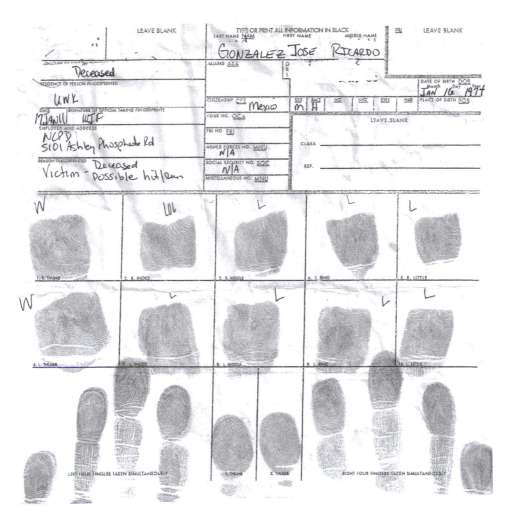

FIGURE 4-11 Fingerprints of victim.

Statement of Detective Robert A. Storey, continued
19 January 2011

0930: I reviewed Sergeant Bill Fulmer's crime scene investigation report. Physical and trace evidence from the scene indicated the color of the car was blue. The chain-of-custody form thoroughly documented the status of all physical evidence collected.

Crime Stoppers Reports

0930-1500: I returned three Crime Stoppers calls, none of which offered substantive information.

CRIME STOPERS OF KENTUCKY
P.O. Box 559 North Collins, KY
PH: (859) 333.1313   FAX: (859) 333.1515
CONFIDENTIAL – DO NOT INCLUDE IN CASE FILE

Report #	001	Received:	19 Jan 11 JS
Alt. ID		Date of Report:	19 Jan 11
Case No:	2011 CNL FH 0005		
Taken By:	Jolene Smith	Time Taken:	0935
Offense Type:	Homicide, H+R		
Location:			
Agency:	NCPD	Officer:	Det. Storey

Information:

Anonymous caller advised Osama Ben Laden was driving a checkered cab which hit him and his dog in a crosswalk on Broad Street.

Information Transmitted to _NCPD_ (Agency)
on _19 Jan 11   1105_ (Date, Time)
Individual transmitting information: _J Smith_

FIGURE 4-12 Crime Stoppers Tip #1.

CRIME STOPERS OF KENTUCKY
P.O. Box 559 North Collins, KY
PH: (859) 333.1313   FAX: (859) 333.1515
CONFIDENTIAL – DO NOT INCLUDE IN CASE FILE

Report #	002	Received:	19 Jan 11 Rhode
Alt. ID		Date of Report:	19 Jan 11
Case No:	2011 CNC FH0005		
Taken By:	Rhonda Rhode	Time Taken:	1220
Offense Type:	Hit and Run		
Location:			
Agency:	NCPD	Officer:	Det. Storey

Information:

Mrs Mary Lou Christman, 601 South Magnolia St. 859-832-0115 said her neighbor's green Volkswagon had a smashed in front fender. The neighbor's name is Christopher Hurt at 603 South Magnolia Street. Mrs. Christman also inquired as to whether or not we could do something about Mr. Hart's barking dogs.

Information Transmitted to _NCPD_ (Agency)
on _Jan 19, 2011   1300_ (Date, Time)
Individual transmitting information: _R Rhode_

FIGURE 4-13 Crime Stoppers Tip #2.

CRIME STOPERS OF KENTUCKY
P.O. Box 559 North Collins, KY
PH: (859) 333.1313 FAX: (859) 333.1515
CONFIDENTIAL – DO NOT INCLUDE IN CASE FILE

Report #	003	Received:	19 Jan 11 JS
Alt. ID		Date of Report:	19 Jan 11
Case No:	2011 CNL FH005		
Taken By:	Glenn Smith	Time Taken:	1452
Offense Type:	H+R		
Location:			
Agency:	NCPD	Officer:	Det Story

Information:

Wanda Sue Ramos, 746 Riviss Avenue, said she saw a gold Honda car swerving on Ashley Phosphate Rd. on Monday January 17. She thinks it hit something, then drove off. She can be reached at 859-941-1411

Information Transmitted to ___NCPD___ (Agency)
on __19 Jan 11___ __1510___ (Date, Time)
Individual transmitting information: ___J Smith___

FIGURE 4-14 Crime Stoppers Tip #3.

Investigating Auto Shops
19 January–21 January 2011

I called the following auto repair shops to inquire about repairs made to vehicles in the previous two days. All calls resulted in negative responses.

AAA's Chop Shop
Moore's Paint and Body
Norton and Richardson Body Shop
Precision Collision, Inc.
Richard's Corvette
Summerville Collision Center, Inc.

Fingerprints

22 January 2011

The fingerprints (Figure 4-11) taken from the victim hit a match in the Automated Fingerprint Identification System (AFIS). The victim's name is Jose Ricardo Gonzalez. He is an illegal alien from Mexico City. He was in jail in Florida for possession of a controlled substance and burglary. He was out on probation pending return to Mexico when he traveled to North Collins. The victim has no known relatives.

Potential Witness Interviews

Lisa Jeffers

1 February 2011

1030: I interviewed Lisa T. Jeffers, a guidance counselor at Porter-Gaud school, regarding her Crime Stoppers call. Ms. Jeffers advised that one of her students, Zachary Sanford, may have some information regarding the hit and run.

CRIME STOPPERS OF KENTUCKY
P.O. Box 559 North Collins, KY
PH: (859) 333.1313 FAX: (859) 333.1515
CONFIDENTIAL – DO NOT INCLUDE IN CASE FILE

Report #	004	Received:	Feb 11 JHall
Alt. ID	6131-BC	Date of Report:	1 Feb 11
Case No:	2011 CAX.F H005		
Taken By:	Jessie Hall	Time Taken:	0830
Offense Type:	Possible Hit + Run		
Location:			
Agency:	NCPD	Officer:	Det. Story

Information:

Ms. Lisa Jeffers called to say one of her students at Porter Gaud may have some information regarding the HtR on Ashley Phosphate Rd. a couple of weeks ago. Please call her at the school @ 859-402-4775 before 3:00 pm.

Information Transmitted to ____NCPD____ (Agency)
on __1 Feb 11__ __0900__ (Date, Time)
Individual transmitting information: __JHall__

FIGURE 4-15

Zachary Sanford

1100: I interviewed nine-year-old Zachary Sanford. Because of the nature of his information, I interviewed him at the school in the presence of Ms. Jeffers. Zachary relayed that on the evening of his birthday, January 16, while driving from the Sonic Restaurant on Rivers Avenue to his home in Coosaw Creek, his father hit something, which cracked the windshield of their car. Zachary indicated that his parents were arguing while his father was driving, leading me to believe there might be a domestic problem in the home.

Investigation of Suspect
Background Check

1330: I ran a criminal background check on Dr. and Mrs. Sanford. Both criminal histories are clean; however, Mrs. Sanford has extensive traffic violations on her DMV record. Dr. Sanford's DMV record is clean.

Second Interview with Delta Waring Sanford

1630: After rights advisement, I interviewed Zachary's mother, Mrs. Delta Waring Sanford. Mrs. Sanford denied any domestic abuse and was not cooperative. After answering a few questions, she requested a lawyer, at which time I concluded the interview.

Interview with Dean Stanford

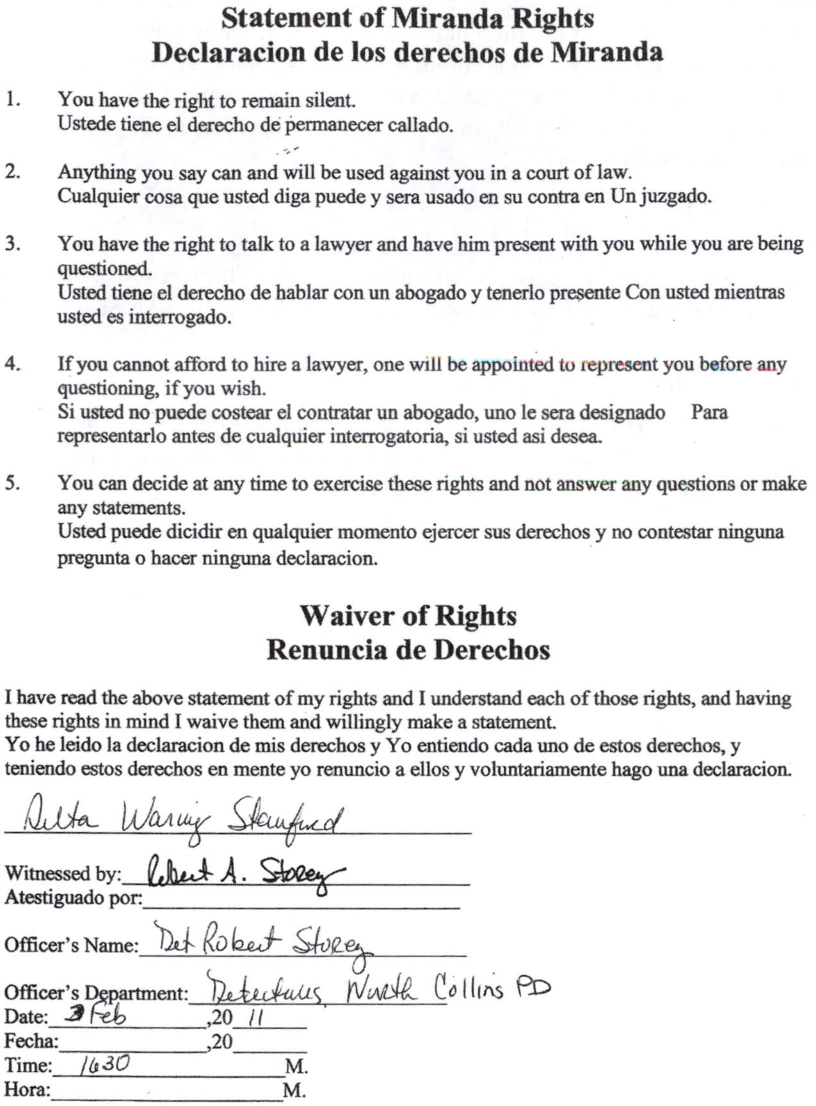

Statement of Miranda Rights
Declaracion de los derechos de Miranda

1.   You have the right to remain silent.
      Ustede tiene el derecho de permanecer callado.

2.   Anything you say can and will be used against you in a court of law.
      Cualquier cosa que usted diga puede y sera usado en su contra en Un juzgado.

3.   You have the right to talk to a lawyer and have him present with you while you are being questioned.
      Usted tiene el derecho de hablar con un abogado y tenerlo presente Con usted mientras usted es interrogado.

4.   If you cannot afford to hire a lawyer, one will be appointed to represent you before any questioning, if you wish.
      Si usted no puede costear el contratar un abogado, uno le sera designado   Para representarlo antes de cualquier interrogatoria, si usted asi desea.

5.   You can decide at any time to exercise these rights and not answer any questions or make any statements.
      Usted puede dicidir en qualquier momento ejercer sus derechos y no contestar ninguna pregunta o hacer ninguna declaracion.

Waiver of Rights
Renuncia de Derechos

I have read the above statement of my rights and I understand each of those rights, and having these rights in mind I waive them and willingly make a statement.
Yo he leido la declaracion de mis derechos y Yo entiendo cada uno de estos derechos, y teniendo estos derechos en mente yo renuncio a ellos y voluntariamente hago una declaracion.

Delta Waring Stanford

Witnessed by: *Robert A. Storey*
Atestiguado por:

Officer's Name: *Det Robert Storey*

Officer's Department: *Detectives, North Collins PD*
Date: *3 Feb* ,20 *11*
Fecha: ,20
Time: *1630* M.
Hora: M.

FIGURE 4-16 Miranda waiver for Delta Waring Sanford.

1700: After rights advisement, I interviewed Zachary's father, Dr. Dean J. Sanford. Dr. Sanford was quite cooperative but denied driving on Ashley Phosphate Road the evening of January 16. He stated that his wife drives a GL450 Mercedes SUV, light blue in color with a Kentucky vanity tag that reads, "Miss Delta."

Search of the Vehicle
1 February 2011

2100: I applied for a search warrant for Dr. Sanford's GL450 Mercedes. Judge Einsteiner granted the warrant.

2200: The Sanfords' GL450 Mercedes SUV was seized from the Sanfords' driveway at 4300 Club Course Boulevard after crime scene investigators took photos and video and reviewed the exterior for evidence. Although the SUV was red in color, the VIN numbers matched. Acme Tow and Go towed the vehicle to the NCPD impound lot.

Follow-up Investigation on the Vehicle
2 February 2011

0800-1000: I called the following repair shops seeking info on repairs on a 2010 GL450 Mercedes. All inquiries met with negative responses.

Harold Arnold's Sentry Buick Pontiac	J & L Auto Body Inc.
C & L Body Repair	JT's Paint and Body Shop
Dent Express	Jeff's Auto
Paintless Dent Removal	MAACO Collision Repair and Service
Home Town Paint and Body	Miles Road Paint and Body Service

Financial Investigation

1015: I obtained the Sanfords' credit card receipt from the Coosaw Creek Crab Shack, verifying that the Sanfords ate dinner there Sunday evening, January 16, 2011, from approximately 1900 to 2000. Two glasses of white wine were ordered; however, no dessert was ordered. The manager of the Crab Shack voluntarily gave me the receipt.

Follow-up Investigation of the Vehicle
3 February 2011

0800: I called Boone's Auto Repair and Detailing Shop, inquiring about body work done on a 2010 GL450 Mercedes SUV. The owner, Kenny A. Boone, said he had done some work on a similar vehicle a few weeks ago and agreed to meet with me.

1000: I interviewed Kenny Boone; he provided me information and a repair receipt for repairs made to a 2010 GL450 light blue Mercedes SUV registered to Dr. Dean J. Sanford. Mr. Boone said the owner, Dean Sanford, paid in cash for the repairs and requested the vehicle be painted red. Mr. Boone replaced the windshield and the front grill and repaired several dents/scratches before painting the vehicle. Mr. Boone agreed to give me the receipt and the Mercedes' grill. The grill will be tested for the victim's DNA. Mr. Boone had destroyed the windshield, which was the only other part he replaced on the SUV.

Detective Robert A. Storey Narrative, continued

1045: Dr. Sanford called and requested a meeting, which we set up for 1400. Dr. Sanford stated that he needed to talk. While I was on the phone with him, I requested to re-interview his wife, setting that meeting for 1630.

Arrest Warrant

1130: Believing that I had enough evidence to arrest Dr. Sanford at our meeting, I obtained an arrest warrant from Judge Gantery.

Interview with Suspect

1400: After rights advisement, I spoke with Dr. Sanford. During this interview, Dr. Sanford admitted to hitting something with his car on Ashley Phosphate Road the evening of January 16.

Statement of Miranda Rights
Declaracion de los derechos de Miranda

1.   You have the right to remain silent.
      Ustede tiene el derecho de permanecer callado.

2.   Anything you say can and will be used against you in a court of law.
      Cualquier cosa que usted diga puede y sera usado en su contra en Un juzgado.

3.   You have the right to talk to a lawyer and have him present with you while you are being questioned.
      Usted tiene el derecho de hablar con un abogado y tenerlo presente Con usted mientras usted es interrogado.

4.   If you cannot afford to hire a lawyer, one will be appointed to represent you before any questioning, if you wish.
      Si usted no puede costear el contratar un abogado, uno le sera designado   Para representarlo antes de cualquier interrogatoria, si usted asi desea.

5.   You can decide at any time to exercise these rights and not answer any questions or make any statements.
      Usted puede dicidir en qualquier momento ejercer sus derechos y no contestar ninguna pregunta o hacer ninguna declaracion.

Waiver of Rights
Renuncia de Derechos

I have read the above statement of my rights and I understand each of those rights, and having these rights in mind I waive them and willingly make a statement.
Yo he leido la declaracion de mis derechos y Yo entiendo cada uno de estos derechos, y teniendo estos derechos en mente yo renuncio a ellos y voluntariamente hago una declaracion.

Dean J. Sanford

Witnessed by: *Robert A. Storey*
Atestiguado por: _____

Officer's Name: *Det Robert Storey*

Officer's Department: *Detectives, North Collins' PD*
Date: *1 Feb* _____ ,20 *11*
Fecha: _____ ,20 _____
Time: *1700* _____ M.
Hora: _____ M.

FIGURE 4-17 Miranda waiver for Dr. Dean J. Sanford.

1630: After rights advisement, I re-interviewed Mrs. Delta Sanford, with her attorney present. Mrs. Sanford denied anything happening on Ashley Phosphate Road on January 16 and refused to answer further questions. Mrs. Sanford was released without arrest.

Arrest

1645: I arrested Dr. Sanford on violation of KY Codes 56-5-1210, 56-5-1230, and 56-5-1260. He was booked into the North Collins Police Department annex at 1700.

BOOKING REPORT

DATE/TIME OF AR. 3 Feb 11, 1900

CASE NUMBER 2011CNCFH0005

PERSONAL DATA

DEFENDANT NAME (LAST, FIRST, MIDDLE): Sanford Dean James | RACE: W | SEX: M | DATE OF BIRTH: 8 Dec 66 | DOCKET NUMBER:

AGE: 44 | ETH.: C | HEIGHT: 5'11 | WEIGHT: 170 | HAIR: Brown | EYES: Blue | SOCIAL SECURITY NUMBER: 098-77-6543 | VISIBLE SCARS AND MARKS: None | NCIC: ✓ | I.D. NUMBER:

ADDRESS (NUMBER AND STREET): 4300 Club Course Drive | CITY: North Collins | STATE: KY | ZIP CODE: 40243 | RESIDENT: • J (S) O U | PHONE NUMBER: 859-555-1111

ALIAS: N/A | PLACE OF BIRTH: Boone NC | DRIVERS LICENSE NUMBER: #005040967 | STATE: KY

EMPLOYER OR OCCUPATION: Dentist-Sanford Dental | NEXT OF KIN: Delta Waring Sanford | ADDRESS (CITY AND STATE): Same

B... OFFICER'S NAME: Officer Nia Callaway | NUMBER: 625 | ARRESTING OFFICER: Det Robert Storey | AGENCY: NCPD | NUMBER: 242

ARRESTEE ARMED ☐ YES ☑ NO WEAPON TYPE: ☐ SEMI-AUTO ☐ FULL-AUTO ☑ ON VIEW ARREST ☐ SUMMONED ☐ CUSTODY

JUVENILE DISPOSITION: 1. ☐ HANDLED, RELEASED 2. ☐ REFFERED TO OTHER AUTHORITY *J — This Jurisdiction. S — State. O — Out of State. U — Unknown

ADDITIONAL CASE NUMBERS MORE IN REMARKS ☐

IF HOLDING FOR ANOTHER AGENCY, CIRCLE CHARGE - A, B, C

	A	B	C
CHARGE I.D.	H-64493		
CHARGE	Accident Resulting in Death	Failure to Render Aid	Failure to Report Accident
STATUTE	56-5-1210	56-5-1230	56-5-1260
BOND AMOUNT	#100,000 TO BE SET	TO BE SET	TO BE SET
BOND TYPE	GSC	GSC	GSC
RET. DATE	TBD	TBD	TBD
DISPOSITION	H-64493	H-64493	H-64493

	A DAYS	A AMOUNT	B DAYS	B AMOUNT	C DAYS	C AMOUNT
SENTENCE						
TIME SERVED						
GOOD TIME						
BALANCE						
PAID						
RECEIPT NUMBER						

RELEASE DATE | TIME | RELEASING OFFICER | NUMBER | AGENCY RELEASED TO

SIGNATURE OF RECEIVING OFFICIAL X [signature] LIST ANY REMARKS BELOW

REMARKS:

DEFENDANTS PERSONAL PROPERTY RECEIPT TOTAL CASH AT TIME OF ARREST→ $62.45

QUANTITY	ITEM	QUANTITY	ITEM
1	Wallet		
1 set	keys - Mercedes, BMW, home		

I HEREBY STATE THAT THE PROPERTY LISTED ABOVE CONSTITUTES ALL CLAIMS TO PROPERTY ON MY PERSON AT THE TIME OF MY ARREST.

X Dean J. Sanford — DEFENDANT'S SIGNATURE AT TIME OF ARREST

Robert A Storey NCPD Detective — OFFICER

I HEREBY STATE, ON THE DATE OF MY RELEASE, THAT THE ABOVE LISTED PROPERTY WAS RETURNED TO ME, IN SATISFACTION OF ALL CLAIMS TO PROPERTY ON MY PERSON AT THE TIME OF MY ARREST.

X

FIGURE 4-18 Booking report.

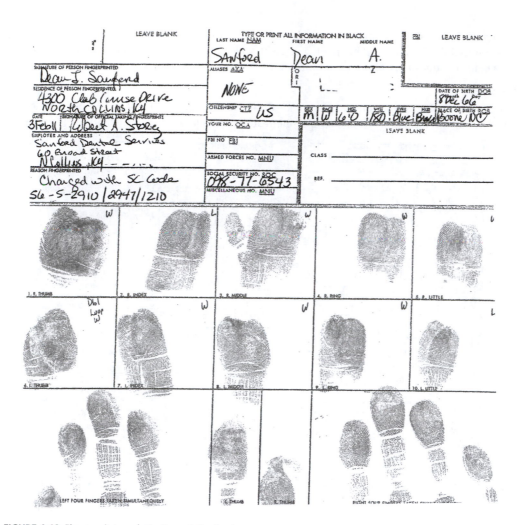

FIGURE 4-19 Fingerprint card, Dr. Dean J. Sanford.

DORCHESTER COUNTY SHERIFF'S OFFICE

BOND REQUEST

DCSO CASE NUMBER (S): _2011 CWC FH 0005_

DEFENDANT'S NAME: _Dean James Sanford_

DATE OF BIRTH: _8 Dec 66_   SSN: _098-77-6543_

PRIOR ARREST: YES (NO)   SID #: _____   FBI #: _____

ARREST CHARGE # 1: _Accident Resulting in Death_ WARRANT # _H-644938_

BOND RECOMMENDATION: _____ _TO BE SET_

ARREST CHARGE # 2: _Failure to Render Aid_ WARRANT # _H-644938_

BOND RECOMMENDATION: _TO BE SET_

ARREST CHARGE # 3: _Failure to Report Accident_ WARRANT # _H-644938_

BOND RECOMMENDATION: _TO BE SET_

ARREST CHARGE # 4: _____ WARRANT # _____

BOND RECOMMENDATION: _____

ADDITIONAL INFORMATION: _____

_____

_____

_____

_____

ARRESTING OFFICER: _ROBERT STOREY_   _Robert Storey — 3Feb 11_
                     Print Name   Signature and Date

FIGURE 4-20 Bond request form.

Discussion Questions

1. Construct a timeline for this incident and the subsequent investigation. What additional information might you need to substantiate the timeline?
2. How does the fact that no witnesses have been located impact the investigation?
3. Explain how you established the credibility of Zachary Sanford's statement.
4. List the information that was necessary to obtain a search warrant for Delta Sanford's SUV.
5. What are the elements of the crime(s) committed if this offense occurred in your state?
6. What evidence can link the suspect to the scene of the crime?
7. If you have found discrepancies in the paperwork, list them and explain what information is incorrect.

Reference

[1]   Reith, C. (1956). *A New Study of Police History*. London: Oliver and Boyd.

5 A Serial Arsonist?

OBJECTIVE

All criminal investigations should follow a systematic and logical process. Unlimited time and resources are not available to law enforcement officers or detectives. This chapter provides the sources where statutes can be found and identifies various types of evidence that will be encountered in all types of investigations. This case file deals with arson.

KEY TERMS

beyond a reasonable doubt	preponderance of the evidence	standard of proof
circumstantial evidence	profiling	statute of limitations
Code of Federal Regulations	real evidence	testimonial evidence
direct evidence	reasonable suspicion	United States Code

What You Will Learn

LEARNING OUTCOMES

- Compare and contrast various types of evidence
- Examine case documentation to establish links
- Demonstrate knowledge of how cases are cleared
- Become familiar with the investigative strategy decision tree

CRITICAL THINKING

- Elements of the crime
- Types of physical evidence
- Key investigative strategies

Overview

This chapter links several areas of interest together as you have now learned how to create case files and document the investigation from the time the call is reported until all leads have been thoroughly investigated. As you begin to conclude case investigations—whether or not they result in prosecution—there are additional aspects that must be considered throughout the process.

Crime Statistics

The Federal Bureau of Investigation (FBI) collects monthly reports from approximately 18,000 agencies. These data are provided on a voluntary basis and are used to provide an overall view of crime trends in the United States. The results are published annually in a report titled *Crime in the United States* [1]. The results are available at www.fbi.gov/about-us/cjis/ucr/crime-in-the-u.s/2010/crime-in-the-u.s.-2010.

FBI Uniform Crime Report

Not every criminal offense is solved by an arrest. Many weeks, months, or years may pass between the time a crime was committed and the time a suspect is charged. There is virtually no way to link that data accurately. The FBI's *Uniform Crime Report* has two methods of "clearing a crime."

First, the crime can be cleared by arrest. Three specific conditions have to be met and at least

- One person has been arrested.
- One person has been charged with commission of the offense.
- One person has been turned over to the court for prosecution (this can be following arrest, court summons, or police notice).

The arrest of one person may clear several crimes, and the arrest of many people may clear only one crime.

Second, the case may be cleared by exceptional means, and the agency must have met the following four conditions:

- Identified the offender.
- Gathered enough evidence to support an arrest, make a charge, and turn the offender over to the court for prosecution.
- Identified the offender's exact location so that the suspect could be taken into custody immediately.
- Encountered a circumstance outside the control of law enforcement that prohibits the agency from arresting, charging, and prosecuting the offender; this may include the death of a suspect.

Standards of Proof

According to the United States Supreme Court, the **standard of proof** in a criminal trial is beyond a reasonable doubt. The standard of proof is a duty to prove or disprove a fact in dispute. The burden is on the government to prove guilt of the allegations, not on the defendant to prove innocence. Remember, in the American criminal justice system, all are innocent until proven guilty. The standard of **beyond a reasonable doubt** requires the evidence to be so strong there is no reasonable doubt that the defendant committed the crime. Proof beyond a reasonable doubt is the highest standard and is a determination that there is no other logical explanation for the facts that are presented. The prosecutorial case must prove beyond a reasonable doubt the defendant is guilty of each element of the crime in order to win a conviction in a criminal proceeding.

A **preponderance of the evidence** may be the standard of proof for grand jury indictments—this can vary according to statutory limitations in different states. A preponderance finding is a determination that the charges are more likely to be true than not true. This standard of proof is also used in civil proceedings. A preponderance of the evidence is more convincing than an opposite point of view and is used in civil proceedings. It demonstrates the superiority in weight that is more convincing than the opposing side. That means that only 51 percent of the evidence can determine the decision in a noncriminal trial versus the requirement of beyond a reasonable doubt in a criminal proceeding.

Reasonable suspicion is the rational and reasonable belief that the facts warrant an investigation of a crime and is less than probable cause. Reasonable suspicion leads an officer to proceed in an attempt to establish probable cause that a crime has been committed and that the subject under investigation is the probable offender.

In all criminal and civil legal actions, **statutes of limitations** are established by the state legislatures. In criminal proceedings almost every criminal offense with the exception of murder and other heinous crimes has a time limit for prosecution. These statutes restrict the time in which legal actions may be brought against defendants. In civil actions, this generally means there is a time limit for filing a lawsuit. Once the statute of limitations has passed, the judicial system loses jurisdiction. The reason for establishing a statute of limitations is that evidence and witnesses can be lost or corrupted, which will prevent timely disposition of the actions. Every state has its own timelines established.

Statutory Basis for Criminal and Civil Proceedings

The **United States Code** (USC) gathers all the general and permanent federal laws enacted by Congress. Title 18 deals with federal crimes, penalties and prisons. The USC can be accessed via www.gpo.gov/fdsys/browse/collectionUScode.action?collectionCode=USCODE. The **Code of Federal Regulations** (CFR) is the compilation of general rules and regulations of offices of the federal government. The electronic version is updated annually and is available at www.gpo.gov/fdsys/browse/collectionCfr.action?collectionCode=CFR. Consult the CFR for federal administrative law. Cornell University Law School maintains a useful website linking the U.S. Constitution, the U.S. Code, and individual state constitutions and statutes at www.law.cornell.edu/statutes.html#state.

Investigative Due Diligence

An investigation involves the examination, study, search, tracking and collection of facts. A continual gathering of facts resolves problems and answers questions. At the same time, new questions arise and the investigation can take on different aspects. As the case evolves, you must develop hypotheses and draw conclusions based on the information that is revealed. A home burglary investigation may be linked to an organized band of thieves through the *modus operandi* identified by your review of the scene. There may be a serial offender committing crimes across jurisdictional lines. Following the investigative strategy developed at the onset of your case should yield associative linkages to other cases that were previously unresolved. All officers must conduct a thorough and unbiased case investigation and work collaboratively to solve cases.

Profiling of the individuals who are committing the offenses enables the investigator to utilize a process to identify the general characteristics of the most likely suspect(s). Although criminal profiling has risen to new heights on television shows, it is really a skill based on the ability of the investigator to analyze statistical and psychological data revealed through close examination of case facts. Criminals do not observe jurisdictional lines, so it is very important to communicate with surrounding agencies to identify similar offenses. Again, diligent observation and accurate case files will contribute to solving crimes against people and property offenses.

Types of Evidence Admissible in Court

Although most students would agree the criminal investigator is most interested in physical evidence when completing a case analysis, there are other types of evidence that can be collected and utilized to solve a crime. Objects, such as weapons, clothing, latent fingerprints, or hair, are considered physical or **real evidence**. Statements of credible and competent sworn witnesses are **testimonial evidence**. The observations of eyewitnesses are considered by the court to be **direct evidence** and when true can establish a fact. Any information that tends to prove or disprove a point is considered **circumstantial evidence**. The burden of proof remains with the prosecution as prosecutors utilize these various types of evidence to prove guilt beyond a reasonable doubt. The evidence accepted by the court must be relevant, competent, and material. Accurate case files can substantiate the prosecutorial assertions and lead to a conviction. The observations, evaluation, and assessment that the investigators document throughout the case files can be critical in establishing guilt beyond a reasonable doubt.

■ ■ ■ ▬▬▬▬▬▬▬▬▬▬▬▬▬▬▬▬▬▬▬▬▬▬▬▬▬▬▬▬▬▬▬

Case File: Arson

Case File Elements

- Incident/offense report
- Supplemental reports
- Crime scene investigation reports
- Arson reports
- Rights waivers and statements
- Follow-up

Critical Questions and Activities

As you go through the case file, think about the following questions:

1. Who first noticed the fire?
2. Who called in the fire?
3. What color were the flames and smoke?
4. Was there any kind of explosion before the fire?
5. Were there any suspicious or unusual conditions or circumstances?
6. Was anyone killed or injured?
7. Who had access to the site?

7 p.m.—10 September 2010: Randolph Police Department

At 7 p.m. on September 10, 2010, Detective Bentley and her partner Detective Dalton reported for duty at the Randolph Police Department. About two and a half hours into the shift, they received a call to report to Central High School to investigate a fire.

"Well, it looks like the rivalry has begun early this season," said Bentley, "In a small town where football is taken almost as seriously as going to church every Sunday, it's a wonder we don't get more calls like this."

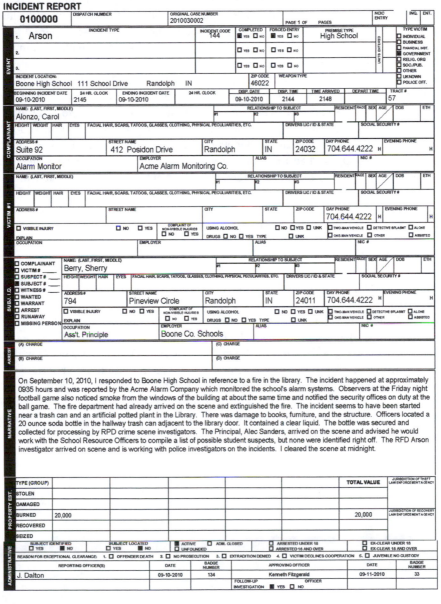

FIGURE 5-1 Incident report for the fire at Central High School.

9:30 p.m.—10 September 2010: Central High School

When the detectives arrived at the scene, three officers, four firefighters, and the school administrators were standing by. The three officers gave Detective Bentley and her partner a brief account of whom they had interviewed and who had been on scene. This briefing included a login sheet of every person who had been on scene. The officers told the detectives they were already on the school property, working security for the home football game against Jefferson High School. During the halftime show, the school's fire alarm started sounding. Following the school's fire policy, all school buildings were evacuated. Because the football game was located in the outdoor stadium, the fire did not interrupt the game. The officers realized the origin of the fire was in the library, so their main focus was securing the scene for further investigation. The officers reported that within minutes of their arrival on scene, the fire department also arrived. The firefighters immediately searched for possible victims and quickly extinguished the fire.

"So do we have any witnesses?" Detective Bentley asked. One of the officers pointed to Sherry Berry, the assistant principal. Mrs. Berry told the officers that during the half-time show, she heard the fire alarms sounding. She then walked north toward the school buildings to determine if a fire really had started or if someone had falsely sounded the alarm. According to the school's policy, the fire department is immediately dispatched when the alarm sounds, whether it is a false alarm or not. As Mrs. Berry approached the library, Detective Dalton and Detective Bentley met her. Mrs. Berry stated, "I could smell smoke coming from the front doors as I approached the library entrance." At this point Detective Bentley began asking some serious questions of the only witness she had.

"You said you heard the alarm during the halftime show, is that right, Mrs. Berry?" asked Detective Bentley.

"Yes," replied Mrs. Berry.

"It's so noisy during the halftime show, how could you hear the alarms, Mrs. Berry?"

Mrs. Berry, clearly nervous answered, "Well, I heard the alarms in between the songs while the band was playing."

Detectives Bentley and Dalton exchanged looks, and Dalton stepped in, "We'll finish this up at the station, Mrs. Berry. Bentley, I'll meet you there."

Bentley watched as they walked toward the cruiser. She recalled that the school's budgets were being cut and wondered if there was any money to be made from a library fire. Then again, the whole town had been talking lately about Mrs. Berry and her extracurricular activities when her husband was out of town. Bentley made sure to write down her two theories in her notes so that she could ask about them in more detail later. For now, she turned her focus back to the crime scene inspection.

PAGE __1 of 1__

017

COMPLAINT # __2010-01__

WITNESS STATEMENT

STATEMENT OF __Sherry Berry__   DATE OF BIRTH __11/4/59__   AGE __52__

HOME ADDRESS __794 PineView Cir Lebanon IN 46052__ HOME PHONE _____ BUS. PH. __221-1111__

EMPLOYER __Boone Co. Schools__   BUS. ADDRESS __111 School Drive__

THIS STATEMENT IS IN REFERENCE TO __Arson at employer__

WHICH OCCURS AT __10 pm__   , ON OR ABOUT __Sept. 10, 2010__

AT APPROXIMATELY __2200 hrs__ HOURS, IN NORTH CHARLESTON, SOUTH CAROLINA.

THIS STATEMENT IS GIVEN _____ B.H.S. (DATE) AT __2200 hrs__   (TIME), AT __Sept 10, 2010__

_____ (LOCATION)

On September 10th, 2010, I was working
the varsity football game and heard
fire alarms sounding. I then walked
to the building to determine if it was false,
cut. As I approached the library I was
met by Det. Dalton & Det. Bentley in which
they informed me a fire had been set
to the library. They then asked me to step
outside so they could secure the scene and
I was later asked to provide a statement

end of statement

Sherry Berry

I HAVE READ THE FOREGOING STATEMENT OR HAVE HAD IT READ TO ME AND IT IS TRUE AND CORRECT TO THE BEST OF MY KNOWLEDGE. I HAVE GIVEN THIS STATEMENT FREELY AND VOLUNTARILY AND HAVE BEEN PROVIDED A COPY OF MY STATEMENT.

WITNESS: _____

WITNESS: _____   SIGNATURE: _____

FIGURE 5-2 Sherry Berry's witness statement.

9:50 p.m.—10 September 2010: Library, Crime Scene Walkthrough

As Bentley began to assess the crime scene, she noted that the south entrance serves as the primary entrance to the library. The firefighter proceeded to show Bentley the burn patterns coming from a trash can on the north wall of the library. The evidence technician was already working on taking carpet samples from around the trash can and a row of books along with several control samples. V patterns were used to determine the point of origin for the fire in the trash can located on the north wall. As is procedure, Bentley began taking photographs, sketching the area where the fire occurred, and collecting any relative physical evidence. Bentley noticed a twenty-ounce soda bottle, which she carefully placed in the evidence bag to be analyzed later at the lab.

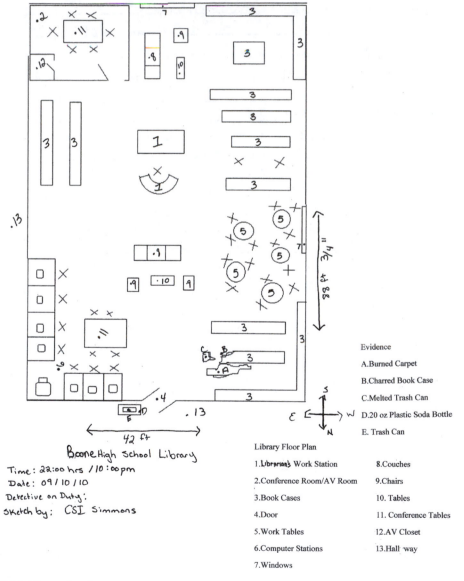

FIGURE 5-3 Library sketch.

10 a.m—12 September 2010: Randolph Police Department

"Hey, Bentley!" Dalton bellowed from across the room, "Got a fingerprint off the bottle you brought in."

Bentley spun around, eager to see if they matched Mrs. Berry's prints, since she did not give the most convincing story of her exact whereabouts during the high school game. Bentley strode over to meet Bailey, only to be let down by the news that there were no matches in the database or to Mrs. Berry. After talking with Dalton, they both decided that it was just kids being kids at a football game where a high school rivalry ran back for generations. As for Mrs. Berry, they both had their theories as to what she was doing the night the fire broke out.

FIGURE 5-4 Pictures of latent prints.

Crime Scene Log

** This crime scene log should be maintained by the initial Uniform officer at the scene of a major crime until that officer is properly relieved of responsibility for that scene. The completed log should then be immediately forwarded to the Crime Scene Unit. **

Name	Org./Address	Purpose	Time Arrived	Time Departed
Dalton	RPD	Police	21:48	2400
Jones	RPD	Police	21:49	2400
SGT. Johnson	RPD	Police SGT	21:53	2340
Lt. Smith	RPD	Police Sup.	21:59	2340
Det. Miller	RPD	Police Det.	22:00	2320
Det. Wright	RPD	Police Det	22:00	2320
P. Carter	RFD	Fire	2148	2320
R. Jacobs	RFD	Fire	2148	2320
S. Silly	RFD	Fire	2148	2320
L. Hot	RFD	Fire	2148	2320
P. Smok Capt.	RFD	Fire Capt	2200	2330
Det P. Arson	RFD	Arson FireDet.	22 15	2330
CSI M. Bentley	RPD	Police CSI	2230	2330
J. Bogstad	RPD	Pol. CSI	2230	2330
S. Simmons	RPD	Police CSI	2230	2330

Case Number _2010 -01_
Incident Type _Arson_
Incident Date _9-10-10_

OFFICER(s) MAINTAINING LOG

1. _Dalton   134_   IN _2148_   OUT _2400_

2. _____   IN _____   OUT _____

3. _____   IN _____   OUT _____

FIGURE 5-5 Entry/exit log.

CHAIN OF CUSTODY SHEET

CASE NUMBER	EVIDENCE TAG #
2010 - 01	

Revised 12/05

CITY COURT DATE	PAGE # / OF /
GSC	

OFFICER NAME/BADGE #	DATE	TIME	PROPERTY CLASSIFICATION (Mark one box only)	
Bentley, M / 135	09-10-10	2200		
DEFENDANT/OWNER NAME and ADDRESS			X	GSC EVIDENCE
Unknown at the time of the Incident				CITY COURT EVIDENCE
				FAMILY COURT EVIDENCE
				FOUND PROPERTY
				SAFEKEEPING (RETURN TO OWNER)

(ONLY PROPERTY THAT <u>CANNOT</u> BE PHOTOGRAPHED AND RETURNED TO THE OWNER SHALL BE TURNED IN)

ITEM #	DESCRIPTION (Caliber, brand, model, serial number, color - Currency Amount & Denominations, Etc.)
1	Burnt Carpet from library
2	Sample of Carpet from library
3	20oz MTN. DEW bottle from Trash Can at library door

PROPERTY RECEIPT (OWNER/DEFENDANT SIGNATURE)

ITEM #	DATE	RELEASED BY	RECEIVED BY	PURPOSE: (Do Not Write In This Column)
1-3	9-10-10	NAME Det Bentley ORGANIZATION CSI SIGN B—	NAME Joan Carol ORGANIZATION Crime Evidence Room SIGN	9-11-10
		NAME ORGANIZATION SIGN	NAME ORGANIZATION SIGN	
		NAME ORGANIZATION SIGN	NAME ORGANIZATION SIGN	
		NAME ORGANIZATION SIGN	NAME ORGANIZATION SIGN	

White Copy: Evidence   Green Copy: Case Disposition   Blue Copy: Case File/Officer   Pink Copy: Defendant/Owner

FIGURE 5-6 Chain-of-custody sheet.

9:30 p.m.—17 September 2010: Randolph Police Department

Dalton tossed a football in the air to himself and sighed, "Man, I hate the nightshift. I'm ready for some full-fledged action. You know, like you see on TV where they go from sitting in the office to a drug bust in a matter of minutes of getting on shift."

Bentley chuckled, "You do know that you work at the town of Lebanon where the biggest crime is not going to the football game on Friday nights."

"I just wish there was more action!" Dalton went on to say.

Bentley shook her head, "Settle down, Rook, there's enough action out there for you. Think of this quiet town as a stepping-stone. After all, everyone has to start somewhere, and being in a small town isn't all that bad. You get to really know the people you are working every day to protect." Bentley stood and snatched the football out of the air as Dalton tossed it again. "Come on. If you're that anxious, we'll make a couple of rounds around the block."

As they were getting on their coats, the radio sounded. There had been another fire, this time at Stall High School. Bentley took a deep breath and said to Dalton, "Be careful what you wish for. You might just get it." Dalton could hardly hold in his excitement. This would be the second fire in a week, and that could only mean one thing—a serial arsonist. The two loaded up in the cruiser and headed over to Stall High School.

9:41 p.m.—17 September 2010: Stall High School

The officers who arrived before Dalton and Bentley gave them a rundown on who had been on scene and what had been done to secure the scene. The officers explained they were patrolling the school during the football game. During the halftime show, they heard the fire alarms sounding. The officers then split up and walked toward the school buildings, located on the other side of the school property from the stadium, to locate the fire. Because the football stadium was away from all the school buildings, the fires did not interrupt the game. Officer Jones told the detectives that as he approached the library, he noticed thick dark smoke coming from the front doors. As soon as he saw the smoke, he called the fire in to dispatch and then contacted the principal, David Goforth, to report to the front entrance of the school for questioning. Goforth was waiting at the front of the school. Bentley questioned him and took his witness statement.

INCIDENT REPORT

| 0100000 | DISPATCH NUMBER | | ORIGINAL CASE NUMBER 201009172145 | | PAGE 1 OF | PAGES | NCIC ENTRY | INQ. | ENT. |

	INCIDENT TYPE	INCIDENT CODE	COMPLETED	FORCED ENTRY	PREMISE TYPE	TYPE VICTIM
1.	Arson	144	☑ YES ☐ NO	☑ YES ☐ NO	High School	☐ INDIVIDUAL ☐ BUSINESS ☐ FINANCIAL INST. ☑ GOVERNMENT ☐ RELIG. ORG ☐ SOC./PUB. ☐ OTHER ☐ UKNOWN ☐ POLICE OFF.
2.			☐ YES ☐ NO	☐ YES ☐ NO		
3.			☐ YES ☐ NO	☐ YES ☐ NO		

INCIDENT LOCATION: Stall High School   800 Westport Lane   Randolph   IN   ZIP CODE 46022   WEAPON TYPE

| BEGINNING INCIDENT DATE 09-17-2010 | 24 HR. CLOCK 2130 | ENDING INCIDENT DATE 09-17-2010 | 24 HR. CLOCK | DISP. DATE 2300 | DISP. TIME 2130 | TIME ARRIVED 2145 | DEPART TIME | TRACT # 57 |

COMPLAINANT

NAME: (LAST, FIRST, MIDDLE) Jones, Samuel   RELATIONSHIP TO SUBJECT #1 #2 #3   RESIDENT RACE SEX AGE DOB ETH

HEIGHT WEIGHT HAIR EYES   FACIAL HAIR, SCARS, TATOOS, GLASSES, CLOTHING, PHYSICAL PECULIARITIES, ETC.   DRIVERS LIC / ID & STATE   SOCIAL SECURITY #

ADDRESS # Office 54   STREET NAME 800 Westport Lane   CITY Randolph   STATE IN   ZIP CODE 46022   DAY PHONE 704.300.6010 H   EVENING PHONE H

OCCUPATION School Resource Officer   EMPLOYER Boone Co. School System   ALIAS   NIC #

VICTIM #1

NAME: (LAST, FIRST, MIDDLE)   RELATIONSHIP TO SUBJECT #1 #2 #3   RESIDENT RACE SEX AGE DOB ETH

HEIGHT WEIGHT HAIR EYES   FACIAL HAIR, SCARS, TATOOS, GLASSES, CLOTHING, PHYSICAL PECULIARITIES, ETC.   DRIVERS LIC / ID & STATE   SOCIAL SECURITY #

ADDRESS #   STREET NAME   CITY   STATE   ZIP CODE   DAY PHONE 704.300.6010 H   EVENING PHONE H

☐ VISIBLE INJURY   ☐ NO ☐ YES   COMPLAINT OF NON-VISIBLE INJURIES ☐ NO ☐ YES   USING ALCOHOL ☐ NO ☐ YES ☐ UNK   DRUGS ☐ NO ☐ YES TYPE   ☐ UNK   ☐ TWO-MAN VEHICLE ☐ DETECTIVE SPLASH'T ☐ ALONE ☐ ONE-MAN VEHICLE ☐ OTHER ☐ ASSISTED

EXPLAIN   OCCUPATION   EMPLOYER   ALIAS   NIC #

SUBJ. I.D.

☐ COMPLAINANT ☐ VICTIM # ___ ☐ SUSPECT # ___ ☑ SUBJECT # ___ ☐ WITNESS # ___ ☐ WANTED ☐ WARRANT ☐ ARREST ☐ RUNAWAY ☐ MISSING PERSON

NAME: (LAST, FIRST, MIDDLE) Goforth, David   RELATIONSHIP TO SUBJECT #1 #2 #3   RESIDENT RACE SEX AGE DOB ETH

HEIGHT WEIGHT HAIR EYES   FACIAL HAIR, SCARS, TATOOS, GLASSES, CLOTHING, PHYSICAL PECULIARITIES, ETC.   DRIVERS LIC / ID & STATE   SOCIAL SECURITY #

ADDRESS # 63   STREET NAME Pikes Place   CITY Lebannon   STATE IN   ZIP CODE 46001   DAY PHONE 704.300.6010 H   EVENING PHONE H

☐ VISIBLE INJURY   ☐ NO ☐ YES   COMPLAINT OF NON-VISIBLE INJURIES ☐ NO ☐ YES   USING ALCOHOL ☐ NO ☐ YES ☐ UNK   DRUGS ☐ NO ☐ YES TYPE   ☐ UNK   ☐ TWO-MAN VEHICLE ☐ DETECTIVE SPLASH'T ☐ ALONE ☐ ONE-MAN VEHICLE ☐ OTHER ☐ ASSISTED

EXPLAIN   OCCUPATION Principal   EMPLOYER Boone Co. School System   ALIAS   NIC #

ARREST

(A) CHARGE   (C) CHARGE

(B) CHARGE   (D) CHARGE

NARRATIVE

On September 17, 2010, I responded to Stall High School in reference to a fire in the library. The incident was reported around 2145 hours by SRO Samuel Jones who was patrolling the school grounds during the Friday night football game. Officer Jones saw black smoke coming from the school library and called 911. The RFD responded and extinguished the fire. No victims were located and stated the trash can seemed to be the place where the fire was started. A 20 oz. soda bottle with liquid was recovered by the CSI and secured for analysis at the crime lab. The bottle will also be processed for latent fingerprints and comparison to a similar fire last week at Boone High School. There was no forced entry to the library doors. Books, carpet and furniture were damaged. The RFD arson investigator arrived and I turned the scene over to the detectives at 2347 hours.

PROPERTY EST.

TYPE (GROUP)						TOTAL VALUE	JURISDICTION OF THEFT LAW ENFORCEMENT AGENCY
STOLEN							
DAMAGED	10000					10,000	
BURNED	20000					20,000	JURISDICTION OF RECOVERY LAW ENFORCEMENT AGENCY
RECOVERED							
SEIZED							

ADMINISTRATIVE

| SUBJECT IDENTIFIED ☐ YES ☑ NO | SUBJECT LOCATED ☐ YES ☑ NO | ☑ ACTIVE ☐ UNFOUNDED | ☐ ADM. CLOSED | ☐ ARRESTED UNDER 18 ☐ ARRESTED 18 AND OVER | ☐ EX-CLEAR UNDER 18 ☐ EX-CLEAR 18 AND OVER |

REASON FOR EXCEPTIONAL CLEARANCE: 1. ☐ OFFENDER DEATH   2. ☐ NO PROSECUTION   3. ☐ EXTRADITION DENIED   4. ☐ VICTIM DECLINES COOPERATION   5. ☐ JUVENILE NO CUSTODY

REPORTING OFFICER(S)	DATE	BADGE NUMBER	APPROVING OFFICER	DATE	BADGE NUMBER
J. Dalton	09-17-2010	134	J Fitsgerald	09-18-2011	100
			FOLLOW-UP INVESTIGATION ☐ YES ☐ NO	OFFICER	

FIGURE 5-7 Incident report for fire at Stall High School.

PAGE _1 of 1_   COMPLAINT # 2010-02

WITNESS STATEMENT

STATEMENT OF _David Goforth_ DATE OF BIRTH _3/2/51_ AGE _50_

HOME ADDRESS _PO Box 784_ HOME PHONE _____ BUS. PH. _704-524-7206_

EMPLOYER _Stall High School_ BUS. ADDRESS _800 Westport Lane_

THIS STATEMENT IS IN REFERENCE TO _fire @ Stall High_

WHICH OCCURS AT _9/17/10 Stall High School_, ON OR ABOUT _9-17-10_

AT APPROXIMATELY _22:__ HOURS, IN NORTH CHARLESTON, SOUTH CAROLINA.

THIS STATEMENT IS GIVEN _Stall High_ (DATE) AT _9/17/10_ (TIME), AT _2230_ (LOCATION)

_I was met by two officers as
I was approaching the library. I was
called to this location over my walkie talkie
and noticed a fire had started. Officer
Bentley then asked me to walk with
her to the front entrance for
questioning. I did not see anyone
suspicious._

end of statement
D. Gof

I HAVE READ THE FOREGOING STATEMENT OR HAVE HAD IT READ TO ME AND IT IS TRUE AND CORRECT TO THE BEST OF MY KNOWLEDGE. I HAVE GIVEN THIS STATEMENT FREELY AND VOLUNTARILY AND HAVE BEEN PROVIDED A COPY OF MY STATEMENT.

WITNESS: _R=t Benl_

WITNESS: _Rot Dal_   SIGNATURE: _D Goforth_

FIGURE 5-8 Witness statement from David Goforth, principal of Stall High School.

Firefighter Statements

The firefighters gave Dalton a detailed briefing of what they saw and did when they arrived on scene. They were dispatched to a fire at Stall High School at 9:38 p.m. When they arrived, Officer Jones directed them to the school library, which was the scene of the fire. Once they were on scene, the firefighters searched for possible victims and extinguished the fire. They reported that no victims were found on the scene. After the fire was extinguished and no victims were confirmed on the scene, the officers resecured the area around the crime scene and waited for the detectives to arrive.

Crime Scene Inspection

During the crime scene inspection, Bentley and Dalton both noted that the trash can seemed to be where the fire started and that there was a soda bottle located inside it. They couldn't help but notice the similarities to the fire that occurred the previous Friday night at Boone High School. Both detectives immediately zeroed in on preserving the bottle, hoping that it too would provide some fingerprints that would match the previous case.

"So what do you think we have on our hands, Detective?" Goforth asked. "Just a couple of kids fooling around or something more?"

Bentley shrugged her shoulders, "You know as well as I do you can't assume anything until you examine all of the evidence."

Goforth scoffed, "Well, if you ask me, if it looks like a duck, walks like a duck, and sounds like a duck…"

"I'm open to any suggestions," Bentley said. "Think about it tonight and meet us early in the morning to compile a list of suspects." Bentley slammed the car door and watched as Goforth started scribbling down names in a notepad. She had known Goforth all her life, and if there was one thing he loved, it was a good mystery. She had no doubt she would have a full list of students on her desk in the morning.

Crime Scene Log

** This crime scene log should be maintained by the initial Uniform officer at the scene of a major crime until that officer is properly relieved of responsibility for that scene. The completed log should then be immediately forwarded to the Crime Scene Unit. **

Name	Org./Address	Purpose	Time Arrived	Time Departed
Dalton	RPD	Police	21:48	24:00
Jones	RPD	Police	21:49	24:00
SGT. Johnson	RPD	Police SGT	21:53	23:40
Lt. Smith	RPD	Police Sup.	21:59	23:40
Det. Miller	RPD	Police Det.	22:00	23:20
Det. Wright	RPD	Police Det	22:00	23:20
F. Carter	RFD	Fire	21 50	23:20
R. Jacobs	RFD	Fire	2150	23:20
S. Silly	RFD	Fire	21 50	23:20
L. Hot	RFD	Fire	2150	23:20
P. Smok Capt.	RFD	Fire Capt	2200	23:30
Det P. Arson	RFD	Arson Fire Det.	22:15	23:30
CSI M. Bentley	RPD	Police CSI	22:30	23:30
J. Bogstad	RPD	Police CSI	22:30	23:30
S. Simmons	PPD	Police CSI	22:30	23:30

Case Number ____2010 -01____

Incident Type ____Arson____

Incident Date ____9 | 17 | 10____

OFFICER(s) MAINTAINING LOG

1. __Dalton   134__   IN ____   OUT ____

2. __Bentley   135__   IN ____   OUT ____

3. _____   IN ____   OUT ____

FIGURE 5-9 Entry/exit log for Stall High School crime scene.

CHAIN OF CUSTODY SHEET

CASE NUMBER	EVIDENCE TAG #
2010-02	

Revised 12/05

CITY COURT DATE
GSC

| PAGE # 1 | OF 1 |

OFFICER NAME/BADGE #	DATE	TIME	PROPERTY CLASSIFICATION (Mark one box only)
Bentley, M 135	9/17/10	22:00	

DEFENDANT/OWNER NAME and ADDRESS		PROPERTY CLASSIFICATION
Stall High School 800 Westport		X GSC EVIDENCE
		CITY COURT EVIDENCE
		FAMILY COURT EVIDENCE
		FOUND PROPERTY
		SAFEKEEPING (RETURN TO OWNER)

(ONLY PROPERTY THAT CANNOT BE PHOTOGRAPHED AND RETURNED TO THE OWNER SHALL BE TURNED IN)

ITEM #	DESCRIPTION (Caliber, brand, model, serial number, color - Currency Amount & Denominations, Etc.)
1	Burnt carpet from library
2	Sample of carpet from library
3	20 oz Mtn. Dew bottle from trash can at library door.

PROPERTY RECEIPT (OWNER/DEFENDANT SIGNATURE)

ITEM #	DATE	RELEASED BY	RECEIVED BY	PURPOSE: (Do Not Write In This Column)
1-3	9-17-10	NAME Det. Bentley ORGANIZATION CSI SIGN M Bentley	NAME Joan Carol ORGANIZATION Crime Evidence Room SIGN	9-18-10
		NAME ORGANIZATION SIGN	NAME ORGANIZATION SIGN	
		NAME ORGANIZATION SIGN	NAME ORGANIZATION SIGN	
		NAME ORGANIZATION SIGN	NAME ORGANIZATION SIGN	

White Copy: Evidence   Green Copy: Case Disposition   Blue Copy: Case File/Officer   Pink Copy: Defendant/Owner

FIGURE 5-10 Chain of custody sheet for Stall High School.

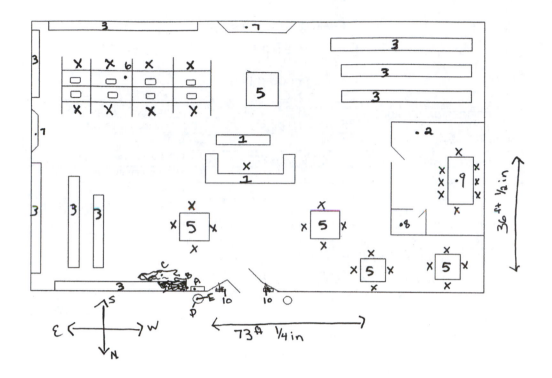

Library Floor Plan

1. Librarian's Work Station   8. Conference Table

2. Conference Room/AV Room   9. AV Closet

3. Book Cases   10. Plants

4. Door

5. Work Tables

6. Computer Stations

7. Windows

Evidence

A. Melted Trash Can

B. Charred Book Case

C. Burned Carpet

D. Trash Can

E. 20 oz Plastic Soda Bottle

Stall High School Library
Time: 22:15 / 10:15 pm
Date: 09/17/10
Detective on Duty:
Sketch by: CSI Simmons

FIGURE 5-11 Crime scene sketch of the Stall High School library.

8 a.m.—18 September 2010, Randolph Police Department

Just as Bentley had suspected, Principal Goforth was waiting for her to arrive that morning. Although she wished she had a few more minutes to gather her thoughts before beginning the day, she had to admit they had no leads, so any information they could get would be helpful. Out of the list of students Goforth gave her, three names stood out: Jeremy Davidson, Tommy Johnson, and Scott Miller. Jeremy Davidson was well known around the community. He was a smart kid with a scholarship to college but he was no saint. Jeremy used to stay in trouble with the cops for petty stuff like toilet papering someone's home, throwing eggs at people, and being a real smart aleck whenever he got picked up. Tommy Johnson was also known to the people of Lebanon. His father was a cop in the next town over, and he thought he could use his dad's job to get him out of trouble. The last suspect was one worth taking a look into as well. Scott Miller was recently released from the football team, and he had made it well known that the coach was going to pay for that decision. To Scott, the football team was everything; it was his ticket to college as well as to getting out of this town forever. After talking with Principal Goforth, Bentley knew her only shot of linking any one of these boys with the crime relied on the fingerprints that the CSI lifted from the soda bottle.

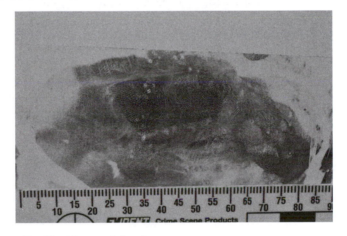

FIGURE 5-12 Latent prints lifted from soda bottle.

10:15 a.m.—21 September 2010, Randolph Police Department

Bentley just shook her head in disbelief; none of the three boys' fingerprints matched the soda bottle. She and Dalton just looked at each other, wondering what clue they missed.

"I just don't get it. I thought we had the case in the bag for sure," Dalton said as he banged his head against the wall. "I mean, I already got my dress uniform pressed and everything for the big press conference to announce we caught the guy."

Bentley couldn't help but smile despite her disappointment. Poor Dalton was so ready to see himself in the papers. "Look, we still have a few games left. Don't think it's too late yet. The person who did this will mess up, and when that happens, we will be there to collar him."

8:30 a.m.—14 June 2011, Randolph Police Department

Sergeant Lori Torres and Detective Dalton were on patrol in the center of town. Sergeant Torres had transferred from the big city and had only been on the job in this town for a few months. Torres was having a hard time adjusting to life in such a small town. She thought Dalton had been nice enough, but if he didn't stop asking her questions about what it was like to work CSI in a big city, she thought she would explode. Just when she thought she couldn't take any more, they received a call to respond to a house fire, possibly arson related.

8:37 a.m.—14 June 2011, Darcy Avenue

Inside the home, Torres noticed that a window had been broken because a brown bottle had been thrown through it. Torres found the bottle and handled it carefully, thinking there might be fingerprints on the bottle. Torres heard a car door slam and obscenities being yelled. She immediately headed out to assist Dalton.

Torres recognized David Johnson from a DUI checkpoint the previous month. Mr. Johnson was yelling and berating Detective Dalton, who was calmly trying to talk him down when Torres walked up.

"I'm really sorry that this has happened, Mr. Johnson, but you yelling and carrying on isn't going to help us solve anything," Torres said calmly.

"I know you're right. I'm sorry. It's just that, it's all I've got to my name," Mr. Johnson ran his fingers through his hair, which now matched his erratic behavior. When asked if he could think of anyone who would do this, he yelled, "Jeremy, that bastard neighbor kid did it!" After talking with David Johnson more, Torres learned that Jeremy had been verbally aggressive toward David's son Tommy.

After Mr. Johnson calmed down and started talking more reasonably, Torres left Dalton to continue talking with Johnson while she worked the crime scene. She noticed a matchbox and in the trash can, on top, she saw an empty bottle of nail polish remover. This didn't seem to fit in, because Mr. Johnson had just told them that his wife and family had been on vacation for a few days now. Something wasn't sitting right here. All there was left to do now was to get the witness statements from the neighbor, Jeremy Davidson, and Mr. Johnson. Torres was particularly interested to see what exactly was in this brown bottle.

I₁ Structure Type ☆

If fire was in an enclosed building or a portable/mobile structure, complete the rest of this form.

1 ☒ Enclosed building
2 ☐ Portable/mobile structure
3 ☐ Open structure
4 ☐ Air-supported structure
5 ☐ Tent
6 ☐ Open platform (e.g., piers)
7 ☐ Underground structure (work areas)
8 ☐ Connective structure (e.g., fences)
0 ☐ Other type of structure

I₂ Building Status ☆

1 ☐ Under construction
2 ☐ Occupied & operating
3 ☐ Idle, not routinely used
4 ☐ Under major renovation
5 ☒ Vacant and secured
6 ☐ Vacant and unsecured
7 ☐ Being demolished
0 ☐ Other
U ☐ Undetermined

I₃ Building Height ☆

Count the roof as part of the highest story.

| 0 | 0 | 8 |

Total number of stories at or above grade

| 0 | 0 |

Total number of stories below grade

I₄ Main Floor Size ☆

|__|,|____|,|____| Total square feet

OR

| 0 | , | 2 | 0 | 0 | BY | 0 | , | 1 | 0 | 0 |
Length in feet   Width in feet

NFIRS–3 Structure Fire

J₁ Fire Origin ☆

| 0 | 0 | 5 | ☐ Below grade
Story of fire origin

J₂ Fire Spread ☆

If fire spread was confined to object of origin, do not check a box (Ref. Block D3, Fire Module)

2 ☐ Confined to room of origin
3 ☒ Confined to floor of origin
4 ☐ Confined to building of origin
5 ☐ Beyond building of origin

J₃ Number of Stories Damaged by Flame

Count the roof as part of the highest story.

| 0 | 0 | 1 | Number of stories w/minor damage (1 to 24% flame damage)

| 0 | 0 | 0 | Number of stories w/significant damage (25 to 49% flame damage)

| 0 | 0 | 0 | Number of stories w/heavy damage (50 to 74% flame damage)

| 0 | 0 | 0 | Number of stories w/extreme damage (75 to 100% flame damage)

K Type of Material Contributing Most to Flame Spread

☒ Check if no flame spread OR if same as Material First Ignited (Block D4, Fire Module) OR if unable to determine → Skip to Section L.

K₁ |__|__|__| Item contributing most to flame spread

K₂ |__|__|__| Type of material contributing most to flame spread   Required only if item contributing code is 00 or <70.

L₁ Presence of Detectors ☆
(in area of the fire)

N ☐ None Present → Skip to Section M
1 ☒ Present
U ☐ Undetermined

L₂ Detector Type

1 ☒ Smoke
2 ☐ Heat
3 ☐ Combination smoke and heat
4 ☐ Sprinkler, water flow detection
5 ☐ More than one type present
0 ☐ Other
U ☐ Undetermined

L₃ Detector Power Supply

1 ☐ Battery only
2 ☐ Hardwire only
3 ☐ Plug-in
4 ☒ Hardwire with battery
5 ☐ Plug-in with battery
6 ☐ Mechanical
7 ☐ Multiple detectors & power supplies
0 ☐ Other
U ☐ Undetermined

L₄ Detector Operation

1 ☐ Fire too small to activate
2 ☐ Operated → Complete Block L5
3 ☒ Failed to operate → Complete Block L5
U ☐ Undetermined

L₅ Detector Effectiveness
Required if detector operated

1 ☐ Alerted occupants, occupants responded
2 ☐ Alerted occupants, occupants failed to respond
3 ☒ There were no occupants
4 ☐ Failed to alert occupants
U ☐ Undetermined

L₆ Detector Failure Reason
Required if detector failed to operate

1 ☒ Power failure, shutoff, or disconnect
2 ☐ Improper installation or placement
3 ☐ Defective
4 ☐ Lack of maintenance, includes not cleaning
5 ☒ Battery missing or disconnected
6 ☐ Battery discharged or dead
0 ☐ Other
U ☐ Undetermined

M₁ Presence of Automatic Extinguishing System ☆

N ☐ None Present
1 ☒ Present
2 ☐ Partial System Present → Complete rest of Section M
U ☐ Undetermined

M₂ Type of Automatic Extinguishing System
Required if fire was within designed range of AES

1 ☒ Wet-pipe sprinkler
2 ☐ Dry-pipe sprinkler
3 ☐ Other sprinkler system
4 ☐ Dry chemical system
5 ☐ Foam system
6 ☐ Halogen-type system
7 ☐ Carbon dioxide (CO_2) system
0 ☐ Other special hazard system
U ☐ Undetermined

M₃ Operation of Automatic Extinguishing System
Required if fire was within designed range

1 ☐ Operated/effective (go to M4)
2 ☐ Operated/not effective (go to M4)
3 ☐ Fire too small to activate
4 ☐ Failed to operate (go to M5)
0 ☐ Other
U ☒ Undetermined

M₄ Number of Sprinkler Heads Operating
Required if system operated

| 0 | 0 |
Number of sprinkler heads operating

M₅ Reason for Automatic Extinguishing System Failure
Required if system failed or not effective

1 ☐ System shut off
2 ☐ Not enough agent discharged
3 ☐ Agent discharged but did not reach fire
4 ☐ Wrong type of system
5 ☐ Fire not in area protected
6 ☒ System components damaged
7 ☐ Lack of maintenance
8 ☐ Manual intervention
0 ☐ Other
U ☐ Undetermined

NFIRS–3 Revision 01/01/06

FIGURE 5-13 Fire department report at 108 Darcy Avenue.

A | 0743M | SC | 06 | 14 | 2011 | A9 | 1106140 | 001 | ☐ Delete ☐ Change ☐ No Activity | NFIRS-1 Basic
FDID ☆   State ☆   Incident Date ☆   Station   Incident Number ☆   Exposure ☆

B Location Type ☆   ☐ Check this box to indicate that the address for this incident is provided on the Wildland Fire Module in Section B, "Alternative Location Specification." Use only for wildland fires.   Census Tract | 10661011

- ☒ Street address — 108 | Prefix | Daecy — A.V.E | 6
  Number/Milepost   Street or Highway   Street Type   Suffix
- ☐ Intersection
- ☐ In front of — Lebanon
  Apt./Suite/Room   City   — IN 54300 —   State ZIP Code
- ☐ Rear of
- ☐ Adjacent to
- ☐ Directions — DavenPort St
- ☐ US National Grid   Cross Street, Directions or National Grid, as applicable

C Incident Type ☆ 1001 | Fire
Incident Type

D Aid Given or Received ☆   ☒ None
1 ☐ Mutual aid received
2 ☐ Auto. aid received
3 ☐ Mutual aid given
4 ☐ Auto. aid given
5 ☐ Other aid given
Their FDID | Their State
Their Incident Number

E1 Dates and Times   Midnight is 0000
Check boxes if dates are the same as Alarm Date.

	Month	Day	Year	Hour	Min
Alarm ☆	06	14	2011	0829
Arrival ☐	06	14	2011	0831
Controlled ☐	06	14	2011	0855
Last Unit Cleared ☐	06	14	2011	1030

ALARM always required
ARRIVAL required, unless canceled or did not arrive
CONTROLLED optional, except for wildland fires
LAST UNIT CLEARED, required except for wildland fires

E2 Shifts and Alarms   Local Option
C | 3 | A
Shift or Platoon   Alarms   District

E3 Special Studies   Local Option
Special Study ID#   Special Study Value

F Actions Taken ☆
11 | Extinguished the Fire
Primary Action Taken (1)
12 | Overhauled the scene
Additional Action Taken (2)
41 | identify hazardous mat
Additional Action Taken (3)

G1 Resources ☆
☐ Check this box and skip this block if an Apparatus or Personnel Module is used.

	Apparatus	Personnel
Suppression	1	4
EMS	1	2
Other	1	1

☐ Check box if resource counts include aid received resources.

G2 Estimated Dollar Losses and Values
LOSSES: Required for all fires if known. Optional for non-fires.   None
Property $ | 20,000 | ☐
Contents $ | | ☐
PRE-INCIDENT VALUE: Optional
Property $ | | ☐
Contents $ | | ☐

Completed Modules
☒ Fire–2
☒ Structure Fire–3
☐ Civilian Fire Cas.–4
☒ Fire Service Cas.–5
☐ EMS–6
☐ HazMat–7
☐ Wildland Fire–8
☐ Apparatus–9
☐ Personnel–10
☒ Arson–11

H1 ☆ Casualties   ☒ None

	Deaths	Injuries
Fire Service		
Civilian		

H2 Detector   Required for confined fires.
1 ☐ Detector alerted occupants
2 ☒ Detector did not alert them
U ☐ Unknown

H3 Hazardous Materials Release   ☐ None
1 ☐ Natural gas: slow leak, no evacuation or HazMat actions
2 ☐ Propane gas: <21-lb tank (as in home BBQ grill)
3 ☐ Gasoline: vehicle fuel tank or portable container
4 ☐ Kerosene: fuel burning equipment or portable storage
5 ☐ Diesel fuel/fuel oil: vehicle fuel tank or portable storage
6 ☒ Household solvents: home/office spill, cleanup only
7 ☐ Motor oil: from engine or portable container
8 ☐ Paint: from paint cans totaling <55 gallons
0 ☐ Other: special HazMat actions required or spill > 55 gal (Please complete the HazMat form.)

I Mixed Use Property   ☐ Not mixed
10 ☐ Assembly use
20 ☐ Education use
33 ☐ Medical use
40 ☐ Residential use
51 ☐ Row of stores
53 ☐ Enclosed mall
58 ☐ Business & residential
59 ☐ Office use
60 ☐ Industrial use
63 ☐ Military use
65 ☐ Farm use
00 ☐ Other mixed use

J Property Use ☆   ☐ None
Structures
131 ☐ Church, place of worship
161 ☐ Restaurant or cafeteria
162 ☐ Bar/tavern or nightclub
213 ☐ Elementary school, kindergarten
215 ☐ High school, junior high
241 ☐ College, adult education
311 ☐ Nursing home
331 ☐ Hospital

341 ☐ Clinic, clinic-type infirmary
342 ☐ Doctor/dentist office
361 ☐ Prison or jail, not juvenile
419 ☒ 1- or 2-family dwelling
429 ☐ Multifamily dwelling
439 ☐ Rooming/boarding house
449 ☐ Commercial hotel or motel
459 ☐ Residential, board and care
464 ☐ Dormitory/barracks
519 ☐ Food and beverage sales

539 ☐ Household goods, sales, repairs
571 ☐ Gas or service station
579 ☐ Motor vehicle/boat sales/repairs
599 ☐ Business office
615 ☐ Electric-generating plant
629 ☐ Laboratory/science laboratory
700 ☐ Manufacturing plant
819 ☐ Livestock/poultry storage (barn)
882 ☐ Non-residential parking garage
891 ☐ Warehouse

Outside
124 ☐ Playground or park
655 ☐ Crops or orchard
669 ☐ Forest (timberland)
807 ☐ Outdoor storage area
919 ☐ Dump or sanitary landfill
931 ☐ Open land or field

936 ☐ Vacant lot
938 ☐ Graded/cared for plot of land
946 ☐ Lake, river, stream
951 ☐ Railroad right-of-way
960 ☐ Other street
961 ☐ Highway/divided highway
962 ☒ Residential street/driveway

981 ☐ Construction site
984 ☐ Industrial plant yard

Look up and enter a Property Use code and description only if you have NOT checked a Property Use box.   ⇒ Property Use | Code
Property Use Description

NFIRS-1 Revision 01/01/05

FIGURE 5-14

K1 Person/Entity Involved
Local Option

Business Name (if applicable)

Area Code   Phone Number

☑ Check this box if same address as incident Location (Section B). Then skip the three duplicate address lines.

Mr. David   Johnson
Mr., Ms., Mrs.   First Name   MI   Last Name   Suffix

108   Darcy   Ave
Number   Prefix   Street or Highway   Street Type   Suffix

Post Office Box   Apt./Suite/Room   City   Lebanon

IN   54300 -
State   ZIP Code

☐ More people involved? Check this box and attach Supplemental Forms (NFIRS–1S) as necessary.

K2 Owner
Local Option

☐ Same as person involved? Then check this box and skip the rest of this block.

Business Name (if applicable)

Area Code   Phone Number

☑ Check this box if same address as incident Location (Section B). Then skip the three duplicate address lines.

Mr., Ms., Mrs.   First Name   MI   Last Name   Suffix

Number   Prefix   Street or Highway   Street Type   Suffix

Post Office Box   Apt./Suite/Room   City

State   ZIP Code

L Remarks:
•Local Option

Suspected arson case, Fire Investigators called to evaluate scene

Fire Module Required?

Check the box that applies and then complete the Fire Module based on Incident Type, as follows:

☐ Buildings 111	Complete Fire & Structure Modules
☐ Special structure 112	Complete Fire Module & Section I, Structure Module
☐ Confined 113–118	Basic Module Only
☐ Mobile property 120–123	Complete Fire Module
☐ Vehicle 130–138	Complete Fire Module
☐ Vegetation 140–143	Complete Fire or Wildland Module
☐ Outside rubbish fire 150–155	Basic Module Only
☐ Special outside fire 160	Complete Fire or Wildland Module
☐ Special outside fire 161–163	Complete Fire Module
☐ Crop fire 170–173	Complete Fire or Wildland Module

ITEMS WITH A ☆ MUST ALWAYS BE COMPLETED!

☐ More remarks? Check this box and attach Supplemental Forms (NFIRS–1S) as necessary.

M Authorization

Check box if same as Officer in charge. ⇨

098014	Stan Clark	Captain	Fire Supres	06	14	2011
Officer in charge ID	Signature	Position or rank	Assignment	Month	Day	Year
☐ 0716	John Hart	Firefighter	Fire Supres	06	14	2011
Member making report ID	Signature	Position or rank	Assignment	Month	Day	Year

FIGURE 5-15

K1 Person/Entity Involved
Local Option

Business Name (if applicable)   Area Code   Phone Number

☒ Check this box if same address as incident Location (Section B). Then skip the three duplicate address lines.

Mr. | David | Johnson
Mr., Ms., Mrs. First Name   MI   Last Name   Suffix

108 | | Darcy   AVE
Number Prefix Street or Highway   Street Type Suffix

| | Lebanon
Post Office Box   Apt./Suite/Room   City

IN 54300 – | | |
State ZIP Code

☐ More people involved? Check this box and attach Supplemental Forms (NFIRS–1S) as necessary.

K2 Owner
Local Option

☐ Same as person involved? Then check this box and skip the rest of this block.

Business Name (if applicable)   Area Code   Phone Number

☒ Check this box if same address as incident Location (Section B). Then skip the three duplicate address lines.

Mr., Ms., Mrs. First Name   MI   Last Name   Suffix

Number Prefix Street or Highway   Street Type Suffix

Post Office Box   Apt./Suite/Room   City

State ZIP Code –

L Remarks:
•Local Option

Suspected arson case. Fire Investigators called to evaluate scene

Fire Module Required?

Check the box that applies and then complete the Fire Module based on Incident Type, as follows:

☐ Buildings 111	Complete Fire & Structure Modules
☐ Special structure 112	Complete Fire Module & Section I, Structure Module
☐ Confined 113–118	Basic Module Only
☐ Mobile property 120–123	Complete Fire Module
☐ Vehicle 130–138	Complete Fire Module
☐ Vegetation 140–143	Complete Fire or Wildland Module
☐ Outside rubbish fire 150–155	Basic Module Only
☐ Special outside fire 160	Complete Fire or Wildland Module
☐ Special outside fire 161–163	Complete Fire Module
☐ Crop fire 170–173	Complete Fire or Wildland Module

ITEMS WITH A ★ MUST ALWAYS BE COMPLETED!

☐ More remarks? Check this box and attach Supplemental Forms (NFIRS–1S) as necessary.

M Authorization

☐ Check box if same as Officer in charge ⇨

098019	Stan Clarey	Captain	Fire Supres	06	19	2011
Officer in charge ID	Signature	Position or rank	Assignment	Month	Day	Year
☐ 1315	John Hart	Fire fighter	Fire Supres	06	19	2011
Member making report ID	Signature	Position or rank	Assignment	Month	Day	Year

FIGURE 5-16

WITNESS STATEMENT

Case Number 110614○

Statement of Agatha Miller   Date of Birth 03/23/1945   Age 66

Home Address 104 Darcy Ave   Home Phone 675-6758 Bus.Phone

Employer Retired   Bus.Address

The statement is in reference to Suspected Arson

Which occurred at 108 Darcy Ave   On or about   14 June 2011

At approximately 0820 hours

The statement is given 14 June 2011 (Date) at 0845 (Time) at

104 Darcy Ave (Location)

Section.21-193. False reports or complaints to the police department.
   No person shall knowingly make or file or cause to be made or filled a false or misleading report, allegation or complaint with the police department.

At 08:18 in the Morning I went to let my dog out
to go to the bathroom and I smelled smoke.
After a few seconds I noticed smoke coming from
the Johnson's house at 108 Darcy ave. That is when
I went inside and called 911. I think the family
is on vacation in Florida this week.

I have read the forgoing statement or have had it read to me and it is true and correct to the best of my knowledge. I have given this statement freely and voluntarily.

Signature: Agatha Miller

Witness: SGT Torres

I have received a copy of this statement   AM

FIGURE 5-17 Agatha Miller's witness statement.

PAGE ___1 of 1___   COMPLAINT # 1106140

RANDOLPH METRO POLICE DEPT.
STATEMENT

STATEMENT OF ___Jeremy Davidson___

HOME ADDRESS __103 Darcy Ave. Lebanon, IN__   HOME PHONE __944.753.4311__

EMPLOYER ___N/A___   BUSINESS ADDRESS ___N/A___

BUS. PHONE ___N/A___   OCCPUATION ___Student___

THIS STATEMENT IS GIVEN __6/15/11__ (DATE) AT __11:10 am__ (TIME)

__103 Darcy Ave. Lebanon, IN__

On June 14th I was still sleeping in, since it is
summertime. My mom can verify that I was home
all morning. She kept trying to wake me up to put
out the trash. I know that Mr. Johnson doesn't
like me because I'm always skating up and down
the road. His kid and I don't get along either, he's
always acting like a punk and talking trash. I
don't like Mr. Johnson or his kid but I wouldn't
set the fire to his house. I have a scholarship
waiting on me and no way I would screw
that up.

——————————— end of statement ———————————

I HAVE READ THE FOREGOING STATEMENT OR HAVE HAD IT READ TO ME AND IT IS TRUE AND CORRECT TO THE BEST OF MY KNOWLEDGE. I HAVE GIVEN THIS STATEMENT FREELY AND VOLUNTARILY AND HAVE BEEN PROVIDED A COPY OF MY STATEMENT.

WITNESS: _Lori Jones_

WITNESS: _____   SIGNATURE: _Jeremy Davidson_

FIGURE 5-18 Jeremy Davidson's witness statement.

PAGE 1 of 1

RANDOLPH METRO POLICE DEPARTMENT
STATEMENT

STATEMENT OF David Johnson

HOME ADDRESS 108 Darcy Ave Lebanon, IN   HOME PHONE 944.753.8977

EMPLOYER self employed   BUSINESS ADDRESS same as above

BUS. PHONE 944.753.8977   OCCPUATION plumber

THIS STATEMENT IS GIVEN 14 June 2011 (DATE) AT 1000 (TIME)

108 Darcy Ave (LOCATION) Lebanon, IN

On the 14th of June, I left my house at 0630 to go fishing. I arrived at Fisher Creek, in Summerville at about 0700. I got a call at 0845 that my house was on fire. Shortly after I got the call, I drove back home. I made it back to my home at 0910. I know I didn't leave any appliances on. I feel strongly that the neighbor kid, Jeremy, set my house on fire. My son, Andrew has been constantly harassed by Jeremy. Jeremy has threatend my son's life and I actually got into an altercation, verbally with him. He is a trouble-maker. My wife and two kids are both in Florida on vacation. I was planning on driving to Florida tommorow morning. Other than Jeremy, I have no idea who would set my house on fire

I HAVE READ THE FOREGOING STATEMENT OR HAVE HAD IT READ TO ME AND IT IS TRUE AND CORRECT TO THE BEST OF MY KNOWLEDGE. I HAVE GIVEN THIS STATEMENT FREELY AND VOLUNTARILY AND HAVE BEEN PROVIDED A COPY OF MY STATEMENT.

WITNESS: _Lou Torres_

WITNESS: _____

SIGNATURE: _David Johnson_

FIGURE 5-19 David Johnson's victim statement.

CRIM 212   Entry/Exit Log

Case Number: _____1106140_____
Photographer: _____Taylor Davidson_____ID No. 69813
Detective: _____SGT Lori Torres_____ID No. 70273____
Crime Classification: Arson Investigation_____

Log Maintained by: _____Wanda Jones_____   ID No. ____82535____

Date	Time In	Time Out	Last Name	First Name	Agency	Badge/ID No.	Reason for Entry
6-14-11	8:27am	10:12am	Hart	John	FD	1715	Firefighter/Lead Fireman
6-14-11	8:27am	10:12am	Clarey	Stan	FD	098014	Firefighter/Captain
6-14-11	8:27am	10:12am	Johnson	Christopher	FD	70278	Firefighter
6-14-11	8:27am	10:12am	Crawford	Trey	FD	94159	Firefighter
6-14-11	8:27am	10:12am	Gard	Alexander	FD	77702	Firefighter
6-14-11	8:32am	1:20pm	Small	Timothy	PD	7269	Supervisor
6-14-11	8:32am	1:20pm	Torres	Lori	PD	70273	SGT/CSI
6-14-11	8:32am	1:20pm	Jones	Wanda	PD	82535	Officer
6-14-11	11:10am	1:20pm	Davidson	Taylor	PD	69813	CSI Photographer
6-14-11	11:10am	1:20pm	Carter	Ray		N/A	Insurance Arson Investigator

Date 6-14-11   Time: 1:30   Lori Torres   Page 1 of 1

FIGURE 5-20 Entry/exit log for 108 Darcy Avenue.

CHAIN OF CUSTODY SHEET

CASE NUMBER	EVIDENCE TAG #
1106140	0041311
CITY COURT DATE	PAGE # 1 OF 1
06-16-2011	

OFFICER NAME/BADGE #	DATE	TIME	PROPERTY CLASSIFICATION (Mark one box only)	
SGT Lori Torres 70273	06-14	1:16 PM	✓	GSC EVIDENCE
DEFENDANT/OWNER NAME and ADDRESS				CITY COURT EVIDENCE
				FAMILY COURT EVIDENCE
				FOUND PROPERTY
				SAFEKEEPING (RETURN TO OWNER)

(ONLY PROPERTY THAT <u>CANNOT</u> BE PHOTOGRAPHED AND RETURNED TO THE OWNER SHALL BE TURNED IN)

ITEM #	DESCRIPTION (Caliber, brand, model, serial number, color - Currency Amount & Denominations, Etc.)
1	Fire alarms (3)
2	Matches (1) box
3	Nail Polish Remover Bottle (1)
4	Broken Brown Bottle (1)
5	Ten Print Card - Suspect 1
6	Ten Print Card - Suspect 2

PROPERTY RECEIPT (OWNER/DEFENDANT SIGNATURE)

ITEM #	DATE	RELEASED BY DE1015691-Warrant	RECEIVED BY	PURPOSE: (Do Not Write In This Column)
1	06-14	NAME David Johnson ORGANIZATION per warrant SIGN David Johnson	NAME Lori Torres ORGANIZATION R.P.D SIGN Lori Torres	transportation to Randolph P.D. evidence locker
2	06-14	NAME David Johnson ORGANIZATION per warrant SIGN David Johnson	NAME ORGANIZATION Lori Torres SIGN	" "
3	06-14	NAME David Johnson ORGANIZATION per warrant SIGN David Johnson	NAME ORGANIZATION SIGN	
4	06-14	NAME David Johnson ORGANIZATION per warrant SIGN David Johnson	NAME ORGANIZATION SIGN	

White Copy: Evidence   Green Copy: Case Disposition   Blue Copy: Case File/Officer   Pink Copy: Defendant/Owner

FIGURE 5-21 Chain of custody.

FIRST FLOOR PLAN - 1,178 S.F.

SECOND FLOOR PLAN - 1,178 S.F.

Case # 1106140
Incident date : 06-14-2011
Scale Not to Scale
Sketch Drawn By: Lori Torks
Location : 108 Darcy Ave

N ➤

FIGURE 5-22 Crime scene sketch.

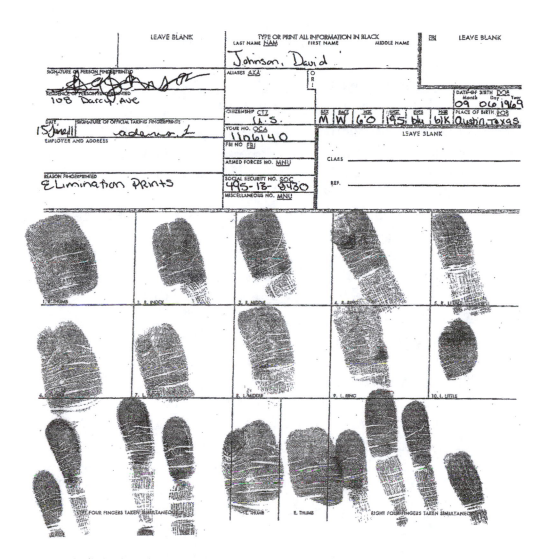

FIGURE 5-23 Elimination prints.

6:15 a.m.—15 June 2011: Torres Residence

When the phone rang, Torres nearly jumped out of her own bed. Sleepily she answered, "Hello?"

Dalton could hardly hold himself together "Judge signed it. Let's go check it out now! I'll be there in two minutes. Move it, Torres!" Torres couldn't believe it, normally things like this in a big city take a while, she thought to herself. It really does matter who you know in a small town. She was thankful the judge had signed off on the search warrant for the Johnson residence; she couldn't wait to get in there and really take a good look around. As with anything dealing with insurance claims, both the bank and insurance company were notified of the fire and were also issued search warrants.

PAGE 1 of 2

COMPLAINT # 11 06 14 0

RANDOLPH METRO POLICE DEPT
STATEMENT

STATEMENT OF __John Hart, lead Firefighter, Engine 1__
HOME ADDRESS __312 Lovers lane, Westport, IN__   HOME PHONE __944.522.1485__
EMPLOYER __Randolph Metro PD__   BUSINESS ADDRESS __911 Main Ave.__
BUS. PHONE __863-9123__   OCCUPATION __Firefighter__
THIS STATEMENT IS GIVEN __14 June 2011__ (DATE) AT __0900__ (TIME)
__108 Darcy Ave, Lebanon, IN__

Upon arrival at the scene, myself and three other
firefighters from Engine 1, shift A, evaluated
the scene for safety hazard. We established
safety zones and proceeded to extinguish the
fire. While we suppressed the fire we
made sure to preserve the fire scene to
preserve transient evidence. During the
process of overhaul and salvage, I observed
evidence at the scene that made me think,
the fire was set intentionally. All doors to
the home were locked and secure. The
window on the rear of the house was
shattered. A brown glass bottle was found
3 feet away from the shattered window near
the leg of a burned sofa leg. The bottle
seemed out of place. I also observed
all (3) fire alarms were disarmed and
missing batteries. I informed SGT Torres to →

I HAVE READ THE FOREGOING STATEMENT OR HAVE HAD IT READ TO ME AND IT IS TRUE AND CORRECT TO
THE BEST OF MY KNOWLEDGE. I HAVE GIVEN THIS STATEMENT FREELY AND VOLUNTARILY AND HAVE BEEN
PROVIDED A COPY OF MY STATEMENT.

page 1 of 2

WITNESS: _Lori Torres_

WITNESS: _____   SIGNATURE: _John Hart_

FIGURE 5-24 John Hart's witness statement.

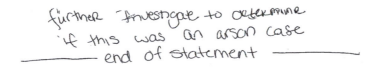

further investigate to determine
if this was an arson case
———— end of statement ————

page 2of 2
Statement of John Hart, June 14, 2011

FIGURE 5-25 Page 2 of John Hart's witness statement.

SEARCH WARRANT
Home Insurance-Fire Records of Customer
Gov. Code ∼ 7460 et. seq.

THE PEOPLE OF THE STATE OF INDIANA to any peace officer in Boone County
Warrant No. DE 1015690

Order: The affidavit below, sworn to and subscribed before me on this date, has established probable cause for this search warrant which you are ordered to execute as follows:

Home Insurance-Fire: 234 Holly Lane, Lebanon IN 46058, GEICO Home Insurance

Customer: David Johnson 108 Darcy Ave, Lebanon IN 46058

Execution by custodian of records: This warrant will be deemed executed if the custodian of records or other designated employee causes the listed records to be delivered to the affiant within ten days of service.

Time Extension: None or Date:_____
15 June 2011, Honorable Henry Scott
Date and time issued Judge of the Superior Court

Affiant's name and agency: SGT Lori Torres, Randolph Police Department

Statement of Probable Cause: The facts in support of this warrant are contained in the Statement of Probable Cause, which is filed herewith and incorporated by reference. David Johnson is suspected of causing fire to his dwelling for home insurance money. His fingerprints were found at the crime scene.

Evidence type: The listed records tend to show, (1) that a felony has been committed, or (2) that a particular person has committed a felony.

Time extension: I have been informed by Geico that, because of the number and nature of the records to be seized the listed records cannot reasonably be produced within the ten days required pursuant to Gov. Code ∼7475. I therefore request an order extending the compliance date to [date records are to be produced].

Declaration: I declare under penalty of perjury that the information within my personal knowledge contained in this affidavit, including all incorporated documents is true.

15 June, SGT Lori Torres
Date, Affiant

FIGURE 5-26 Search warrant, page 1.

OCA# 2010025358

RETURN

I received the attached Search Warrant _____ OCTOBER 1, 2010 _____ , 2010, and have executed it as follows:

On ___ Oct 1, 2010 ___ , 2010 at _____ 12:15 _____ o'clock __ P __ M, I searched that is described in the warrant and

I left a copy of the warrant with _____ On Kitchen Table _____ with a receipt for the items seized.

The following is an inventory of property taken pursuit to the warrant:

Item	Location	Officer
(#1) Lowes Receipt	Kitchen Table	Dalton
(#2) 20oz Min Dew bottle	Kitchen Table	Dalton
(#3) 1gal Paint Thinner	Kitchen Table	Dalton

This inventory was made in the presence of ___ Det Bentley _____ AND __

___ Det Simmons _____

I swear that this Inventory is a true and detailed account of all the property taken by me on the warrant.

SWORN to before me this __ 11th _____

day of __ Oct. _____ , 2010

__ Nelly Bentley _____
(Signature of Officer Executing Warrant)

___ J. Judy _____ (L.S.)

Signature of Judge

FIGURE 5-27 Search warrant, page 2.

PAGE 1 of 1

COMPLAINT # 1106170

RANDOLPH METRO POLICE DEPARTMENT
STATEMENT

STATEMENT OF Ray Carter

HOME ADDRESS 3456 3rd West, Orango, IN   HOME PHONE 509-1245

EMPLOYER Insurance Corporation   BUSINESS ADDRESS 234 Holly Lane,

BUS. PHONE 579-1230   OCCUPATION Fire Investigator

THIS STATEMENT IS GIVEN 14 June 2011 (DATE) AT 1000 (TIME)

108 Darcy Ave, Lebanon, IN

On June 14, 2011, I received a phone call from the Randolph Metro Police Department about a house fire of: David Johnson, 108 Darcy Ave, Lebanon, IN.

When the scene was made safe, lead firefighter John Hart pointed out evidence that proved the house to be set intentionally.

Ⓐ Batteries missing from (3) fire alarms

Ⓑ Brown glass bottle laying on ground near sofa leg—a liquid was still noticed in the glass bottle—was sent to lab

Ⓒ Insured has BAC Protection yet it didn't respond—Customer called/turned off @0730/14 June

Ⓓ Broken window shows someone threw the glass object through the back house window which caught the SOFA on FIRE

★ Insurance relief money will not be released till further investigation —— end of statement ——

I HAVE READ THE FOREGOING STATEMENT OR HAVE HAD IT READ TO ME AND IT IS TRUE AND CORRECT TO THE BEST OF MY KNOWLEDGE. I HAVE GIVEN THIS STATEMENT FREELY AND VOLUNTARILY AND HAVE BEEN PROVIDED A COPY OF MY STATEMENT.

WITNESS: _Lmi Carter_

WITNESS: _____   SIGNATURE: _Ray Carter_

FIGURE 5-28 Ray Carter's witness statement.

7 a.m.—15 June 2011: Johnson Residence

Torres couldn't stop thinking about the witness statements from the fire investigator and the fire-fighter yesterday. Why would anyone have the batteries out of their fire alarms, not to mention have their BAC (battery backup) protection turned off? When she asked these questions to Mr. Johnson, he had explained that he was going to change the batteries when he returned home from fishing. He said that one of them had beeped and kept him up almost all night, and he was so angry that he took them down and took the batteries out. He also had an explanation for calling the BAC home security system and cutting off the service: they were in a hard spot because of the economy and he was trying to save a few dollars. As a single person, she could appreciate needing to save a few dollars wherever you can. Surprisingly enough, Mr. Johnson had agreed to a polygraph test.

RANDOLPH METRO POLICE DEPT.

POLYGRAPH REPORT

To: Sgt. Lori Torres
           Randolph Metro PD
           Case # 1106140

From: Lt. Alan Sawyer   **Polygraph Examiner**
           Special Investigations Unit

Subject: Polygraph Examination of: David Johnson

           DOB: 09061969

           Race: W

           Sex: M

Results: YES   **DECEPTION INDICATED**

On (June 15, 2011   ) following consent to undergo polygraph examination, the subject was administered a specific polygraph examination. The main issue under consideration was whether or not the subject has any knowledge of, or personal involvement in an ARSON at 108 Darcy Ave.

During the test phase the subject was asked the following questions with responses as indicted:

1.) Did you have any involvement with your house being set on fire DJ: NO
2.) Are you currently on administrative leave from your current employer DJ: (YES) NO
3.) Do you have any idea who would have set your house on fire DJ: neighbor kid, Jeremy
4.) Have you ever committed a crime in which you were not caught DJ: NO
5.) Did you recently purchase home insurance-fire,within last two weeks DJ: YES

Upon completion of the examination, it was the opinion of the examiner that   **DECEPTION** was indicated to the above relevant questions.

Respectfully submitted,

Alan Sawyer

Certified Polygraph Examiner

FIGURE 5-29 Polygraph results.

9:31 a.m.—16 June 2011: Randolph Police Station

"Dalton, Torres, you're never going to believe this!" Detective Bailey said. "So you know that liquid that you found in the brown bottle? It was acetone!" she exclaimed. Torres and Dalton slapped each other on the back. With Johnson's fingerprints all over the nail polish remover bottle, they knew they had the arson case in the bag. "Wait, wait, wait! It gets better. So you know those high school cases that we could never get a match with the fingerprints? Well, you guessed it. Mr. Johnson, as it turns out, also likes to use soda bottles filled up with acetone."

Dalton didn't realize he was holding his breath until he tried to speak, "Bailey, are you 100 percent sure those prints match?"

Bailey rolled her eyes, "I'm always sure. Now, go get your man!" Torres put her hand on Dalton's shoulder, "I know that Bentley would've been proud of you."

"No time for that now," Dalton said sternly. "Let's go get our bad guy. I have a suit that's just been waiting for this day!"

Conclusion

David Johnson was arrested and tried for insurance fraud; the other charges of arson in the school libraries are pending. Mr. Johnson had taken out a large insurance policy against his house and had hoped to collect the money to start over. He and his wife were recently separated, and he had been laid off from his former job as a police officer. He thought he had the perfect crime in mind but wanted to test the waters with the football games. Mr. Johnson should have known there is no such thing as the perfect crime.

ARREST WARRANT

DE 1015691

☐ County/ [XX] Municipality of

THE STATE
against
DAVID LEE JOHNSON

Address: 108 Darcy Avenue
Randolph, IN
Phone: SSN:
Sex: M Race: W Height: 6'0 Weight: 195
DL State: IN DL #: 46022
DOB: 05-01-1967 Agency ORI #: 100800
Prosecuting Agency: Randolph PD
Prosecuting Officer: Dalton
Offense: Arson 1st
Offense Code: 16-11-110
Code/Ordinance Sec.

This warrant is **CERTIFIED FOR SERVICE** in the [X] County/ [X] Municipality of Randolph, IN Boone County. The accused is to be arrested and brought before me to be dealt with according to law.

Signature of Judge (L.S.)
Date: 06-16-2011

RETURN

A copy of this arrest warrant was delivered to defendant David Lee Johnson on 06-16-2011.

134
Signature of Constable/Law Enforcement Officer

RETURN WARRANT TO:

Boone County Sessions Court

☐ County/ [X] Municipality of Randolph, IN

AFFIDAVIT

Personally appeared before me the affiant Det Dalton who being duly sworn deposes and says that defendant David Lee Johnson did within this county and state on June 14, 2011 violate the criminal laws of the State of Indiana (or ordinance of ☐ County/ [X] Municipality of Randolph, IN) in the following particulars:

DESCRIPTION OF OFFENSE: Knowingly and maliciously ignited a residence fire

I further state that there is probable cause to believe that the defendant named above did commit the crime set forth and that probable cause is based on the following facts:

On June 14, 2011, David Lee Johnson distributed an accelerant throughout the livingroom of his residence at 108 Darcy Avenue and then set fire to the accelerant in an effort to cause destruction of the dwelling. No residents were home at the time of the fire and the Randolph Fire Dept. was able to extinguish the fire. An arson investigation revealed the fire was intentionally set and evidence was found linking Mr. Johnson to the point of origin of the fire.

Sworn to and subscribed before me on (L.S.)
Signature of Issuing Judge
Signature of Affiant
Affiant's Address
Affiant's Telephone 544-0000

☐ County/ [X] Municipality of

ARREST WARRANT

TO ANY LAW ENFORCEMENT OFFICER OF THIS STATE OR MUNICIPALITY OR ANY CONSTABLE OF THIS COUNTY:

It appearing from the above affidavit that there are reasonable grounds to believe that on June 14, 2011 defendant did violate the criminal laws of the State of Indiana (or ordinance of [X] County/ [X] Municipality of Randolph, IN Boone Co.) as set forth below:

DESCRIPTION OF OFFENSE: Arson, Class B Felony IC 35-43-1-1

Now, therefore, you are empowered and directed to arrest the said defendant and bring him or her before me forthwith to be dealt with according to law. A copy of this Arrest Warrant shall be delivered to the defendant at the time of its execution, or as soon thereafter as is practicable.

(L.S.)
Signature of Issuing Judge
Judge Code:
Judge's Address 0000 Bridgeview
Judge's Telephone 654-0000
Issuing Court: [X] Magistrate ☐ Municipal ☐ Circuit

ORIGINAL

FIGURE 5-30 Arrest warrant.

Police Prosecutive Case Folder Checklist

ORIGINAL CASE NUMBER	1106140		DATE	06-16-2011	

DEFENDANT	Johnson	David	W	M	44	05-01-67
	Last Name	First Name	Race	Sex	Age	DOB

THE FOLLOWING PAPERWORK MUST BE COMPLETED, PLACED IN THE CASE FOLDERS AND CHECKED BY THE DUTY SUPERVISOR BEFORE BEING SUBMITTED.

- [X] PROSECUTIVE SUMMARY
- [X] INCIDENT REPORT (1 COPY) BOOKING REPORT (3 COPIES)
- [X] AFFIDAVIT (4 COPIES) TICKET (ALL COPIES)
- [X] N.C.I.C. PRINTOUT (1 ORIGINAL)
- [X] ADVISEMENT OF RIGHTS FORM (1 ORIGINAL)
- [ ] VICTIM NOTIFICATION FORM (IF NOT A BUSINESS) (JAIL RECEIVES YELLOW AND PINK)

CHECK ANY OF THE FOLLOWING PAPERWORK THAT IS INCLUDED IN CASE FOLDER

- [X] DEFENDANT(S) STATEMENT(S) (ORIGINALS)
- [X] CHAIN OF CUSTODY SHEET (EVIDENCE BLUE COPY)
- [X] OTHER EVIDENCE INFORMATION (EXPLAIN) ON SCENE LINE UP FORMS
- [X] INVESTIGATOR SUPPLEMENTS (ORIGINALS)
- [X] SEARCH WARRANTS/RETURNS
- [X] LAB ANALYSIS REQUEST
- [X] LAB ANALYSIS RESULTS
- [ ] CORONERS REPORT
- [X] PHOTOS AND MISCELLANEOUS INFORMATION

FIREARM CASES/VIOLENT OFFENSES

- [X] **CRITERIA FOR DETECTIVE NOTIFICATION OR CALL-OUT**

  Evidence of a unique nature that has been located at the scene and could possibly be linked to recent incidents. For example: bullet resistant vests, masks, clothing, photographs, or other weapons...etc. Type of firearm or ammunition that may be similar to recently documented crimes.

- [ ] **COMPLETE HABITUAL VIOLENT OFFENDER FORM**

  Forward to Crime Analysis Supervisor

- [ ] **CHECK PROBATION AND PAROLE STATUS OF SUSPECT(S)**

  Forward a copy of incident to I.L.P. Unit

  If applicable, contact Probation and Parole and report the incident involving suspect.
  . **Probation and Parole** ⋅

- [ ] **BOND STATUS OF SUSPECT(S)**

  Question suspect about bond status. If on bond, contact appropriate court for possible bond cancellation.

- [ ] **COMPLETE TRACE FORMS AND FORWARD TO A.T.F. TASK FORCE/INV.SEC.**

  OFFICER'S SIGNATURE AND BADGE: _____

FIGURE 5-31 Prosecutive case file checklist.

POLICE DEPARTMENT PROSECUTIVE SUMMARY REPORT

DATE OF REPORT: 06-16-2011	**CASE NUMBER:** 1106140
DATE/TIME INCIDENT: 06-14-2011	**LOCATION INCIDENT:** 108 Darcy Ave.
DATE/TIME ARREST: 06-16-2011	**LOCATION ARREST:** 411 City Hall Dr.

DEFENDANT INFORMATION

DEF	LAST	FIRST	MID	DOB	AGE	SSN	STATEMENT
#1	Johnson	David	Lee	05-01-1967	44	*1733	No
#2							
#3							
#4							

DEF	DEFENDANT(S) CHARGES	WARRANT/SUMMONS
#1	Arson 1st degree	DE 1015691
#2		
#3		
#4		

VICTIM INFORMATION

VIC	LAST	FIRST	ADDRESS	PHONE	DOB
#1	GEICO Insurance	(Ray Carter)	234 Holly Lane	704.579.1230	Corp.

WHAT IS DEFENDANT(S) ACCUSED OF DOING
(WHO, WHAT, WHEN, WHERE, HOW, AND WHY?)

On June 14, 2011, David Johnson deliberately set fire to his personal residence at 108 Darcy Ave. by utilizing an incendiary device to ignite the fire. The purpose was to destroy the residence. No occupants were at home at the time of the fire.

EVIDENCE
INDICATE IF SUBMITTED FOR ANALYSIS

clear fluid used as accelerant, soda bottle, fingerprint card and latent prints

WITNESS #1

LAST NAME	FIRST	MIDDLE	PHONE NUMBER
Dalton	John		704.521.1200

ADDRESS / STREET NUMBER/NAME/ CITY/ STATE/ZIP CODE
123 Candy Lane, Lebanon, IN 46058
WHAT WITNESS CAN TESTIFY TO:
Investigation on 6-14-2011 at 108 Darcy Ave.

STATEMENT TAKEN: YES ( ) NO (X)

WITNESS #2

LAST NAME	FIRST	MIDDLE	PHONE NUMBER
Bentley	Mary		704.521.1200

ADDRESS/STREET NUMBER/NAME/CITY/STATE/ZIP CODE:
123 Candy Lane, Lebanon, IN 46058
WHAT WITNESS CAN TESTIFY TO:
Investigation on 6-14-2011 at 108 Darcy Ave.
STATEMENT TAKEN: YES ( ) NO (X)

SUBMITTING OFFICER: Det. J. Dalton	
APPROVING OFFICER: Lt. J. Fitzgerald	

FIGURE 5-32 Prosecutive case file report.

Discussion Questions

1. Review the case narrative and all the documentation. What, if any, inconsistencies did you note in the case file?
2. Establish the timeline, and explain how the house fire was linked to the school arson investigations.
3. How did Mrs. Berry enter into the school arson investigations? At any point was she considered a suspect during the investigation? Why was she not a significant personality in this case?
4. Is it significant that the perpetrator had recently obtained a new fire insurance policy on his residence? Explain your answer.
5. How can David Johnson be linked to the school arson fires?
6. Is the investigation complete? When a suspect confesses to a crime, is that the end of the investigation? What can happen that will cause this investigation to remain in active status?
7. What, if any, unanswered questions did you develop as you reviewed the narrative and the case files? Are you satisfied that the suspect, David Johnson, has not committed any other arsons as he was preparing and practicing for the house fire? Why or why not?

Reference

[1]   U.S. Department of Justice. Crime in the United States. Federal Bureau of Investigation, <http://www2.fbi.gov/ucr/cius2009/offenses/clearances/index.html>; 2012.

6

Homicide or Suicide

OBJECTIVE

This case file examines witnesses and suspects, interviews, and interrogations. The physical evidence will be used to corroborate the witness statements and lead to a determination of motive, intent, and opportunity. The case investigates whether a death was a homicide or a suicide.

KEY TERMS

CSI effect	interview	preliminary investigation
gunshot residue	investigative strategy	scientific method of inquiry
initial survey	latent fingerprints	trace evidence
interrogation	Miranda rights	waiver statement

What You Will Learn

LEARNING OUTCOMES

- Distinguish facts from misperceptions
- Appraise situations and circumstances present at crime scenes
- Develop alternative explanations for incidents
- Assess forensic analysis findings when conflicting statements are presented

CRITICAL THINKING

- Elements of the crime
- Types of physical evidence
- Key investigative strategies

Introduction

The primary goal of every investigation is to find the truth and let the facts prove or disprove any allegations. This case file is an excellent example of police officers arriving on a scene and finding the alleged perpetrator still there with compelling physical evidence to indicate this is an "open and shut" case. In fact, the *corpus delicti* is obvious when law enforcement officers are summoned to the scene. A deceased white male is lying on the ground with a handgun nearby, and a sobbing female is in the vicinity. In fact, the investigators are notified by the responding officers that there is a homicide and they have a suspect in custody. However, when the detectives arrive to conduct their **initial survey**, a walkthrough of the crime scene that assists in determining the scope of the investigation, they are aware that perception is not always reality, and the young woman who is present with the body of the victim may or may not be the perpetrator.

A thorough investigation must be conducted. Detectives are trained to discern facts from opinions. Whereas a rookie police officer could mistake this type of incident as one that only requires completing paperwork and then arresting the woman on the scene for homicide, seasoned investigators must carefully examine all aspects of the case and process the scene as if there are no witnesses; they will have to rely on physical evidence analysis to assist in determining the facts of the case.

The Steps of an Investigation

The first officers on the scene will complete the **preliminary investigation** and an offense report to establish that a crime has been committed. This report will become the face sheet for the case file. Great attention must be given to the completion of the offense or incident report so that anyone reviewing the case can determine the initiation of events, the actions of the first responders, and who assumed responsibility for the investigation of the case. The questions who, what, where, when, and how must all be addressed during the preliminary investigation and contained in the offense report. When completing the report, officers must ensure they provide a fundamental understanding of the conditions at the scene upon arrival. Photographs and sketches are important elements for documenting the crime scene, but the offense or incident report will link all the facts to the photos and diagrams and present a complete depiction of the scene when officers first arrived.

Throughout the entire investigation, officers and detectives will rely on the **scientific method of inquiry**, which means that data will be collected through observing, analyzing physical evidence, formulating theories, and then testing those theories against the various statements from witnesses, victims, analysts, legal representatives, and previous investigative experience. As more data are gathered and facts are established, those hypotheses can be reexamined until the truth is discerned. In the American criminal justice system, this means the data and the investigative case files will be presented to a judicial authority for a final determination.

The CSI Effect

For most investigations where forensic evidence analysis must occur, there is a long waiting period. This is in direct conflict with how television shows present the progress of investigations; the phenomenon is known as the **CSI effect**. The idea that there is an instant examination and determination of the "guilty party" was created by television producers and has led to unreasonable expectations that criminal investigations will be resolved in a very short time

---

VIOLENT CRIME STATISTICS FROM THE UNIFORM CRIME REPORT

Nationwide in 2011, there were an estimated 1,203,564 violent crimes.

- The numbers in each of the four categories of violent crime offenses decreased when compared with the 2010 reports. Robbery had the largest decrease at 4.0 percent, followed by aggravated assault with a 3.9 percent decline, forcible rape with a 2.5 percent decrease, and murder with a 0.7 percent decline.
- Nationwide in 2011, there were an estimated 9,063,173 property crimes.
- The two-year trend showed that property crime decreased 0.5 percent in 2011 compared with the 2010 report. The five-year trend, comparing 2011 data with that of 2007, showed an 8.3 percent drop in property crime.
- Collectively, victims of property crimes lost an estimated $15.6 million in 2011.
- The FBI estimated that in 2011, agencies nationwide made about 12,408,899 arrests, excluding traffic violations.
- The 2011 arrest rate for violent crimes was 534,704 per 100,000 inhabitants; for property crime the rate was 1,639,883 per 100,000 inhabitants.
- By violent crime offense, the arrest rate (including murder and non-negligent manslaughter, forcible rape, robbery, and aggravated assault) was 172.3 per 100,000 inhabitants, and the arrest rate for property crime (burglary, larceny – theft, motor vehicle theft, and arson) was 531.3 per 100,000 inhabitants.
- In 2011, there were 14,633 law enforcement agencies that reported their staffing levels to the Federal Bureau of Investigation (FBI).
- The rate of sworn officers was 2.4 per 1,000 inhabitants in the nation in 2011. The rate of full-time law enforcement employees (civilian and sworn) per 1,000 inhabitants was 3.4.

Source: http://www.fbi.gov/about-us/cjis/ucr/ucr.

---

frame. Witnesses or victims may not be able to provide statements to the case detectives. The backlogs of physical evidence waiting to be examined by a very limited number of crime lab resources may result in delays of several months before the results are available to detectives. Although modern police work has been able to blend scientific theories of crime detection into the practical aspects of investigation, detectives are working multiple cases simultaneously, and many times, confessions are acquired by perpetrators who simply get tired of being under suspicion or finally cave in to a guilty conscience. Witnesses and victims lose their desire to persevere in the investigation throughout long delays and the appearance of a lack of progress by the agency in solving the case.

Planning a Successful Investigation

When detectives are asking questions, they are seeking the facts of the case. A successful **investigative strategy** includes a methodical plan that involves prioritizing the leads gathered during the preliminary investigation. Setting objectives and establishing an organized list of defined activities may include interview strategies, suspect identification and arrest strategies, a method for gathering intelligence, and even handling the media may be included in the overall plan. As new information and facts are developed, the original investigative strategy must be constantly reviewed for accuracy. Follow-up statements, corroborating statements from various aspects of the case, comparisons of the results of scientific analysis of the physical evidence to the statements, and determining additional steps to be taken are all ongoing processes that may impact the investigative strategy.

Interview or Interrogation?

Conducting interviews will assist in gathering the critical information, developing the timeline that reflects the sequence of events before and after a crime was committed, and identifying the scope and focus of the investigation. An effective **interview** also eliminates improbable suspects while developing additional leads or suspects. It is nonaccusatory and can assist in identifying proper interrogation strategies.

Although all interviews have the potential to reveal useful information, even more strategic planning is invested into conducting an interrogation. Both interviews and interrogations are used for gathering information and seeking the truth. However, an **interrogation** is much more focused and will eventually lead to the accusations made by detectives against the suspect. Interviews are conducted with subjects; interrogations are focused on a specific suspect. Interrogations should be recorded and the event preserved via digital files. Before an interrogation begins, the detective must read the **Miranda rights** and **waiver statement** to the suspect, who must sign the forms before formal questioning may begin. While the Miranda rights are used to notify a suspect of the obligations of the legal entity to safeguard constitutional rights, the waiver statement is used when suspects are willing to waive their rights and to give a statement to the detectives or officers investigating the crime. If at any time during the interrogation the suspect requests an attorney, the interrogation must end.

Visible and Hidden Physical Evidence

Crime scene technicians are trained to recognize the potential presence of **trace evidence**, which refers to small particulates used to link victims, suspects, objects, and crime scenes. The types of trace evidence range from hairs and fibers, to DNA, soil, and chemical residues. This is a limited list of trace evidence; however, extreme care must be taken during the preliminary report and initial walkthrough to prevent the disappearance or destruction of trace evidence. This evidence can be analyzed by the crime lab and compared to databases for identification and matching. In the following case, the trace evidence is a critical component for determining the perpetrator. **Gunshot residue** (GSR) is formed when the firing pin of a weapon strikes the primer of a cartridge, sending a bullet through the barrel of a gun. Gunshot residue travels both forward (with the bullet) and backward from the rear of the gun and will deposit on both the shooter and the target that is within a few inches of the discharged weapon. The presence of gunshot residue can accurately define the distance of the victim from the barrel of the gun. GSR found on the hands or clothing of an individual can reveal that the person either fired a weapon or handled one that was recently fired. This is particularly useful when investigating a scene that is a potential suicide. However, GSR can be detected for only a limited time, so the absence of GSR on hands or clothing does not completely rule out a suspect.

There are many types of physical evidence and forensic analyses that can be requested for physical evidence. **Latent fingerprints** are the most common type of physical evidence. CSI technicians apply powders or chemicals that adhere to the friction ridge impressions made by fingers, hands, or feet. Those patterns are created by deposits of sweat and other secretions and are unique to each human being. No two fingerprints are alike. The presence of a latent print belonging to a suspect who denies ever being at the scene of a crime is difficult for the suspect to explain. The absence of a suspect's fingerprints does not exonerate the suspect. The same can be said for DNA and other trace evidence.

■ ■ ■ ━━━━━━━━━━━━━━━━━━━━━━━━━━━━━

Case File: Homicide or Suicide

Case File Elements

- Incident/offense report
- Witness statements
- Crime scene files

Critical Questions and Activities

As you read the following case file, create a timeline that accurately sequences the events that occurred. Examine the statements of the witnesses, and determine if the physical evidence supports those statements. What was the investigative strategy for this case, and how did it work to identify motive, intent, and opportunity?

Call to the Scene

6:10 p.m.—Friday, 22 October: John's Island Police Department, Detective Bureau

A cool breeze hung in the air as a light rain drizzled across the early evening sky. The phone rang, and Detective Kirkpatrick looked at it hesitantly, glancing at the clock that displayed less than an hour remaining on his shift, before finally deciding to pick it up. One of the duty officers, Partridge, greeted him on the other end of the line.

"Detective Kirkpatrick?" Officer Partridge asked. "Sorry to call just before you get off, but we've got a…situation here." Kirkpatrick, a homicide detective, could only assume they had a corpse on their hands.

"Who killed who?" Kirkpatrick asked, picking up a pen and a pad of paper from his desk.

"We're not exactly sure anyone killed anyone. We can't tell if it's a homicide or a suicide," Officer Partridge said. Kirkpatrick was intrigued.

"Start at the beginning," he said.

"Yes sir," said Officer Partridge, "I responded to a 911 dispatch at 210 Maine Road. When I arrived on scene at 5:40 p.m., I found a woman doubled over crying at the feet of a deceased male victim with a single gunshot wound to the head. The body position indicated the man had shot himself."

"What makes you think it could be homicide?" Kirkpatrick asked.

"Well, the female is covered in a great deal of blood, and I don't think it's hers. Could be some kind of lovers' quarrel gone too far, sir."

"Humph," sighed Kirkpatrick. "How's the woman doing?"

"She's upset, sad. Doesn't seem angry. She hasn't said much to anyone so far," the officer replied.

"Call for some backup to help secure the scene and start logging traffic in and out. I'll call the coroner and be down within the hour. Thanks, Partridge."

The Walkthrough
6:40 p.m.—Friday, 22 October: 210 Maine Road, John's Island, Georgia

The road to the crime scene was isolated; from the looks of it, there wasn't a neighbor for half a mile at least. Red and blue lights flickered through the trees lining the street as Kirkpatrick pulled into the driveway. The detective parked the car and walked over to his partner, Detective Perez, who had arrived on the scene just moments before. The two exchanged light-hearted gripes about the longest calls always coming in right at shift change; then they walked over to Officer Partridge, who had just finished stringing police tape around the scene that included the body of a young white male. Blood seeped from a smallish wound on the victim's forehead while the back of his head appeared to have been blown nearly off by the force of the bullet's exit. Blood, bone, and brain matter littered the grass around the corpse's head.

"Officer Partridge," said Kirkpatrick, "you ready to take us through it?"

"Yes, sir, "Partridge answered, motioning for the detectives to join him next to the body. "The victim is Everett Grant, a twenty-six-year-old white male. This is his home. The young lady over there," Partridge said, pointing to a woman standing by an ambulance wrapped in an emergency blanket and talking to paramedics between sobs, "is Emilia Williams. She was the woman on the scene when I arrived. The victim also has a wife, Jacqueline Grant, whom we have yet to locate."

Detective Perez knelt to examine the body, but Kirkpatrick hesitated. "Wait a minute," Kirkpatrick said to Partridge, "A young woman who is not his wife is this upset and the only other person here? Let me guess, girl on the side?" Officer Partridge shrugged and nodded. "*Always* right before shift change."

"You're starting to sound like a broken record," said Detective Perez. "Come here, look at this." Kirkpatrick knelt beside Perez, who motioned to the pistol in the victim's right hand. "A .38. Looks like it could've made the entry and exit wounds," Perez said pointing to the hole in the right temple of the victim with the eraser end of his pencil. "Shirt's damp, too," Perez continued, "But that could just be from the rain."

"What about these holes?" Kirkpatrick asked, pointing to several tears in the victim's shirt. "Could be sign of a struggle."

"Or just an old shirt," Perez said.

The crime scene photographer, Officer Carl Robinson, arrived on scene at 7 p.m. and began taking pictures of the location as he approached the area.

FIGURE 6-1 Male victim face-down on his stomach—photographer facing north.

Kirkpatrick directed the photographer to take pictures of the entry and exit wounds, the gun, the full body, as well as the area in which the body was found.

Johns Island PD Photo Log

Case Number: _____102210_____

Photographer: ___Carl Robinson_____ ID No. 74191_____

Detective: ____Kirkpatrick and Perez_____ ID No. 84437/74191_____

Crime Classification: Homicide_____

Log Maintained by: __CSI C. Robinson_____ ID No. ___88112_____

Item No.	Date	Time	Description	Location	Notes
1	10-22-11	1904	Male victim laying face down on stomach – photographer facing North	210 Maine Rd	Adjacent to the home
2	10-22-11	1910	Male victim laying face down on stomach – photographer facing West	210 Maine Rd	
3	10-22-11	1911	Male victim -- photographer facing East	210 Maine Rd	
4	10-22-11	1916	Midrange view of victim and gun	210 Maine Rd	
5	10-22-11	1917	Midrange view showing travel document	210 Maine Rd	
6	10-22-11	1918	Close-up of victim's face and location of gun	210 Maine Rd	
7	10-22-11	1919	Close-up of victim's head – photographer facing East	210 Maine Rd	
8	10-22-11	1920	Close-up of victim's head – photographer facing Southeast	210 Maine Rd	
9	10-22-11	1920	Closer view of wound	210 Maine Rd	
10	10-22-11	1922	Midrange view of travel document	210 Maine Rd	
11	10-22-11	1923	Close-up view of weapon proximity to victim's hand	210 Maine Rd	

Date _____10-22-11_____   Time: _____1925_____   Page _1___ of __1___

FIGURE 6-2 Photo log from 210 Maine Road.

FIGURES 6-3–6-13 Match these scene photos to the photo log.

Upon completion, Kirkpatrick directed Robinson to photograph Ms. Williams and to recruit a female officer to collect her bloody clothes. CSI Robinson bagged and labeled the gun to be sent to the crime lab for further analysis. Robinson then placed paper bags on the hands of the victim so that they could be tested for gunshot residue (GSR) when the coroner arrived.

FIGURES 6-3–6-13 (Continued) Match these pictures to the entries on the photo log.

Kirkpatrick left the body and walked up to the house. The side door was wide open. He noted a small hole in the doorframe, which likely contained the bullet from the exit wound, and directed CSI Robinson to recover the evidence. Inside the house, the detective found a whiteboard immediately to the right of the door with a photograph taped to it of Mr. Grant and another woman who did not

FIGURES 6-3–6-13 (Continued) Determine how the physical evidence is documented in the photo log.

resemble the woman outside. Under the picture was a note that read: "I will be with Giselle helping her watch the children. Love you honey. Jackie."

"I knew it," Kirkpatrick said. A sudden chill ran down his spine as he realized he might have a double homicide on his hands. He summoned CSI Robinson, and they carefully searched the

FIGURES 6-3–6-13 (Continued) Why is it important to accurately show placement of physical evidence in photographs?

remainder of the house. There was no one else at the residence. Kirkpatrick directed CSI Robinson to the board and walked back outside.

While they worked, Officer Partridge returned to the detectives. "I knew I'd heard Grant's name before. I just realized, I know the victim's receptionist. Her name is Rebecca Hart." Officer Partridge gave the detectives Ms. Hart's address and contact information.

"Great. Thanks, Partridge. I found a note inside saying the wife is at Giselle's house. See if you can find out who that is and turn up that address for us," Kirkpatrick said.

"I'm on it," Partridge replied, turning to leave.

"I'll deal with the coroner and interview Ms. Williams if you want to go interview Ms. Hart," Kirkpatrick said.

"Sounds like a plan," Perez replied, standing. He walked down the drive and got into his car, backing slowly out of the rural driveway.

Coroner's Onsite Investigation

7:47 p.m.—Friday, 22 October: 210 Maine Road, John's Island, Georgia

The coroner, Dr. Anita Illysen, arrived on the scene and began by issuing a case number and a gunshot residue number. Detective Kirkpatrick watched as she examined the body for additional

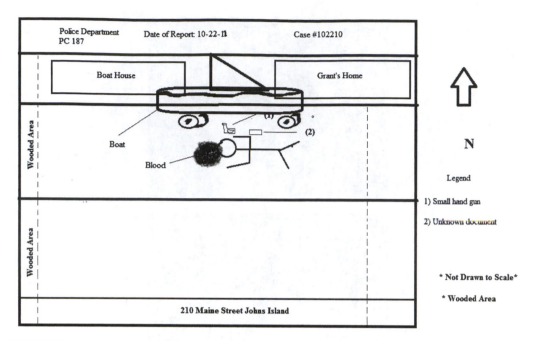

FIGURE 6-14 Final crime scene sketch.

wounds to the victim. "The victim," she stated, "appears to have been shot once with a medium-caliber round—one entry wound to the right temple and one exit wound behind the left ear are visible." She took the corpse's body temperature by puncturing the liver with a thermometer. "Ninety-two degrees, Detective. Your victim was breathing less than 4 hours ago."

Using various collection materials, Dr. Illysen proceeded to take samples from the victim, including fingernail scrapings and hair and fiber samples. Then the doctor processed the victim's hands for gunshot residue.

The coroner continued to examine the body. "Preliminary examination indicates that there are no defensive wounds, but you'll know better when the body gets a more thorough exam at autopsy."

The coroner stood and withdrew her car keys. "We'll put him in the freezer for now, and he will be first on the table Monday morning. I'll have the report sent over as soon as I'm done." Kirkpatrick thanked the doctor for her help and waved as she turned to leave the scene.

Interview 1

Rebecca Hart (Receptionist) and Caleb Black (Ms. Hart's Boyfriend)
8:37 p.m.—Friday, 22 October: 17 Flamingo Street, John's Island, Georgia

Detective Perez arrived at the home of Rebecca Hart to find lights on inside the house. Hoping she would still be awake, Perez exited his car and approached the front door. A young woman answered on the third knock, and the detective introduced himself.

"Good evening, ma'am. I'm Detective Perez. Are you Rebecca Hart?"

"I am," Hart replied.

"Ms. Hart, there's been an incident. Would you mind if I came inside?"

"Oh yes, of-of course," she stammered, letting the detective pass her. She directed him into the living room where he sat in a chair and Rebecca Hart took the sofa next to him. "What has happened?"

"Ms. Hart, you work for Mr. Everett Grant, correct?" Hart nodded. "Ms. Hart, could you account for Mr. Grant's whereabouts today?"

"Why?" she asked, "What is this regarding?"

"Ms. Hart, Everett Grant was found dead this evening," Perez said solemnly.

"Oh my god…" Hart started, trailing off into a series of sobs.

Hearing the commotion, another man entered the room from the hall. "What's going on here?" Detective Perez introduced himself and explained the situation to the man, who introduced himself as Caleb Black, Ms. Hart's boyfriend. The two sank into the couch as Mr. Black tried to console Ms. Hart, who eventually managed to get her weeping under control.

"Ms. Hart," Perez began, "can you account for Mr. Grant's schedule today?"

"Y-yes," she said in a feeble voice. "I mean, it was a light day at the office so Mr. Grant left around 3:15 p.m. to have a late lunch with his wife before he left on his business trip this weekend. I-I didn't see him again after that."

"Did anything unusual happen? Anything out of the ordinary?"

"No, no I don't think so…," she said.

"Yeah it did," Caleb Black interrupted, "I came down to the office just as Grant was leaving. You see, when he leaves early he lets her go home early too, so I was coming down to pick her up. Grant and I said 'hey' to each other before I opened the door to the office. While I was waiting for Rebecca to get her things together, she received…"

"A phone call!" Hart interrupted. "That's right! I answered a call from a woman looking for Mr. Grant. I didn't think anything about it, so I told her that Mr. Grant was out to lunch with his wife. I asked for her number so he could call her back, but she yelled angrily that she would be seeing him soon and hung up."

"Yeah, it was so loud I could hear it," Black added.

"I just didn't think much of it," Hart said, "We get angry customers sometimes. It happens. Do you think it could be related?"

"Maybe," Perez evaded. "Did you get the name of the person who called?" Hart pursed her lips and clinched her eyes shut, concentrating, before looking up.

"Yes!" she exclaimed, "Emilia Williams. That's what she said her name was."

Detective Perez reached into his pocket and withdrew a business card. Thank you very much, Ms. Hart, Mr. Black," he said, nodding to each and offering Rebecca Hart the card. "If you think of anything else that might be helpful, please give me a call. Thank you for your time."

Interview 2

Emilia Williams

9:14 p.m.—Friday, 22 October: 210 Maine Road, John's Island, Georgia

Detective Kirkpatrick walked over to the ambulance. The young woman who had been dressed in blood-soaked jeans and a T-shirt was now wearing a pair of scrubs several sizes too large for her and still wrapped in an emergency blanket. A female officer offered the detective a sealed paper evidence bag with the woman's bloody clothes inside, and he motioned for her to take them to CSI Robinson to be logged in as evidence.

"Ma'am," Kirkpatrick said, "My name is Detective Kirkpatrick."

"Emil-Emilia Williams," the woman stammered. Detective Kirkpatrick tried to question her, but once she started talking, Williams did not stop. She rambled and sobbed, stating several times that she was unsure what happened and that she had just shown up to find him lying dead on the ground. Williams's voice broke and she began to cry uncontrollably.

Kirkpatrick was able to calm her down, albeit briefly, until she saw the body again and began crying hysterically. The detective realized the environment was not conducive to questioning and decided to move to a more neutral location.

"Ms. Williams, would you be willing to ride down to the station with one of our officers so we can get a little more information?" Emilia Williams suppressed a whimper and then nodded in agreement. Kirkpatrick motioned the female officer back over and asked her to drive Ms. Williams to the police station. She coaxed Williams out of the ambulance and into her squad car.

Officer Partridge walked over to the ambulance. "Got the information you were looking for. Wife is still alive and all right. Here's the address." Partridge handed the detective a piece of paper.

"Thanks, Partridge," he said, taking the information. Kirkpatrick's phone rang.

Johns Island PD Entry/Exit Log

Case Number: _____102210_____

Photographer: ____Carl Robinson_____   ID No. 74191_____

Detective: ____Kirkpatrick and Perez_____   ID No. 84437/74191____

Crime Classification: Homicide_____

Log Maintained by: ___Officer Senegal_____   ID No. __85493_____

Date	Time In	Time Out	Last Name	First Name	Agency	Badge/ID No.	Reason for Entry
10-22-11	1740	2201	Partridge	Christopher	JIPD	19931	Responded to 911 Call
10-22-11	1741	2159	Smith	Patricia	JI EMS	874	Responded to 911 Call
10-22-11	1741	2159	Adams	Nate	JI EMS	715	Responded to 911 Call
10-22-11	1745	2100	Ricard	Tony	JI Vol FD	23	Responded to 911 Call
10-22-11	1840	2250	Kirkpatrick	John	JIPD	84437	Detective assigned to case
10-22-11	1840	2037	Perez	Miguel	JIPD	94830	Detective assigned to case
10-22-11	1858	2250	Robinson	Carl	JIPD	88112	CSI assigned to case
10-22-11	1947	2130	Illysen	Anita	Lamar Co Coroner	44123	Coroner assigned to case

Date ____10-22-11____   Time: ___2250____   Page _1___ of __1___

FIGURE 6-15 Entry and exit log for 210 Maine Road.

"Kirkpatrick. Go ahead."

"Hey, it's Perez. Apparently our witness Emilia made some sort of angry threat about seeing our victim tonight."

"Oh, she did?" Kirkpatrick asked. "I couldn't get anything out of her here so I had her taken down to the station. I was getting ready to head back and question her myself."

"Locate the wife yet?" Perez asked.

"Yeah, we did. You want to do the notification?"

"Sure. See you at the station."

Interview 3

Jacqueline Grant (Victim's Wife), Giselle Woods, and Tristan Woods

10:30 p.m.—Friday, 22 October: 1117 Glenwood Drive, John's Island, Georgia

Perez hated this part of the job. Notifying next-of-kin was one of those things that never got any easier. Perez braced himself as he strode up the porch steps. A young woman opened the door on the second ring of the bell.

"Jacqueline Grant?" Detective Perez asked.

"No, no. I'm Giselle Woods, her sister."

"Ms. Woods, my name is Detective Perez. I'm looking for Jacqueline Grant. Is she here?"

"She is," Ms. Woods replied, "Please, come inside."

Detective Perez went into the living room and had a seat as Jacqueline Grant entered with a man who identified himself as Tristan Woods, Giselle's husband.

"Ms. Grant, I'm afraid your husband has been involved in a shooting," Perez said.

"Shooting? Is he all right?" she asked nervously.

"Ma'am, I'm sorry to have to break this to you," Perez began, "but I'm afraid that your husband didn't make it."

The news seemed to devastate Jacqueline Grant, and she broke into uncontrollable sobs as her sister tried to console her. Perez waited patiently for several minutes until she was able to get her crying under control.

"Ms. Grant, I'm sorry to have to do this to you, but I'm hoping you can answer some questions." Grant wiped at her eyes and sniffed, trying to contain more sobs.

"I'll try my best," she replied.

"Ms. Grant, can you think of anyone who might want to harm your husband?"

"No, no," she said, "Everyone loved him. I don't know anyone who had any problems with him."

"Ms. Grant, I was wondering if you could account for your schedule today?" Perez asked.

"Now wait a minute," Tristan Woods said, speaking up for the first time. "You can't possibly think that Jacqueline had anything to do with this."

"No, no," Perez said, "I'm not accusing anyone. We just need to collect as much information as we can."

"I'll answer," Ms. Grant said, silencing more protest from Tristan Woods. "I came here from work to spend time with my sister before picking up her kids from after school camp. We've been here since about 4 p.m."

Detective Perez questioned Ms. Grant and the Woods couple for another 20 minutes, but he did not note anything suspicious or any change in their demeanor. At the end of the interview, Ms. Grant agreed, against the Woods' protest, to come down to the police station for a gunshot residue test.

Interview 4

Emilia Williams: Follow-up

10:49 p.m.—Friday, 22 October: John's Island Police Department, Detective Bureau

"Ms. Williams," Detective Kirkpatrick began, "Have you ever contacted Mr. Grant at work before?"

"S-sure," she stammered, off-balance from the question, "I'd call him at work."

"What about today? Did you call him today?" Kirkpatrick asked. Emilia Williams hesitated.

"Yes," she said, resignation in her voice.

"Who did you talk to on the telephone?" he asked.

"The receptionist answered the phone and told me Everett was not there. He had left to go to lunch with his wife."

Kirkpatrick was seeking more information and asked, "Did you say anything to the receptionist when you were told Everett was not in the office?"

"Yes," Williams started sobbing again, "I said I would see him soon and I did not need to leave a message."

"Can you tell me what you meant when you told the receptionist at his office that you would 'see him soon'?"

Tears welled up in her eyes.

Johns Island PD Evidence Log

Case Number: _____102210_____

Photographer: ___Carl Robinson_____ ID No. 74191_____

Detective: ___Kirkpatrick and Perez____ ID No. 84437/74191

Crime Classification: Homicide_____

Log Maintained by: ___CSI C. Robinson_____ ID No. ___88112_____

Item No.	Date	Time	Description	Location	Notes
1	10-22-11	1945	Smith & Wesson .38 CA single shot revolver SN 23435646	Next to victim's right hand	Process for latent fingerprints
2	10-22-11	1950	Travel document	Next to victim's right hand	Process for latent fingerprints
3	10-22-11	2150	Dental stone impression of shoe marks on ground	Next to victim's body	Hold for comparison
4	10-22-11	2133	Black knee length skirt size 8	Emilia Williams clothing	Hold for GSR processing
5	10-22-11	2133	White long sleeve blouse size 8	Emilia Williams clothing	Hold for GSR processing
6	10-22-11	2133	1 pair panty hose	Emilia Williams clothing	Hold
7	10-22-11	2133	Black Steve Madden high heel ladies shoes size 6	Emilia Williams clothing	Hold for comparison
8	10-25-11	1200	White cotton men's shirt size medium	Victim's clothing	Removed by pathologist at autopsy
9	10-22-11	1200	3 hairs removed from Item 13	On victim's clothing	Removed by pathologist at autopsy
10	10-22-11	1200	Multicolor plaid men's shorts size 32	Victim's clothing	Removed by pathologist at autopsy
11	10-22-11	1200	Men's size 11 leather sandals	Victim's clothing	Removed by pathologist at autopsy
12	10-25-11	0900	GSR report from on male victim	From Crime Lab	Place in case file
13	10-25-11	0900	GSR report from Emilia Williams	From Crime Lab	Place in case file

Date ____10-25-11____   Time: ____1600____   Page _____ of _2___

FIGURE 6-16 Page 1 of the evidence log.

Johns Island PD Evidence Log

Case Number: _____102210_____

Photographer: ___Carl Robinson_____ ID No. 74191

Detective: ___Kirkpatrick and Perez_____ ID No. 84437/74191

Crime Classification: Homicide_____

Log Maintained by: ___CSI C. Robinson_____ ID No. __88112_____

Item No.	Date	Time	Description	Location	Notes
13	10-25-11	0900	GSR report on Jacqueline Grant	From Crime Lab	Place in case file
14	10-25-11	1200	Fingerprint card – victim Everett Grant	Taken at morgue	Hold for comparison
15	10-25-11	1230	Fingerprint card – Emilia Williams	Taken at JIPD	Hold for comparison
16	10-25-11	1300	Fingerprint card – Jacqueline Grant	Taken at JIPD	Hold for comparison
17	10-25-11	1330	Latent prints lifted from S&W handgun	From Crime Lab	Compare to items 14 – 15- 16
18	10-25-11	1540	Black & White Converse tennis shoes size 9	From J. Grant residence	Hold for comparison
19	10-25-11	1545	Black Johnston & Hardy shoes size 9	From J. Grant residence	Hold for comparison
20	10-25-11	1550	iPhone SN 879909988h6777j	From J. Grant residence	Have forensics check phone records

Date ____10-25-11_____   Time: ____1600_____   Page_____ of _2___

FIGURE 6-17 Page 2 of the evidence log.

"I just found out that Everett was married!" she whined. "I wanted to confront him! He'd been lying to me this whole time!" She broke down crying, and the detective offered her a tissue. "I loved him! I'd never hurt him!"

Kirkpatrick saw Perez through the window on the door. "Take a moment to calm down. I'll be back in just a second." Kirkpatrick left the interview room. "What have you got?"

"Ms. Grant is down here. She consented to a GSR test. We're waiting on the results."

"Same for Ms. Williams. She claims that she just found out about the wife and didn't know he was married."

"This just doesn't sit right," Perez said. "I'm going to take another run at the wife, find out if she knew about the affair."

Interview 5

Jacqueline Grant: Follow-up

10:56 p.m.—Friday, 22 October: John's Island Police Department, Detective Bureau

Perez entered the interview room where Ms. Grant was seated. He smiled and sat next to her.

"Ms. Grant," he said, offering her the cup of coffee he'd picked up after speaking with Kirkpatrick, "were you and your husband having any problems?"

Jacqueline Grant thought over the question for a moment. "No, no problems," she said.

"Do you think your husband would ever have an affair?" he asked. Grant glared at the detective.

"Why do you ask?" she said, her voice turning hard.

Perez sighed.

"We're interviewing a woman found at the scene of Mr. Grant's death. She's claiming to be Mr. Grant's girlfriend."

Perez watched her reaction to the news. She bit her lip, shook her head slowly, and put a hand to her forehead in disbelief. "No, no, he wouldn't...," she whispered. "Detective, I don't think I have anything else to say tonight. I need...time."

"You can go on home. Thank you for your time, Ms. Grant. I will be in touch with you tomorrow," Perez said.

Evidence Analysis
11:33 a.m.—Monday, 25 October: John's Island Police Department, Detective Bureau
Coroner's Findings

The coroner's report confirmed that the victim was shot one time. X-rays were used to determine the bullet's trajectory prior to the autopsy. The shot penetrated at the temple and traveled through the back of the victim's head on the left side, exiting behind the left ear. The angle of the bullet's trajectory through the victim's skull was noted as "improbable" for a self-inflicted wound.

Gunshot residue testing of the victim's hands was negative. None of the samples collected from the victim's body or clothing indicated he had fired a weapon, and there were no powder burns around the wound. The report also confirmed that there were no defensive wounds or any other signs of a struggle; however, several ribs were fractured, and bruises on the chest were found in what appeared to be attempts to perform cardiopulmonary resuscitation (CPR) on the victim.

Ballistics

The bullet found in the doorframe at the home was confirmed to be the bullet that killed Mr. Grant. The bullet was a match to the bullet casing found at the scene and was fired from the .38 revolver found in Mr. Grant's hand.

Fingerprints

Latent prints for three persons were recovered from the firearm found at the scene. The victim's fingerprints were found on the grip of the gun, but not at an angle consistent with having held the weapon. Emilia Williams's prints were located around the barrel of the gun, and Jacqueline Grant's fingerprints were found on the grip of the gun, suggesting she had held the weapon properly to have fired it.

Gunshot Residue (GSR)

Gunshot residue was present on the hands of Jacqueline Grant. No traces were found on Emilia Williams's hands.

Johns Island Police Department Supplemental Report

CHEMICAL PROCESSING EXAMINATION REPORT
Scientific Services Bureau
Identification Section
Chemical Processing Unit
7250 Albany Rd.
Johns Island, GA 60101

Agency:	Johns Island PD	**File Number:**	1231
Investigator:	John Kirkpatrick	**Coroner Case No.**	102210
	Miguel Perez	**Date Received:**	10.23.11
Charge:	GA 17-19-30, Murder	**Report Date:**	10.25.11
Victim:	Everett Grant		
Suspects:	Jacqueline Grant		
	Emilia Williams		

Evidence Submitted:

Item 1:   One Smith & Wesson .38 Ca. single shot handgun Serial Number #234356546
Item 2:   One travel document detail sheet
Item 3:   Ten print fingerprint card from victim Everett Grant
Item 4:   Ten print fingerprint card from suspect Jacqueline Grant
Item 5:   Ten print fingerprint card from suspect Emilia Williams

Results:

Item 1 was processed for latent fingerprints and three separate sets with identifiable ridge characteristics were developed. Latent lift (A) lifted from magazine matched victim Grant. Latent lift (B) lifted from barrel of handgun matched suspect Williams. Latent lift (C) lifted from the grip of the handgun was matched to suspect Grant.

Item 2 latent fingerprints developed on this paper were matched to victim Grant.

Disposition of Evidence:

All evidence has been forwarded to the Johns Island Police Department Property Division for storage.

FIGURE 6-18 Evidence processing report.

Search of Grant Residence and Property

3:22 p.m.—Monday, 25 October: 210 Maine Road, John's Island, Georgia

Johns Island Police Department   Consent to Search and/or Seizure

BODY ☒ COMPUTER ☒ PREMISES ☒ VEHICLE ☐

OCA# __102210__   Date: ____10-25-11____

Location: __210 Maine Rd. Johns Island, GA 60101__

I, __Jacqueline Grant__, hereby authorize officer(s) __Kirkpatrick / Perez__
(name of person giving consent)   *and computer*

_____ to conduct a complete search of my __premises__ located
(body, computer, premises, vehicle)

at __210 Maine Rd. Johns Island GA__ .

This computer/vehicle has the following indentifying information:

Make____Sony____   Model __Vaio__ , Serial/VIN# __122000145__

Tag # _____ .

☒ These officers are authorized by me to remove from my body the following fluids, hair, and
substances: ____hairs_____ . __(initials)__

☒ These officers are authorized by me to take from my premises my computer, and to duplicate
and/or inspect any information, files, images or data which it may contain within it or on any media or
storage device associated with it. I also authorize the officers to take from my residence or any other
property of interest in reference to this investigation that they may desire that is associated with the
above listed computer. __(initials)__

☒ These officers are authorized by me to take from my premises/vehicle any letters, papers, materials
or other property of interest in reference to this investigation which they may desire. __(initials)__

I have been advised of my Constitutional Right, not to have a search made of my __vehicle__ or
my property seized. This written permission is being given by me to the above named officer(s),
voluntarily and without threats or promises of any kind.

_____   _____
Witness   Signature

_____   W   F   9/21/86
Witness   Race   Gender   DOB

                                                             555-11-0439
                                                    Social Security Number (required for body
                                                                        consent only)

FIGURE 6-19 Consent to search.

A warrant to search the Grant home and property was issued on the basis of Jacqueline Grant's positive gunshot residue test and fingerprints on the murder weapon. As Detective Perez interviewed Ms. Grant onsite, Detective Kirkpatrick discovered shreds of burned clothing under several logs and vines located about 200 yards from the house. Kirkpatrick identified what appeared to be blood on one of the larger sections of the remaining clothing as well. Confronted with this new evidence, Jacqueline Grant confessed to the murder of her husband, Everett Grant.

OFFENSE/INCIDENT REPORT

INSTRUCTIONS ARE PRINTED SEPARATELY. IF ADDITIONAL SPACE IS NEEDED, USE REVERSE OF FORM; IDENTIFY ITEMS.

1. TYPE: X ORIGINAL

2. CODE NO.	2a. SORT	3. TYPE OF OFFENSE OR INCIDENT	4. CASE CONTROL NUMBER
		Homicide	102210

5. BUILDING NUMBER	6. ADDRESS
	210 Maine Rd. Johns Island,

7. NAME OF AGENCY/BUREAU	8. AGENCY/BUREAU CODE	9. SPECIFIC LOCATION	10. LOCATION CODE
	675		

11a. DATE OF OFFENSE/INCIDENT	11a. TIME OF OFFENSE/INCIDENT	12. DAY	13a. DATE REPORTED	13b. TIME REPORTED	14. DAY
October 22, 2011	3:30 PM – 5:00 PM	F	October 22		1022

15. JURISDICTION (X)	16. NO. OF DEMONSTRATORS	17. NO. EVACUATED	a. TIME START	b. TIME END
☐ EXCLUSIVE ☐ CONCURRENT ☐ PARTIAL ☐ PROPRIETARY				

18. PERSONS INVOLVED

ID CODE (a)	NAME AND ADDRESS (b)	AGE (c)	SEX (d)	RACE (e)	INJURY CODE (f)	TELEPHONE (g)
	Last Name, First, Middle Initial: Williams Emilia Z	21	F	H		HOME -501-5010
	Number, Street, Apt. No., City and State: 21st Island Street Johns Island,					BUSINESS 3-897-3218
	Last Name, First, Middle Initial: Grant Jacqueline T	24	F	W		HOME -343-2149
	Number, Street, Apt. No., City and State: 210 Maine Road Johns Island,					BUSINESS

19. VEHICLE

a. STATUS	b. YEAR	c. MAKE	d. MODEL	e. COLOR (Top/Bottom)	f. IDENTIFYING CHARACTERISTICS
STOLEN / SUSPECT / GOV"T / PERSONAL / VANDALIZED / RECOVERED	g. REGIS-TRATION ▶ YEAR / STATE / TAG NO.			h. VIN	i. VALUE

20. ITEMS TAKEN

a. NAME OF ITEM	b. QUANTITY	c. OWNERSHIP	d. BRAND NAME
Smith & Wesson Caliber Single Shot Revolver	1	☐ GOV'T X PERSONAL	Smith & Wesson

e. SERIAL NO.	f. COLOR	g. MODEL
23435646	Black and Ivory	Single Shot Revolver

h. VALUE	i. UNUSUAL OR UNIQUE FEATURES
$300	Ivory handle on the revolver

j. PROPERTY WAS	k. STATUS OF PROPERTY	VALUE RECOVERED
X SECURRED ☐ UNSECURED	X RECOVERED ☐ MISSING ☐ PARTIAL RECOVERY	

l. NAME OF ITEM	m. QUANTITY	n. OWNERSHIP	o. BRAND NAME
		☐ GOV'T ☐ PERSONAL	

p. SERIAL NO.	q. COLOR	r. MODEL

s. VALUE	t. UNUSUAL OR UNIQUE FEATURES

u. PROPERTY WAS	v. STATUS OF PROPERTY	VALUE RECOVERED
☐ SECURRED ☐ UNSECURED	☐ RECOVERED ☐ MISSING ☐ PARTIAL RECOVERY	

21. NARRATIVE *(If additional space is needed, use blank sheet and attach.)*

call came through 911 at 6:10pm male victim
found dead on property 210 maine Johns island
eMS, fire and police dispatened. Arrived on
scene and found female suspect next to victim
victim was ID as Everett Grant and young lady
emilia williams. Crime scene was taped off
and Detectives were called to the scene.

FIGURE 6-20 Offense report from 210 Maine Road.

Johns Island Police Department
Johns Island, Georgia

MIRANDA RIGHTS

PLACE _JIPD Det. Bureau_ DATE ___10-25-11___   TIME ___1500 hrs___

BEFORE WE ASK YOU QUESTIONS, YOU MUST UNDERSTAND YOUR RIGHTS.

You have the right to remain silent.

Anything you say can be used in court as evidence against you.

You are entitled to talk to a lawyer now and have him present now or at any time during questioning.

If you cannot afford an attorney, one will be appointed for you without cost.

If you decide to answer questions now, without a lawyer present, you will still have the right to stop answering at any time. You also have the right to stop answering at any time until you talk to a lawyer.

Do you understand these rights?   _yes_

Do you wish to talk to us at this time?   _yes_

WAIVER OF RIGHTS

I have read this statement of my rights and I understand what my rights are. I am willing to talk now without a lawyer present. I understand and know what I am doing. NO promises or threats have been made to me and no pressure or coercion of any kind has been used against me.

Signed: _Jacqueline Grant_

Witness: _John Kirkpatrick_
Witness: _Miguel Perez_

FIGURE 6-21 Miranda waiver for Jacqueline Grant.

OFFICE OF THE STATE MEDICAL EXAMINER
2250 S. Ankeny Blvd.,
Phone#: 515-725-1400 / FAX#: 515-725-1414

	Central Office Use Only
	(Date of Receipt)
	(DOD Code)

PRELIMINARY REPORT OF INVESTIGATION BY MEDICAL EXAMINER

DECEDENT: _Everett_ _____ _Grant_

(First Name) (Middle Name) (Last Name)

(COD Code)
LAMAR

ADDRESS: _210 Maine Road_ _Johns Island_ _GA_ _LAMAR_

(residence) (Number & Street or Route, Box No.) (City, State) (County)

(County Assigned Case #)

INFORMATION ABOUT DECEDENT AND DESCRIPTION OF BODY

AGE (If less than 2 yrs. give months & days)
_26_
Age: _____
Date of Birth: _10/28/85_

SEX
☒ Male
☐ Female
☐ Undetermined

CLOTHING
☒ Clothed*
☐ Partly Clothed*
☐ Unclothed

BODY TEMPERATURE
☒ Warm ☐ Cool ☐ Cold
If taken: _95.7°_
site: _____

BLOOD
☐ Nose ☐ Mouth
☐ Ears ☐ Clothing
☐ None

OCCUPATION (Please fill in both parts)
TYPE OF WORK: _CEO_
(Example: machinist, typist, fireman, farmer, salesman, homemaker)

MARITAL STATUS
☒ Married
☐ Never Married
☐ Widowed
☐ Divorced
☐ Separated
☐ Unknown

HEAD-HAIR
☐ None
☐ Partly Bald
☐ Blonde
☒ Brown
☐ Red
☐ Black
☐ Gray
☐ White

EYES-Color: _Blue_
R: ___ mm/L: ___ mm

WEIGHT: _191_ lbs.
LENGTH: _74_ inches

RIGOR
☐ Neck: ☐0 ☒1 ☐2 ☐3
☐ Arms: ☐0 ☒1 ☐2 ☐3
☐ Legs: ☐0 ☒1 ☐2 ☐3
"0" = absent, "3" = full

LIVOR
Color: _Pale_
Fixed? ☐ Yes ☐ No
☐ Anterior
☐ Posterior
☐ Lateral (R / L)

FROTH
☐ Present ☒ Absent
Color: _____

OTHER (Dirt, water etc.)
☐ Nose _____
☐ Mouth _____
☒ Ears _____
☐ None

DECOMPOSITION
☐ Early
☐ Advanced
☒ None

INDUSTRY: _Cell Phone Bu_
(Example: textile, banking, fire dept, farming, insurance, home)

☐ No Occupational Information

HISTORY OF DOMESTIC VIOLENCE
☐ Yes
☒ No

RACE
☒ White
☐ Black
☐ Hispanic
☐ Asian
☐ Other

OTHER HAIR
☒ Mustache
☒ Beard

MISCELLANEOUS
☐ _____
☐ _____
☐ Circumcised

INFORMATION ABOUT OCCURRENCE

ITEM	DATE	TIME [military]	LOCATION	COUNTY	TYPE OF PREMISES (Home, farm, highway, hospital, etc.)
INJURY OR ONSET OF ILLNESS	10/22/11	unk	210 Maine Road Johns Island	LAMAR	ON THE JOB? ☐ YES ☒ NO
LAST SEEN ALIVE	10/22/11	1335	(By whom: Name and Address) Rebecca Hart	LAMAR	Office
DEATH (PRONOUNCED)	10/22/11	1833	(By whom: Name and Address) Nate Adams EMS	LAMAR	Crime Scene
FOUND DEAD BY	10/22/11	18:01	(By whom: Name and Address) Emilia Williams	LAMAR	Crime Scene
POLICE NOTIFIED	10/22/11	18:20	POLICE AGENCY: JI PD	OFFICER: Partridge, Chris
M.E. NOTIFIED	10/22/11	18:41	(By whom: Name and Address) Detective Ann Kirkpatrick	
VIEW OF BODY	10/22/11	19:49	Crime Scene	☐ NOT VIEWED
TO HOSPITAL	10/22/11	21:29	ME Office	Donor Network Notified? 1-800-831-4131 ☒ Yes ☐ No
WITNESSES			(Name and Address) None	BLOOD SAMPLE DRAWN: ☒ Yes ☐ No Why Not? ☒ Blood ☐ Urine ☐ Vitreous

MANNER OF DEATH

probable

☐ NATURAL   ☒ HOMICIDE   ☐ ACCIDENT   ☐ SUICIDE   ☐ UNDETERMINED   ☒ PENDING

M.E. AUTOPSY AUTHORIZED
☒ Yes ☐ No

(signature)
PATHOLOGIST

State Case # if applicable
SME _10210_

NON-M.E. AUTOPSY DONE
☐ Yes ☒ No

PROBABLE CAUSE OF DEATH:
1. _Homicide_
2. Due to: _Single shot in right temple_
3. Due to: _____
Contributing factor: _____

I hereby certify that after receiving notice of the death described herein I took charge of the body and made inquiries regarding the cause and manner of death in accordance with Chapter 331.801 and 802 and the information contained herein regarding such death is true and correct to the best of my knowledge and belief.

Anita Ilysen (Signature of Medical Examiner/ Medical Examiner Investigator)

PRINT NAME: _____
_10/23/11_   _LAMAR_
(Date Signed)   (County of Appointment)

I.S.M.E. review: _____

How Injury Occurred (24d. of death certificate): _____

Send *original* to ___ State Medical Examiner. Copies must be forwarded to County Attorney's office(s).

Form ME-1 (revised 02/2011)

FIGURE 6-22 Medical examiner's report.

The Truth Revealed

Everett Grant, twenty-six, was married to Jacqueline Grant, age twenty-four. The couple had been married for three years and resided in John's Island, Georgia. Mr. Grant was the owner and CEO of Grant Cellular Industries, which provides telecommunications services to Fortune 500 companies based in the Southeast. Jacqueline is a fourth grade teacher at a private school on John's Island and had worked there for nearly two years.

The seemingly happy couple were often seen as a "shining example" for other couples and singles in the area, and the two were well known and liked by their neighbors. They were involved in a great number of community services, church projects, and school functions. They were even beginning to plan for their first child. All seemed to be going well for this young couple in love.

On October 1, Mr. Grant was working late and had told his wife that he would not be home for dinner. This was a common enough occurrence that Jacqueline Grant thought nothing of it. While cleaning the house later that evening, Ms. Grant decided to take a short break at the computer and check her e-mail. Mr. Grant, having been the last to use the computer, had forgotten to log out of his e-mail account. Ms. Grant noticed an e-mail with a flirtatious subject line and opened it. This message was from a female whose name Ms. Grant did not recognize—Ms. Emilia Williams. In the letter, the woman stated that she wanted to touch base with him before he left for work, letting him know that she would be running a little late tonight but that she couldn't wait to secure a kiss "and a little more" from him.

Jacqueline Grant read the e-mail over and over in the hope that she had misread it or that it wasn't actually meant for her husband. However, she searched the inbox and found dozens of messages from the same woman, each with romantic and sexual overtones. Clearly this affair had been going on for some time.

Ms. Grant maintained a passing state of denial about the situation for almost three weeks, wondering if more e-mails were coming, where her husband was really spending his late nights, and questioning everything about their relationship. However, on October 21, a strange woman called late at night asking for Everett, and Jacqueline Grant could no longer stand the pressure of her suspicions.

On the morning of October 22, Mr. Grant informed Ms. Grant that he would be leaving on a last-minute business trip that evening. She informed him that she was helping her sister babysit her children and that she wouldn't be home that afternoon when he was packing. After Mr. Grant left for work, Jacqueline Grant called the school where she worked and told them that she was feeling ill and would not be coming to work that day.

Ms. Grant waited all day for her husband to return home. She had taken Mr. Grant's .38 out of the safe and kept it with her the entire day. Mr. Grant pulled back into his driveway at approximately 3:30 p.m., where his wife met him and confronted him with knowledge of the affair. In the heat of the argument, she pulled out the gun and threatened to kill him. The argument continued to escalate and in a moment of blind rage Jacqueline Grant shot Everett Grant once in the head. Shocked by what she had done, Ms. Grant ran over to the body and made a futile attempt to resuscitate Mr. Grant.

Realizing that she was now a murderer, Jacqueline Grant decided to hide the evidence of her involvement. Ms. Grant placed the firearm in Everett Grant's hand. She changed out of her clothes, now covered in blood from attempts to revive Mr. Grant, and placed the clothes in a brown paper bag; then she took the bag out onto the property and set it on fire. Once the fire was extinguished, Ms. Grant moved several logs and vines on top of the area where she had burned the clothing. Ms. Grant then left to pick up her sister's children from their after-school program and arrived at her sister's home at around 4:15 p.m.

Emilia Williams arrived at the Grants' home at approximately 5:25 p.m. to find the body of Everett Grant, victim of an apparently successful suicide attempt. Shocked, she rushed to the body and began touching it, the gun, and the things around the body as she mourned the loss of her lover. She was eventually able to make her way inside the house and call 911.

■ ■ ■

LABORATORY FIELD

GUNSHOT RESIDUE DATA SHEET

Agency _Johns Island PD_ r. Case Number _IO2210_

Collecting Officer _Anita Myers_ Date _10/22/2011_

Adhesive lifts were taken: Date: _10/22/11_ Time: _11:13 pm_

Guns was fired: Date: _10/22/11_ Time: _____

Type of gun: _Smith + Wesson_ _single shot rev._ Caliber: _.38_

Manufacturer of ammunition: _Remington_

*Please advise for .22 caliber ammunition. Check if brand is unknown:

WINCHESTER	REMINGTON	CCI	FEDERAL
(W) or (Super)	(U)	(C)	(F)

Cartridge Base Sketch

REMINGTON Yellow Jacket		SQUIRES BINGHAM	PMC	SEARS-FEDERAL
(*)	(REM)	(S)	(3+)	(S)

Subject's Name _Jacqueline Grant_ Dead or Alive? _Alive_

Did the subject wash up since the shooting? _Yes, hands_

Does the subject have any debris on the hands or face: _NO_
(Dirt, blood, cosmetics, sweat etc.)

Subject's occupation and hobbies _Hunting, boating, fishing, target shooting_

Discharge Location? (Indoors, Outdoors, Vehicle, etc) _Outdoors_

Number of Shots and description of activity between the discharge and sample acquisition _1, unknown_

Has this subject been in around cr in contact with sparklers, fountains, or any other firework devices?   Yes   (No)

**If YES list kinds, types, times and collect dry spent & unspent device(s) in separate bags and retain for future reference.

Anita Myers
Collecting Officer

FIGURE 6-23 GSR report - suspect Jacqueline Grant.

Discussion Questions

1. Develop a timeline for this case. Do you have all the documentation necessary to establish that timeline?
2. As you reviewed the documentation to develop the timeline, did you detect any discrepancies in the paperwork? If so, what were those inconsistencies?
3. What did you learn from the coroner's inspection of the body at the scene?
4. What important information did you receive from Rebecca Hart?
5. When Officer Perez was talking with Giselle Woods, whose statements did she verify? What was that information?
6. What did the forensic analysis of the gunshot residue kits reveal?
7. What were the conclusions of the latent fingerprint examination? Why is this important?
8. Is the investigation over? What might occur that would change the outcome of this case?

Your Turn: Breaking and Entering

OBJECTIVE

After reviewing the information provided, you will assess the data and develop a strategy to identify and interview the involved parties. You will select the proper paperwork to document the investigation and compile your completed work into a case file similar to those contained in previous chapters. There are only two outcomes: either the prosecutor's office will accept the case and proceed with charges or the case will be closed and charges will not be pursued.

KEY TERMS

breaking and entering   Castle Doctrine   duty to retreat

What You Will Learn

Throughout this book you have read case narratives and studied the documentation created to substantiate the investigation. Now it is your turn. This chapter presents the facts of the case and provides you with all the information you need to compile a case file.

LEARNING OUTCOMES

- Integrate all aspects of case facts into a comprehensive case file
- Formulate an investigative strategy that leads to a conclusion of the case
- Identify involved parties, develop a line of questioning, and extract statements from the witnesses, victims, and perpetrator(s)
- Compile data to present a case file to the prosecutor's office
- Complete all necessary paperwork for submission to supervisors

CRITICAL THINKING

- Elements of the crime
- Types of physical evidence
- Key investigative strategies
- Forms required to substantiate probable cause

Introduction

The **Castle Doctrine** permits citizens to protect themselves, other people, and their property. In many states, this means that protection may be through various methods, including deadly force. The Castle Doctrine or a defense of habitation law is based on the English common law stating "a man's home is his castle."

This scenario is based in South Carolina, a state that permits citizens the right to self-protection in their homes, vehicles, and workplaces. Under this specific law (H.4301 enacted in 2006), a citizen does not have a **duty to retreat.** That means if the citizen is in a place where he has a right to be and it is determined that deadly force is necessary to protect life or property, he has the right to stand his ground and no criminal prosecution against the citizen may be pursued.

There are many variations and stipulations to the castle doctrine laws across the United States. The outcomes of this investigation will vary based on your location. One of the steps that must be included in the investigative strategy you are developing for this case is to determine your specific state law and establish the type of crimes you are investigating. Remember, the elements of each crime constitute the *corpus delicti.* Motive, intent, and opportunity must also be considered during your deliberation of the specific crimes and the path this investigation must take. In addition to the castle law, what are the statutory requirements for repossessions in your state?

You must recognize that this case is also an officer-involved shooting. Are there other agencies that must be notified? Officer Arnett has been ordered by his lieutenant to turn over his agency-issued weapon to you and cooperate completely in the investigation. How is this unique scenario going to impact the types of documents that must be included in the case file?

Victim Jimmy Wainwright will be transported to the hospital to receive the proper medical care for a gunshot wound. Are you going to place him under arrest? What charges (if any) do you place against him? These two factors will also play an important role in determining your investigative strategy and the resulting documentation that must be completed and placed in the case file.

Will there be an investigation as to the validity of the repossession order? What about the failure of the repossession company to comply with the statutes requiring a "peaceful recovery" and the mandatory notification process to Officer Arnett about the issuance of the repossession order and the local law enforcement agency regarding the attempt to repossess?

A partial crime scene diagram has been included for this chapter. Use the information provided in the narrative and the photographs to complete the diagram. Remember that photographs do not always present an accurate representation of the dimensions, but the crime scene diagram can provide the details, including a spatial relationship to the various items and locations contained in the case documents.

■ ■ ■

Case File: Breaking and Entering

Case File Elements

- Incident/offense report
- Supplemental reports
- Victim/witness/suspect statements
- Physical evidence reports
- Follow-up

Critical Questions and Activities

What types of physical evidence are included in this case narrative? What types of documentation will be needed for that physical evidence? All the details may not be provided, so how will you address discrepancies? Remember that if any evidence is moved, even if it was inadvertent, its original location must be documented. Include in your report an explanation of the circumstances that led to the relocation of any moved evidence. You must also focus on addressing any discrepancies that you detect throughout the various statements, observations, and documentation gathered for the case file.

As you reflect on your completed case file, it is important to evaluate the meaning and significance of the data. Is there adequate justification to accept every statement as it was provided? Are the witnesses all telling the truth? If discrepancies are noted, can they be explained? Have all the questions been asked and, finally, have all the questions been answered?

List of Characters

Lead detective: David Williams
Responding officer: Phil Smallwood
CSI officer: Elisha Dockins
Witness/victim I: Daniel Arnett
Witness/victim II: Janet Arnett
Witness/victim III: Jimmy Wainwright
EMS Technician: Jared Robbins
Prosecutor: Jeanette Emporio

10:15 a.m.—16 April 2011: 1410 Castlewood Lane, Winchester, South Carolina

You are homicide detective David Williams. You receive a case assignment directly from your captain and the deputy chief. You are told that an off-duty police officer has shot someone breaking into his house. You are dispatched to the crime scene with specific orders to keep your captain and the chief informed. You know that with this much internal politics, you will have to give the most detailed report of your career. Everyone is watching you.

You arrive on the scene at approximately the same time the crime scene unit arrives, and you see that the responding officers have established a perimeter. A white male is sitting up on a stretcher with his shoulder in bandages. The ambulance does not appear to be in a hurry to leave, as the two EMS techs are standing off to the side smoking cigarettes and waiting your arrival.

What do you do? Who must be interviewed? What do you direct the crime scene investigation (CSI) officer to do? Where do you start? Do you need additional assistance? Who else needs to be notified?

Responding Officer's Statement

On June 15, 2011, at 9:31 a.m., I was dispatched to a residential **breaking and entering** in progress at 1410 Castlewood Lane, Winchester, South Carolina. Under SC law, the act of breaking and entering is the unlawful entry of a structure to commit a felony or theft. Upon arrival at the scene, I observed one white male lying on the ground with a small amount of blood coming from under his shoulder. Daniel Arnett, W/M DOB 04-15-1988, was leaning over the other man applying bandages to the bleeding man's shoulder. Arnett identified himself as a police officer. Arnett stated he had encountered the wounded individual (Jimmy Wainwright, W/M, DOB 12-19-1971) inside the garage of the residence attempting to take a motorcycle. Mr. Wainwright is unknown to the victim and did not have permission to be inside the garage. Janet Arnett, wife of Daniel Arnett, also witnessed some of the events but was on the phone with 911 when the shooting occurred.

Jimmy Wainwright stated he was in the process of repossessing the motorcycle, a black Harley-Davidson Electra Glide Classic S/N 884RE9007FF33335, and that he had a court order for the repossession. The Arnetts were unaware of the existence of the repossession order and deny its validity. Mr. Wainwright was not able to produce any identification to prove he was employed by Duncan Enterprises (the repossession company); however, he did present his driver's license and the court order for the repossession, which appears to be valid.

According to the Arnetts, they were eating a late breakfast when they heard their electric garage door opening. They were the only people at home, so Officer Arnett retrieved his duty weapon and cautiously peered out the door that connected the kitchen to the garage. He observed the white male attempting to roll the motorcycle out of the open garage door. Arnett confronted Wainwright and fired his weapon as the man crossed the threshold between the garage door and the driveway with the motorcycle. Wainwright was hit in the shoulder, but EMS has stated that the wound is superficial. I ran Wainwright's information through NCIC, and he has no outstanding warrants. He does have a permit to carry a concealed weapon. Officer Arnett turned over a Smith & Wesson 9 mm handgun, SN 87994B, to me, which he stated was removed from the victim's holster for safekeeping before he attended to Wainwright's injured shoulder. The weapon has been logged in as evidence by CSI Officer Dockins and secured for transport to the property/evidence unit at the station.

The repossession laws require that a company must notify the local law enforcement agency when they are taking action to complete a repossession court order. The only stipulation is that the event occur peacefully. The repossession company can bring a tow truck to repossess the vehicle from the driveway, the workplace, the street, or a parking lot. The company is not allowed to "breach the peace" or remove a vehicle from a closed garage. I also checked with central dispatch, and the Winchester Police Department did not receive a notification of a repossession effort by Duncan Enterprises on this date.

Photos Taken from the Scene

The following are photos taken from the scene.

FIGURE 7-1 Overall view of the scene from the street.

FIGURE 7-2 Midrange view of the scene.

FIGURE 7-3 Door handle of the truck in the driveway.

FIGURE 7-4 Midrange view of the truck interior.

FIGURE 7-5 Garage door opener on the truck's sun visor.

FIGURE 7-6 The perpetrator had moved the motorcycle across the threshold of the garage.

FIGURE 7-7 Close-up view of motorcycle controls.

FIGURE 7-8 View of garage from the kitchen door.

FIGURE 7-9 View from inside the kitchen door.

FIGURE 7-10 Center doorframe where bullet fragments were located.

FIGURE 7-11 Bullet fragments embedded in the doorframe.

FIGURE 7-12 View from the opposite corner of the garage shows motorcycle and truck.

FIGURE 7-13 View from motorcycle to kitchen door.

FIGURE 7-14 Overall view from opposite corner of garage.

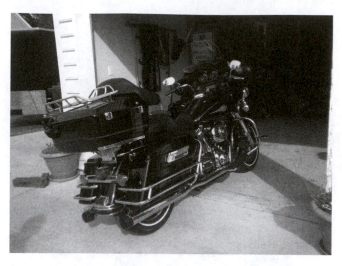

FIGURE 7-15 The Harley-Davidson Electra Glide Classic.

Crime Scene Sketch

Use this template to complete the crime scene sketch.

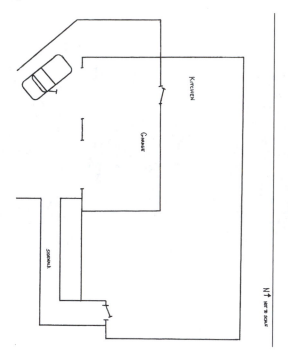

FIGURE 7-16 Blank crime scene sketch.

Statement of Daniel Arnett

My wife and I were sitting in the living room eating breakfast when I heard the garage door open. No visitors were expected, and my wife and I were the only people who had a garage door opener. Fearing a break-in, I retrieved my duty weapon and told my wife to call 911. I went out to the garage, and as I opened the door I saw a white male backing my Harley-Davidson Electra Glide Classic out of the open garage. I shouted, "Stop!" At this time I saw he was wearing a semi-automatic pistol in a holster on his left side. The man refused to obey my command to stop. I pointed my gun at him and fired, hitting him in the shoulder. He went down, and I called to my wife to bring the first aid kit and notify 911 to send an ambulance to our house. The man said that his name was Jimmy Wainwright and that he worked for a repossession company and had a court order to repossess the motorcycle. I took the pistol from his possession and my wife placed it in the house. I dressed his wound while I waited on police and EMS to arrive. The suspect had suffered a minimal loss of blood and was able to continue talking to me while I bandaged the injury. The paramedic team arrived and took over. I advised them I was a police officer and that law enforcement had already been summoned.

The officers arrived and interviewed me and the other man. The man showed them identification as well as the supposed court order to repossess my motorcycle. I've notified my lieutenant of the shooting, and he ordered me to turn over my firearm to the lead detective. I also turned Wainwright's pistol over to Officer Smallwood.

Statement of Janet Arnett

My husband and I were eating breakfast when we heard the garage door open. My husband looked at me and I shook my head, so he went and got his pistol and told me to call 911. As I did, I heard a gunshot. I began to panic, but I heard my husband yell at me to bring the first aid kit and that he was all right. I came out to the garage with the kit and was talking to the 911 operator again on the phone. I told the dispatcher that my husband was a police officer and that he had caught the man breaking into our house and had shot him.

Statement of Jimmy Wainwright

I am an employee of Duncan Enterprises, a towing and repossession company here in town. I received a court order this morning from my employers authorizing the repossession of a black Harley-Davidson Electra Glide Classic S/N 884RE9007FF33335, leased to one Daniel Arnett. The order included Mr. Arnett's current address, 1410 Castlewood Lane, Winchester, South Carolina, so I went directly there.

I did not see the motorcycle in or around the address; however, there was a garage attached to the house with the door closed. The house looked as if no one was home, so I went up to the truck parked in the driveway and saw a garage door opener hanging from the visor. I tried the door on the truck and found it unlocked. I pressed the button on the garage door opener and headed over to the garage as the door went up.

I saw the motorcycle on its kickstand inside the garage. I went up to it and began backing it out when a man came out of the door connecting the garage. He had a gun in his hands. Everything happened so quickly after that. I remember hearing the gunshot and feeling a sharp pain in my shoulder. The next thing I know, the man who pointed the gun at me is leaning over me with bandages trying to stop the bleeding. I tried to tell him I had a court order to repossess the vehicle, but he didn't seem to be paying attention.

When the other officers got here and the paramedics had me patched up, I was able to show them the court order. I left my company ID badge at home, but I did have my driver's license on me and gave it to them as well.

Statement of Jared Robbins (EMS Technician)

We were dispatched to 1410 Castlewood Lane where we were told a police officer had shot a suspect. We were not advised that the situation involved an off-duty police officer who shot someone breaking in to his house until we received a second call from central dispatch. When we arrived, we saw that the police officer, Daniel Arnett, had applied some basic first aid to the victim's shoulder and had stopped the bleeding. Mr. Wainwright was conscious and coherent and appeared to be in relatively good shape. Though he protested that he could walk just fine, we brought Mr. Wainwright by stretcher to the ambulance and assessed his wound. It appeared to be mostly superficial and indirect as the bullet went through flesh only and exited through the victim's shoulder. We redressed the wound and waited for police to arrive. Mr. Wainwright will be transported by ambulance to South Medical Center and turned over to the emergency room staff once you have cleared him to go.

Statement of Elisha Dockins (Crime Scene Technician)

I found one .40 Smith & Wesson casing just outside the door to the house from the garage. The first blood spatter occurred at the threshold between the garage and the driveway, indicating the victim was shot approximately twenty feet from where the shooter was standing. EMS stated the bullet was a flesh wound with a clear exit, and I was able to locate the bullet in the wall opposite the door to the house, approximately five feet from the ground and an inch deep inside the brick. More blood was found on the ground next to where Mr. Wainwright fell and Officer Arnett provided first aid.

I took fingerprints and DNA swabs from all involved parties. I also took fingerprints from the pickup truck parked in the driveway. I located prints all over the steering wheel, handle, and door. However, I can tell you that Wainwright was in this car. I can tell just by eyeballing his prints that they match some of the prints I pulled out of it, namely a handprint on the seat and fingerprints on the garage door opener and the car door handle. It appears the suspect, Wainwright, tried the door then leaned in, putting one hand in the middle of the driver's seat, and used his other to press the button on the garage door opener. Daniel Arnett's fingerprints are the only fingerprints found on his service firearm, a Glock 22 semi-automatic pistol (SN 419119G). I also retrieved a Smith & Wesson 9 mm handgun (SN 87994B) from the custody of Officer Smallwood, which has been logged and will be transported to the property/evidence unit.

Neighbors' Statements

Three nearby neighbors were home during the event, and all reported hearing the gunshot but none were witness to the events except for David Moser, who called police after he saw his neighbor, Daniel Arnett, trying to stop the bleeding of an unknown white male in his garage.

Report Documents

To complete this investigation, view the reports available on the following website: www.elsevierdirect.com/companion.jsp?ISBN=9781455731237.

Discussion Questions

1. Were you presented with sufficient information to accurately develop a case file? If not, what additional data are required to complete this investigation?
2. What crimes were committed?
3. What were the pieces of physical evidence you identified after reading the narrative?
4. How significant is it to the investigation that the victim is an off-duty police officer?
5. What aspects of the investigation could be subject to attack by a savvy defense attorney?
6. What is the outcome of your investigation? Is it over? Why or why not?

Appendix: Blank Forms

☐ ARREST AND ☐ SUPPLEMENTAL BOOKING REPORT

	TIME	**CURRENT DATE**	**DISPATCH NO.**	**ORIGINAL CASE NO.**		**TRACT #**

DEFENDANT NAME (LAST, FIRST, MIDDLE) — RACE | SEX | DATE OF BIRTH

AGE | **ETH.** | **HEIGHT** | **WEIGHT** | **HAIR** | **EYES** | **SOCIAL SECURITY NUMBER** | **VISIBLE SCARS AND MARKS** | **NCIC I.D. NUMBER**

ADDRESS (NUMBER AND STREET | **CITY** | **STATE** | **ZIP CODE** | **RESIDENT** | **PHONE NUMBER**

ALIAS | **PLACE OF BIRTH** | **DRIVERS LICENSE NUMBER/I.D. # & STATE**

EMPLOYER OR OCCUPATION | **NEXT OF KIN** | **ADDRESS (CITY AND STATE)** | **PHONE NUMBER**

TRANSPORTING OFFICERS NAME | **NUMBER** | **ARRESTING OFFICER** | **NUMBER** | **AGENCY**

ARRESTEE ARMED ☐ YES ☐ NO **WEAPON TYPE** ☐ SEMI-AUTO ☐ FULL-AUTO   ☐ ON VIEW ARREST ☐ SUMMONED ☐ CUSTODY

JUVENILE DISPOSITION
1. ☐ HANDLED, RELEASED
2. ☐ REFERRED TO OTHER AUTHORITY

EXAMINED BY HOSPITAL ☐ YES ☐ NO   **VEHICLE TOWED** ☐ YES ☐ NO   **TOWED BY:**

IF HOLDING FOR ANOTHER AGENCY, CIRCLE CHARGE A, B, C

CHARGE

CHARGE I.D.	A	B	C
ADDITIONAL CASE NO.'S			
CHARGE			
STATUTE			
BOND AMOUNT			
WARRANT/TICKET #			
BOND/HEARING DATE			
DATE & TIME OF TRIAL/MAGISTRATE			

REMARKS

THE UNDERSIGNED HEREBY COMMITS TO YOUR CUSTODY THE ABOVE INDIVIDUAL AND SWEARS THAT THE INFORMATION CONTAINED IN THIS SUPPLEMENTAL ARREST & BOOKING REPORT IS TRUE AND CORRECT TO THE BEST OF HIS/HER KNOWLEDGE.   SIGNATURE

I.D. OFF

DATE F.P.	TIME F.P.	I.D. TECHNICIAN	PHOTO ID #	DATE OF PHOTO
DATE	TIME	SEARCHING OFFICER	SUPERVISOR REVIEW AND SIGN	

BOOKING OFFICER

CONDITION AT TIME OF ADMISSION		HOW LONG IN	RELIGION	EDUCATION
EXPLAIN				

LOCAL PRIOR ARREST ☐ YES ☐ NO	WANTED ON WARRANT ☐ YES ☐ NO	MISCELLANEOUS		
ATTORNEY	PERSON TO CALL IN EMERGENCY	ADDRESS		PHONE NUMBER

DISPOSITION

SENTENCE TO DAYS	AND/OR	FINE AMOUNT	COURT	EXPIRATION OF SENTENCE
A.				
B.				
C.				

HOW INMATE RELEASED: ☐ SURETY BOND / COMPANY   ☐ EXPIRATION OF SENTENCE | DATE | TIME
☐ BOND ☐ FINE AMOUNTS   RECEIPT NO.   ☐ BY CLERK OF COURT   ☐ REL. AT COURT

DUTY SGT.

TRANSFERRED OR RELEASED TO: AGENCY: OFFICER: | DATE | TIME

RELEASING OFFICER   SUPERVISOR REVIEW AND SIGN

STATE OF
COUNTY OF

APPLICATION FOR SEARCH WARRANT

Applicant: **Agency:**
Badge: **Date of Application:**
Date of Offense: **Case No.**
Location of Premises to be searched:

Affiant Statement:

_____
Affiant's Signature

STATE OF   )

)   **SEARCH WARRANT**

COUNTY OF   )   _____

TO THE SHERIFF OR BONDED LAW ENFORCEMENT OFFICE OF THIS STATE OR COUNTY OR THE COUNTY OF _____ **OR MUNCIPALITY OF** _____

       It appearing from the attached affidavit that there are reasonable grounds to believe that certain property subject to seizure under provisions of (Statue) of the   , as amended, is located on the following Premises:

DESCRIPTION OF PREMISES (PERSON OR THING)
TO BE SEARCHED

<u>Dwelling or Business Address:</u> _____

<u>City, State, Zip</u> _____

Location Description: _____

       Now, therefore, you are hereby authorized to search the subject premises for the property listed below and to seize such property if found:

DESCRIPTION OF PROPERTY

Item #1 _____

Item #2 _____

Item #3 _____

This Search Warrant shall not be valid for more than ten days from the date of issuance.

A written inventory of all property seized pursuant to this Search Warrant to

_____ <u>Department Property Control & Disposition Officer in Charge</u>

Within ten days from the date of this warrant, such inventory to be signed by the officer executing this warrant, and a copy of such inventory shall be furnished to the person whose premises are searched if demand for such copy is made.

A copy of this Search Warrant shall be delivered to the person in charge of the premises searched at the time of such search if practicable, and, if not, to such person as soon thereafter as is practicable; in the event the identity of the person in charge is not known or if such person cannot be found after reasonable diligence in attempting to locate the person; a copy shall be attached to a prominent place on such premises.

City, State _____

Date _____   _____

                                                              Signature of Judge

Incident Report	Case #	Page Number
Student's Name:	Date	Time:

<u>Description of Incident</u>

MIRANDA RIGHTS WAIVER

Date/Time/Location: _____

I, _____
         (print full name)

have been advised by _____, of the
                              (rank, name, badge number)

_____ that I am suspected of:
         (agency)

      A.   _____

      B.   _____

      C.   _____

I have also been advised that:

1. I have the right to remain silent and make no statement at all;
2. Any statement I do make can be used against me in a court of law or other judicial or administrative proceeding;
3. I have the right to consult with a lawyer prior to any questioning; this lawyer may be a civilian lawyer retained by me at no cost to the United States, or if I cannot afford a lawyer, one will be appointed to represent me at no cost to me.
4. I have the right to have my retained or appointed lawyer present during this interview; and,
5. I may terminate this interview at any time, for any reason.

I understand my rights as related to me and set forth above. With that understanding, I have decided that I do not desire to remain silent, consult with a retained or appointed lawyer, or have a lawyer present at this time. I make this decision freely and voluntarily. No threats or promises have been made to me.

Signature: _____

Date and Time: _____

Witness: _____

Date and Time: _____

At this time, I _____ desire to make the following voluntary statement. This statement is made with an understanding of my rights as set forth above. It is made with no threats or promises having been extended to me.

Page ___ of ____   Complaint # _____

Statement

Statement of: _____

Home Address: _____ Home Phone: _____

Employer: _____ Business Address: _____

Bus. Phone: _____ Occupation: _____

This statement is given: _____ (Date) at _____ (Time)

_____

_____

_____

_____

_____

_____

_____

_____

_____

I have read the foregoing statement or have had it read to me and it is true and correct to the best of my knowledge. I have given this statement freely and voluntarily and have been provided a copy of my statement.

Witness: _____

Witness: _____   Signature: _____

EVIDENCE-PROPERTY RECEIPT

_____ **Police Department**

| 1. _____ Property of Deceased _____ Trial _____ Found _____ Laboratory _____ Stolen-Recovered _____ Secured |

| 2. Case No. | 3. Date-Time Received | 4. Municipal Court (Date & Time) | 5. General Sessions Court |

| 6. Evidence Custodian Use Only | 7. Type of Case |

8. Address where property was impounded (give exact location where found):

9. Found By:	Address	Phone Number
10. Suspect(s) Full Name	Address	Phone Number
11. Victim	Address	Phone Number
12. Owner's Name	Address	Phone Number

13. Item Number	14. Quantity	15.	Description

16. I hereby acknowledge that the above list represents all property taken from my possession and that I have received a copy of this receipt.

17. I hereby acknowledge that the above list represents all property impounded by me in the official performance of my duty as a Police Officer.

SIGNATURE (X) _____

DIVISION _____   ID NO. _____

IMPOUNDING OFFICER (X) _____

18. RECEIVED BY	REASON	DATE AND TIME RECEIVED
RECEIVED BY	REASON	DATE AND TIME RECEIVED
RECEIVED BY	REASON	DATE AND TIME RECEIVED
RECEIVED BY	REASON	DATE AND TIME RECEIVED
RECEIVED BY	REASON	DATE AND TIME RECEIVED
RECEIVED BY	REASON	DATE AND TIME RECEIVED
19. FINAL DISPOSITION	REASON	DATE AND TIME OF DISPOSITION

For Municipal Court _ONLY_

_____ This case has been disposed of. The following evidence can be destroyed: (List by item number) _____

Judge's Signature _____   Date _____

Other (evidence property) can be returned (list by number) _____ Officer's Signature _____

Evidence Log

Case Number: _____ ID No. _____
Photographer: _____ ID No. _____
Detective: _____
Crime Classification: _____

Log Maintained by: _____ ID No. ___

Item No.	Date	Time	Description	Location	Notes

Date _____ Time: _____

Page ____ of ____

Photo Log

Case Number: _____   ID No. _____
Photographer: _____   ID No. _____
Detective: _____
Crime Classification: _____

Log Maintained by: _____   ID No. _____

Item No.	Date	Time	Description	Location	Notes

Date _____ Time: _____

Page _____ of _____

Entry/Exit Log

Case Number: _____ _____ ID No. _____

Photographer: _____ _____ ID No. _____

Detective: _____ _____

Crime Classification: _____

Log Maintained by: _____ ID No. _____

Date	Time In	Time Out	Last Name	First Name	Agency	Badge/ID No.	Reason for Entry

Date _____ Time: _____

Page _____ of _____

CHAIN OF CUSTODY FORM				CASE #		
Chain of Custody						
ITEM NUMBER	QUANTITY	PERSON WHO COLLECTED EVIDENCE:	WHERE EVIDENCE WAS DELIVERED TO:		DATE	TIME

ADDITIONAL CASE INFORMATION

Fingerprint 10-Print Card

NAME OF PERSON FINGERPRINTED (LAST, FIRST, MIDDLE)				DATE
STREET ADDRESS		CITY	STATE	ZIPCODE
MALE/FEMALE	HEIGHT	WEIGHT	EYE COLOR	HAIR COLOR
DATE OF BIRTH		PLACE OF BIRTH (CITY AND STATE)		
SIGNATURE OF PERSON FINGERPRINTED		SIGNATURE OF PERSON TAKING FINGERPRINTS		

1	2	3	4	5
6	7	8	9	10

LEFT HAND	LEFT THUMB	RIGHT THUMB	RIGHT HAND

PROBABLE NATUAL DEATH SCENE QUESTIONS

If an apparent natural death, it is only necessary to contact the Coroners Office (ph) _____.
Obtain the following information to expedite release of the deceased to a funeral home.

Agency Identifier _____ Date _____ Officer on scene _____

Name of Deceased _____

Address of Deceased _____

DOB _____ Age _____ Identification _____

Call Placed By: _____ Phone _____

Deceased Last Seen By: Name _____ Phone _____

　　　　　　　　　　Address _____ Time _____ Date _____

Next of Kin: Name _____ Phone _____ Notified: Yes ☐ _____

　　　　　　Address _____ Relationship _____

Treating Physician _____ Phone _____ Last Seen _____

Treatment in Past Year? Yes ☐   No ☐ For What _____

Medicine Bottles Present Near Deceased? Yes ☐   No ☐ Prescribed by Whom _____

List Medications _____

Alcohol Bottles, Cans, Empty or Partially Empty at Scene? Yes ☐ No ☐

Deceased Lying on? Back ☐   Right Side ☐   Left Side ☐ Abdomen ☐

Deceased in: Bed ☐   Bathroom ☐   Kitchen ☐   Other _____

Is Position Natural Looking? ☐   Awkward Looking ☐

Blood Coming From: Nose ☐   Mouth ☐   Ears ☐

Are there any Electrical Wires or Fixtures Near Deceased?   Yes ☐   No ☐

Is the Deceased Barefooted: Yes ☐   No ☐

Near Water on Floor or Ground? Yes ☐   No ☐

Any Unusual Odor Present? Yes ☐   No ☐

Rigor Present? ☐   Arms ☐   Legs ☐   Neck ☐   Jaw ☐

The Deceased is: Hot ☐   Warm ☐   Cool ☐   Cold ☐

What was the Deceased Doing at the Time of Death? _____

Clothing Description _____

Requested Funeral Home _____

Personal Property Released To _____ by _____

　　　　　　　　　　Date _____ Time _____

CORONER WILL NOTIFY FUNERAL HOME

FORENSIC LABORATORY EXAMINATION REQUEST

1. TO: ☒ ☐ Other *(Specify)*:	2. FROM: 3. RETURN EVIDENCE TO:	4. EXAM PRIORITY ⊙ ROUTINE ○ EXPEDITE ☐ Trial/Article 32/39A (*) ☐ Subject in pre-trial confinement ☐ Subject pending PCS/ Separation/Reenlist (*) ☐ Other (Specify in Block 13) *Date _____	5. LAB USE ONLY a. LAB CASE # b. METHOD OF RECEIPT c. RECEIVED BY/DATE

6. SUBMITTING AGENCY CASE NUMBER	7. TYPE OF OFFENSE

8. PREVIOUS EVIDENCE SUBMITTED
DATE: MAIL METHOD: LAB CASE #:   SUSPECT(S):

9. SUSPECT(S) [*Last, first and middle name(s)*]	10. VICTIM(S) [*Last, first and middle name(s)*]

11. BRIEF DESCRIPTION (SYNOPSIS) OF CASE FACTS THAT MIGHT ASSIST THE LABORATORY IN EXAMINING OR EVALUATING THE EVIDENCE OR ADDITIONAL DOCUMENTATION ATTACHED (*e.g., Summary of investigation, crime scene sketches/photographs, statements*)

12. EVIDENCE SUBMITTED

a. EXHIBIT	b. DESCRIPTION OF EXHIBIT

12. EVIDENCE SUBMITTED *(Continued)*	
a. EXHIBIT	b. DESCRIPTION OF EXHIBIT

13. EXAMINATION(S) REQUESTED *(Briefly furnish any information or instructions that might assist the laboratory in examining the evidence)*

14.a. INVESTIGATOR AND ALTERNATE POC *(Typed or Printed) (Mandatory Information)*	b. TELEPHONE *(Primary/Alt)*:
	c. DSN *(Primary/Alt)*:
	d. Fax:
	e. E-Mail:

15. I CERTIFY EVIDENCE HAS NOT BEEN SUBMITTED TO ANOTHER LABORATORY FOR THE SAME EXAMINATION

a. DATE	b. TYPED/PRINTED NAME OF REQUESTOR	d. TELEPHONE *(Primary/Alt)*:
		e. DSN *(Primary/Alt)*:
	c. SIGNATURE	f. Fax:
		g. E-Mail:

	16. LAB USE ONLY
	LAB CASE #

UNIFORM TRAFFIC ACCIDENT REPORT

PAGE 1 of _____

DOCUMENT CONTROL NUMBER (DO NOT USE)	LOCAL AGENCY USE	REFERENCE NUMBER

REPORTING AGENCY
1 ☐ THP   2 ☐ CPD   3 ☐ SO   4 ☐ OTHER

NAME OF INVESTIGATING AGENCY

HIT AND RUN?   1 ☐ YES   2 ☐ NO
SOLVED?   1 ☐ YES   2 ☐ NO

DATE OF ACCIDENT   MO.   DAY   YR.

DAY OF ACCIDENT
SUN ☐1   M ☐2   T ☐3   W ☐4   THU ☐5   F ☐6   S ☐7

TIME OF ACCIDENT   1 ☐ AM   2 ☐ PM

POLICE NOTIFIED   1 ☐ AM   2 ☐ PM

POLICE ARRIVED   1 ☐ AM   2 ☐ PM

INVESTIGATION COMPLETE?   1 ☐ YES   2 ☐ NO

TYPE ACCIDENT
1 ☐ FATAL   2 ☐ INJURY   3 ☐ PROPERTY DAMAGE

TOTAL VEHICLES	TOTAL KILLED	TOTAL INJURED	TOTAL UNINJURED	PHOTOS TAKEN? 1 ☐ YES 2 ☐ NO	IF YES, BY WHOM? POLICE ☐ OTHER ☐

COUNTY: CODE ____
☐ IN ("X" IF INSIDE CITY LIMITS)
or ____ MILES ☐ N ☐ S ☐ E ☐ W of CITY:
CODE ____
1 ☐ URBAN
2 ☐ RURAL
••••••••••••••
3 ☐ BUSINESS
4 ☐ RESIDENTIAL
••••••••••••••
5 ☐ SCHOOL

OCCURRED ON: STREET, HWY. NAME, OR ROUTE NUMBER   SR. NO.
AT INTERSECTION WITH: SR. NO.

OR: NEAREST INTERSECTION, BRIDGE, RR CROSSING (HOUSE NO - CITY ONLY)
____ FEET   ☐ N ☐ E
OR
____ MILES   ☐ S ☐ W

____ FEET   ☐ N ☐ E
OR
____ MILES   ☐ S ☐ W
MILE POST

0 ☐ NON-INTERSECTION   3 ☐ BRIDGE   4 ☐ UNDERPASS
1 ☐ INTERSECTION   5 ☐ RAMP
2 ☐ RR-XING GRADE XING NO. _____   6 ☐ PRIVATE PROPERTY

TENN. DEPT. OF TRANSPORTATION USE ONLY

CO. NO.	ROUTE NUMBER	SPC CASE	CO. SEQ.	LOG MILE	LOC	FXOB

VEH. 1

YEAR	MAKE	MODEL	COLOR	BODY TYPE	BODY CODE	VIN

LICENSE PLATE NO.   STATE   YEAR
VEH. PULLING TRAILER?   1 ☐ YES   2 ☐ NO
TRAILER CODE
VEH. DISABLED?   1 ☐ YES   2 ☐ NO
VEH. TOWED?   1 ☐ YES   2 ☐ NO
IF TOWED, WHERE?

VEHICLE GOING   ON:
☐ N ☐ S ☐ E ☐ W
POSTED SPEED
OFFICER'S ESTIMATED AMOUNT OF DAMAGE   1 ☐ UNDER $400   3 ☐ OVER $400
"X" POINT OF INITIAL IMPACT (Shade Damaged Areas)

DRIVER'S FIRST   MI   LAST
DOB: MO.   DAY   YR.
DRIVER LICENSE NO.   STATE
NAME

DRIVER'S ADDRESS   CITY   STATE   ZIP   TELEPHONE NUMBER

LICENSE CLASS/TYPE | ENDORSEMENT CODE(S) | ENDORSEMENT COMPLIED WITH? 1 ☐ YES 2 ☐ NO | RESTRICTION CODE(S) | RESTRICTIONS COMPLIED WITH? 1 ☐ YES 2 ☐ NO | SEX 1 ☐ M 2 ☐ F | RACE 1 ☐ WHITE 2 ☐ BLACK 3 ☐ OTHER | DRIVER RESIDENCE 1 ☐ LESS 25 MI. 2 ☐ OVER 25 MI. 3 ☐ OUT OF STATE

OWNER'S NAME   FIRST   MI   LAST   ☐ SAME AS DRIVER
DOB: MO.   DAY   YR.
DRIVER LICENSE NO.   STATE

10 UNDERCARRIAGE
11 UNKNOWN
12 ROLLED
13 NON-CONTACT

OWNER'S ADDRESS   CITY   STATE   ZIP   TELEPHONE NO.
SPECIAL VEHICLE USAGE (Enter Code)
CMV ☐ YES ☐ NO

VEH. 2

YEAR	MAKE	MODEL	COLOR	BODY TYPE	BODY CODE	VIN

LICENSE PLATE NO.   STATE   YEAR
VEH. PULLING TRAILER?   1 ☐ YES   2 ☐ NO
TRAILER CODE
VEH. DISABLED?   1 ☐ YES   2 ☐ NO
VEH. TOWED?   1 ☐ YES   2 ☐ NO
IF TOWED, WHERE?

VEHICLE GOING   ON:
☐ N ☐ S ☐ E ☐ W
POSTED SPEED
OFFICER'S ESTIMATED AMOUNT OF DAMAGE   1 ☐ UNDER $400   3 ☐ OVER $400
"X" POINT OF INITIAL IMPACT (Shade Damaged Areas)

DRIVER'S FIRST   MI   LAST
DOB: MO.   DAY   YR.
DRIVER LICENSE NO.   STATE
NAME

DRIVER'S ADDRESS   CITY   STATE   ZIP   TELEPHONE NUMBER

LICENSE CLASS/TYPE | ENDORSEMENT CODE(S) | ENDORSEMENT COMPLIED WITH? 1 ☐ YES 2 ☐ NO | RESTRICTION CODE(S) | RESTRICTIONS COMPLIED WITH? 1 ☐ YES 2 ☐ NO | SEX 1 ☐ M 2 ☐ F | RACE 1 ☐ WHITE 2 ☐ BLACK 3 ☐ OTHER | DRIVER RESIDENCE 1 ☐ LESS 25 MI. 2 ☐ OVER 25 MI. 3 ☐ OUT OF STATE

OWNER'S NAME   FIRST   MI   LAST   ☐ SAME AS DRIVER
DOB: MO.   DAY   YR.
DRIVER LICENSE NO.   STATE

10 UNDERCARRIAGE
11 UNKNOWN
12 ROLLED
13 NON-CONTACT

OWNER'S ADDRESS   CITY   STATE   ZIP   TELEPHONE NO.
SPECIAL VEHICLE USAGE (Enter Code)
CMV ☐ YES ☐ NO

CITATIONS ISSUED?   1 ☐ YES   2 ☐ NO

DRIVER NO. _____   COURT DIV. _____   COURT DATE _____
CHARGES _____   CITATION NO. _____

DRIVER NO. _____   COURT DIV. _____   COURT DATE _____
CHARGES _____   CITATION NO. _____

INVESTIGATING OFFICER RANK & NAME (Print Name)
BADGE/ID NO.   DIST/ZONE   CAR. NO.
REPORT DATE   MO.   DAY   YR.

DOCUMENT CONTROL NUMBER (DO NOT USE)		LOCAL AGENCY USE	REFERENCE NUMBER

PEDESTRIAN ACTION ("X" all that apply)

Was Pedestrian Involved? 1 ☐ YES   2 ☐ NO

1 ☐ Crossing at intersection-with Signal
2 ☐ Same-Against Signal
3 ☐ Same-No Signal
4 ☐ Same-Diagonally
5 ☐ Crossing Not at Intersection
Was Crosswalk Available? 1 ☐ YES   2 ☐ NO
Was Crosswalk Marked? 1 ☐ YES   2 ☐ NO
Was Pedestrian Within Crosswalk Markings or Extension of Sidewalk Lines? 1 ☐ YES   2 ☐ NO
6 ☐ Coming from Behind Parked Cars
8 ☐ Standing in Safety Zone
9 ☐ Getting On or Off Other Vehicle
10 ☐ Pushing or Working on Vehicle
11 ☐ Other Working in Roadway
12 ☐ Playing in Roadway
14 ☐ Lying in Roadway
7 ☐ Walking in Roadway
  ☐ a. With Traffic
  ☐ b. Against Traffic
Was Sidewalk Available? 1 ☐ YES   2 ☐ NO
16 ☐ Walking Beside Roadway
  ☐ a. With Traffic
  ☐ b. Against Traffic
Was Sidewalk Available? 1 ☐ YES   2 ☐ NO
Was Pedestrian on Sidewalk? 1 ☐ YES   2 ☐ NO
15 ☐ Not in Roadway, Other _____
_____ (explain)

ACCIDENT INVOLVED

1 ☐ Motor Vehicle/Other Motor Vehicle
2 ☐ Motor Vehicle/Railroad Train
3 ☐ Motor Vehicle/Farm Implement
4 ☐ Motor Vehicle/ Animal Drawn Vehicle
5 ☐ Motor Vehicle/Bicycle
6 ☐ Motor Vehicle/Other Pedalcycle
  Type Pedalcycle?_____
7 ☐ Motor Vehicle/Animal
8 ☐ Motor Vehicle/Pedestrian
9 ☐ Motor Vehicle Miscellaneous Actions
  Type Action?_____
10 ☐ Motor Vehicle Overturned in Roadway
Motor Vehicle Ran Off Roadway And
11 ☐ Overturned
12 ☐ Struck Fixed Object
  Type Object?_____
13 ☐ Other _____
(explain)

OTHER PROPERTY DAMAGED?
☐ YES   if Yes: ☐ PUBLIC
☐ NO   ☐ PRIVATE

AMOUNT OF DAMAGE (ESTIMATE)
1 ☐ UNDER $400   3 ☐ OVER $400

OWNER:
NAME _____

ADDRESS _____

DESCRIBE PROPERTY _____

TYPE OF COLLISION
1 ☐ Head-on
2 ☐ Rear end
3 ☐ Angle
4 ☐ Sideswipe-Same Direction
5 ☐ Sideswipe-Opposite Direction
7 ☐ Other
_____ (explain)

LIGHT CONDITIONS
1 ☐ Dawn
2 ☐ Daylight
3 ☐ Dusk
5 ☐ Dark (No Street Lights)
6 ☐ Dark (Street Lights On)
4 ☐ Dark (Street Lights Off)

WEATHER CONDITIONS
1 ☐ Clear
2 ☐ Cloudy
3 ☐ Foggy
4 ☐ Raining
5 ☐ Snowing
6 ☐ Other
_____ (explain)

ROADWAY TYPE-1 ("X" one)

VEH		
1	2	
1 ☐	☐	Interstate
2 ☐	☐	U.S. Route
3 ☐	☐	State Route
4 ☐	☐	County Route
5 ☐	☐	Municipal Route
6 ☐	☐	Other

_____ (explain)

ROADWAY TYPE-2 ("X" all that apply)

VEH		
1	2	
3 ☐	☐	One Way
6 ☐	☐	Ramp (Entrance/Exit)
1 ☐	☐	Two Lane
2 ☐	☐	Four Lane
4 ☐	☐	Divided Lanes
		By What _____
		_____ (explain)
5 ☐	☐	Other

_____ (explain)

ROADWAY HAZARDS ("X" all that apply)

VEH		
1	2	
5 ☐	☐	No Apparent Hazards
1 ☐	☐	Defective Shoulders
2 ☐	☐	Holes, Deep Ruts
7 ☐	☐	No or Obscured Pavement Markings
3 ☐	☐	Loose Material on Surface
8 ☐	☐	Construction/Maintenance Zone
4 ☐	☐	Other Hazards

_____ (explain)

TRAFFIC CONTROLS

VEH		
1	2	
1 ☐	☐	No Controls
2 ☐	☐	Traffic Light
10 ☐	☐	Flashing Yellow (Caution)
11 ☐	☐	Flashing Red (Stop)
12 ☐	☐	Lane Use Control
3 ☐	☐	Stop Sign
8 ☐	☐	4-Way Stop
4 ☐	☐	Yield
13 ☐	☐	Construction Zone Controls
5 ☐	☐	RR Crossbucks
6 ☐	☐	RR Flasher
7 ☐	☐	RR Gates
9 ☐	☐	Other

_____ (explain)

Was Traffic Control Visible?
Veh. 1 ☐ YES ☐ NO
Veh. 2 ☐ YES ☐ NO

Was Traffic Control Functioning Properly?
Veh. 1 ☐ YES ☐ NO
Veh. 2 ☐ YES ☐ NO

ROADWAY SURFACE TYPE

VEH		
1	2	
1 ☐	☐	Asphalt
4 ☐	☐	Concrete
2 ☐	☐	Brick
3 ☐	☐	Gravel
5 ☐	☐	Dirt
6 ☐	☐	Other

_____ (explain)

ROADWAY SURFACE CONDITIONS

VEH		
1	2	
4 ☐	☐	Dry
3 ☐	☐	Wet
2 ☐	☐	Snow
1 ☐	☐	Ice
5 ☐	☐	Mud
6 ☐	☐	Other

_____ (explain)

ROADWAY CHARACTER ("X" two)

VEH		
1	2	
1 ☐	☐	Curve
2 ☐	☐	Straight
3 ☐	☐	Upgrade
4 ☐	☐	Downgrade
5 ☐	☐	Level

DRIVER CONTRIBUTING FACTORS ("X" all that apply)

DRIVER		
1	2	
11 ☐	☐	None
5 ☐	☐	Drinking
6 ☐	☐	Speeding
1 ☐	☐	Failure to Yield
2 ☐	☐	Following too Closely
14 ☐	☐	Reckless Driving
3 ☐	☐	Improper Passing
4 ☐	☐	Improper Turn
8 ☐	☐	Disregard Signal or Sign
9 ☐	☐	Wrong Side of Road
15 ☐	☐	Wrong Way
7 ☐	☐	Weather
13 ☐	☐	Vision Obstructed
		By What?_____
10 ☐	☐	Other _____

_____ (explain)

CONDITION OF DRIVER or PEDESTRIAN
("X" all that apply)

1	2	P	
2 ☐	☐	☐	Had Not Been Drinking
3 ☐	☐	☐	Had Been Drinking
6 ☐	☐	☐	Physical Defect
7 ☐	☐	☐	Ill (Sick)
5 ☐	☐	☐	Ability Not Impaired
4 ☐	☐	☐	Ability Impaired
8 ☐	☐	☐	Apparently Asleep
10 ☐	☐	☐	Apparently Drugged
1 ☐	☐	☐	Apparently Normal
9 ☐	☐	☐	Unknown if Drinking
11 ☐	☐	☐	Other _____

_____ (explain)

TYPE OF ACTION ("X" all that apply)

DRIVER		
1	2	
1 ☐	☐	Going Straight
18 ☐	☐	Negotiating Curve
19 ☐	☐	Passing or Overtaking Another Vehicle
3 ☐	☐	Right Turn to Private Drive
2 ☐	☐	Right Turn to Street
20 ☐	☐	Right Turn on Red Permitted
21 ☐	☐	Right Turn on Red Not Permitted
5 ☐	☐	Left Turn to Private Drive
4 ☐	☐	Left Turn to Street
22 ☐	☐	Turning From Wrong Lane
6 ☐	☐	Slowing or Stopped for Signal or Sign
7 ☐	☐	Slowing or Stopped for Turning Traffic
8 ☐	☐	Slowing or Stopped for Entering Traffic
9 ☐	☐	Slowing or Stopped Other
		_____ (explain)
10 ☐	☐	Starting in Traffic
11 ☐	☐	Starting from Parked Position
12 ☐	☐	Stopped in Traffic Lane
13 ☐	☐	Parked (Legally - 1 ☐ YES 2 ☐ NO)
14 ☐	☐	Backing from Drive
15 ☐	☐	Backing from On-Street Parking Space
17 ☐	☐	Entering from Private Drive
16 ☐	☐	Other _____

_____ (explain)

HAZARDOUS CARGO
Did Accident Involve Hazardous Cargo? 1 ☐ YES   2 ☐ NO
(If yes, "X" all that apply)

VEH				VEH		
1	2			1	2	
0 ☐	☐	NONE		5 ☐	☐	Oxidizers
1 ☐	☐	Explosives		6 ☐	☐	Etiologic Materials
2 ☐	☐	Gases		7 ☐	☐	Radioactive Materials
3 ☐	☐	Flammable Liquids		8 ☐	☐	Corrosives
4 ☐	☐	Flammable Solids		9 ☐	☐	Misc.

_____ (explain)

VEHICLE CONDITION ("X" all that apply)

	VEH. 1	VEH.2
Was vehicle moved prior to investigation?	1 ☐ YES	1 ☐ YES
	2 ☐ NO	2 ☐ NO
Was vehicle burned?	1 ☐ YES	1 ☐ YES
	2 ☐ NO	2 ☐ NO
Was vehicle modified? If yes, explain?	1 ☐ YES	1 ☐ YES
	2 ☐ NO	2 ☐ NO

VEHICLE DEFECTS

	VEH. 1	VEH. 2
Did officer check for defect?	1 ☐ YES	1 ☐ YES
	2 ☐ NO	2 ☐ NO

("X" all that apply)

VEH		
1	2	
6 ☐	☐	No Apparent Defects
1 ☐	☐	Defective Brakes
3 ☐	☐	Defective Steering Mechanism
4 ☐	☐	Defective Tires
8 ☐	☐	Defective Headlights
9 ☐	☐	Defective Signal Lights
10 ☐	☐	Defective Tail Lights
11 ☐	☐	Defective Other Lights

_____ (explain)

5 ☐ Other _____
_____ (explain)

PAGE 2 of _____

DOCUMENT CONTROL NUMBER (DO NOT USE) | LOCAL AGENCY USE | REFERENCE NUMBER

The following block repeats eight (8) times:

NAME _____
VEH NO. _____   ADDRESS   SAME AS: (☐ DRIVER / ☐ OWNER) OF VEHICLE
☐ 1 DRIVER   OR _____ ZIP _____
☐ 2 PASSENGER   TAKEN TO _____ BY _____
☐ 3 PEDESTRIAN   MEDICAL FACILITY (AMBULANCE SERVICE NAME OR PRIVATE PARTY)

Age	Sex	Injury Code	Seating Position	Ejected	Seat Belt	Helmet	ALCOHOL Test	ALCOHOL Result	ALCOHOL Refused	DRUGS Test	DRUGS Result	DRUGS Refused
	M	0										
		1		YES	YES	YES	YES			YES	YES	POS	YES
		2										
	F	3		NO	NO	NO	NO			NO	NO	NEG	NO
		4										

(The above Name/Vehicle block and table is repeated eight times.)

LIST BELOW ALL CHILD PASSENGERS UNDER FOUR (4) YEARS OF AGE

The following block repeats three (3) times:

NAME _____
VEH NO. _____   ADDRESS   SAME AS: (☐ DRIVER / ☐ OWNER) OF VEHICLE
OR _____ ZIP _____
TAKEN TO _____ BY _____
MEDICAL FACILITY (AMBULANCE SERVICE NAME OR PRIVATE PARTY)

Age	Sex	Injury Code	Seating Position	Ejected	Seat Belt	Helmet	Held	CHILD RESTRAINT DEVICE Available	Used	Used Properly
	M	0								
Yrs.		1		YES	YES	YES	YES	YES	YES	YES
		2								
Mos.	F	3		NO	NO	NO	NO	NO	NO	NO
		4								

W I T N E S S E S

(1) Name _____ Age _____ Race _____ Sex _____
Address _____ (Business Phone) _____ (Residence Phone) _____

(2) Name _____ Age _____ Race _____ Sex _____
Address _____ (Business Phone) _____ (Residence Phone) _____

(3) Name _____ Age _____ Race _____ Sex _____
Address _____ (Business Phone) _____ (Residence Phone) _____

DOCUMENT CONTROL NUMBER (DO NOT USE)		LOCAL AGENCY USE	REFERENCE NUMBER

DESCRIBE WHAT HAPPENED: _____

_____

_____

_____

_____

_____

_____

1   2   3   4   5   6   7

COLLISION DIAGRAM

INDICATE NORTH
BY ARROW

1   1

2   2

3   3

4   4

5   5

6   6

1   2   3   4   5   6   7

INVESTIGATOR'S SIGNATURE _____ DATE _____

REPORT REVIEWED BY: _____ DATE _____

Index

Note: Page numbers followed by "*b*" refer to boxes.